Religion and Theology

Religion and Theology

By
Mortimer J. Adler
and
Seymour Cain

Prefaces by
John Cogley, Maurice Friedman
and Wilhelm Pauck

ENCYCLOPÆDIA BRITANNICA, INC.

Chicago • London • Toronto • Geneva • Sydney • Tokyo

PREFACES

JOHN COGLEY

Center for the Study of Democratic Institutions

In his *Idea of a University,* John Henry Newman wrote a chapter called "Knowledge—Its Own End." In it Cardinal Newman said: "To open the mind, to correct it, to refine it, to enable it to know and to digest, master, rule, and use its own knowledge, to give it power over its own faculties, application, flexibility, method, critical exactness, sagacity, resource, address, eloquent expression, is an object as intelligible as the cultivation of virtue, while, at the same time, it is absolutely distinct from it."

Something like that might be said for most of the readings in this collection. With the exception of the Scriptural excerpts, they are not *religious* writings in the full sense of the word. It may even be stretching things a bit to describe some of them as theological. But they all raise questions that the thoughtful religious believer should consider, questions even the nonbeliever has no right to ignore. In this sense, then, reading, studying, analyzing, and discussing what some of the wisest men who ever lived had to say about the religious concern may not be the kind of spiritual contemplation that goes on in a Trappist monastery, but it is "an object as intelligible as the cultivation of virtue, while, at the same time, it is absolutely distinct from it."

Two central ideas from the body of Roman Catholic thought struck me as I read through this little book and the assigned readings from *Great Books of the Western World.* The first was the emphasis Catholic tradition puts on reason. No genuine Catholic thinker has ever held that a man could reason his way into faith, which is always an unmerited gift of God; but no one has been more insistent than Saint Thomas Aquinas that nothing *de fide* can be irrational. Thomas' argument can be simply stated: God is the Author of all truth and He does not contradict Himself; what He teaches through revelation does not conflict with the truth a man can grasp through the use of his own intellect. In the Catholic view, then, faith and reason are not only compatible, they are complementary. When the educated Catholic struggles with the kind of questions raised in these pages—whether they be asked by an Aeschylus or a Freud—he is solidly in the Catholic tradition.

New truths are being discovered all the time, but for the Catholic there can be no alien truths. For every truth—no matter what its immediate source or how secular its uses—proceeds from the Holy Ghost. Saint Thomas, for instance, took truths wherever he found them, whether from the ancient Greeks or the Moslem philosophers of his own day, and related them to the truths he knew by faith, thereby ennobling the truths of reason and enriching the truths of faith. The modern Roman Catholic who absorbs the wisdom found in these readings and is competent to spot the error in them, will come out of the experience more appreciative of his faith and more respectful of his Church's insistence on the primacy of reason over will, emotion, sentiment, or that modern phenomenon, faith-in-faith, belief-in-belief.

The second idea from Catholic theological tradition that struck me was what Cardinal Newman called the development of doctrine. This is the essential Catholic notion that Christian doctrine is ever-expanding and that the riches of the Christian revelation will continue to be manifested throughout time.

Roman Catholics do not look back nostalgically to that

ancient day when dogmas were few, theological knowledge was starkly simple, and intellectual subtleties unknown among religious thinkers. It is Catholic belief that the Church is a living organism and that each generation of Christians is called upon to add to the intellectual capital of the tradition. A Thomas Aquinas built on an Augustine, a Jacques Maritain has been building on an Aquinas. The Church itself, in its *magesterium*, has blessed the efforts of all those who applied themselves to the theological task, and, when the time was ripe, absorbed some of their contributions into the body of its official teachings. Theology for the Catholic, consequently, can never be a "finished" subject, a "completed" task. Presumably, the Church of Rome in five hundred years will teach its ancient doctrines with even more elaboration and subtlety than is now available to it.

The theological enterprise is one to which the Catholic is called. Anything that enriches his understanding of the truths he holds by faith is forever welcome. Of course, those who will be studying these readings and participating in the discussion groups built up around them will not normally be professional theologians. It is not likely that they will stumble across any new theological insights which will later become part of the Catholic heritage. But if, in struggling with the intellectual challenges found here, they strengthen the reason on which their own faith is built, they will in the process give some kind of personal witness to the tradition of reason and faith complementing each other.

It was Thomas À Kempis who said that he would rather feel compunction than know its definition. Taken in themselves, these words are unexceptionable for the religious man. The religious experience always takes precedence over theological speculation. Our God, after all, whether we be Roman Catholics, Eastern Orthodox, Protestants or Jews, is a living God, a Person to be loved rather than a brooding Presence to be studied like a problem in calculus. But, really, there is no conflict between both feeling compunction and knowing its definition. The illiterate Breton peasant may have served for years as a model of simple faith, but would not his faith have been even more impressive if it had been grounded in reason? Somehow, the man of faith has to strike a balance. He must realize that all the intellectual clarity in the world will not of itself lead him one step closer to the knowledge graciously given to those who accept the revelation. At the same time, he has to realize that so intimate are the relations between faith and reason that for men of a certain development not to know the definition of compunction may well impede their feeling it.

The kind of intellectual enterprise suggested by these readings and the questions the editors have added to the text will not do the work of the Church, or the work of prayer, or the work of Grace. It will not produce men of virtue as religious folk understand that word. But men of religious virtue cannot lose by participating in it, and as their intellectual horizons broaden, they will attain another kind of virtue, the kind summed up in Cardinal Newman's chapter head—"Knowledge —Its Own End."

MAURICE FRIEDMAN

Professor of Philosophy, Sarah Lawrence College; author, "Martin Buber: The Life of Dialogue" (New York: Harper's Torchbooks, 1960)

Aeschylus' *Prometheus Bound*, "*Genesis*" and "*Exodus*," the "Sermon on the Mount," St. Augustine's *Confessions*, Dante's *Divine Comedy*, Dostoevsky's "Exhortations of Father Zossima" —these belong to the great classics of religious and devotional literature. Because of them the confrontation with religious experience and reality is a necessity for every man who wishes to possess the heritage which the culture of the West offers him. In the *Great Books of the Western World* religion is a constantly recurring theme bound up with some of the central problems of human experience—how we know, the content and source of morality, the relation of the individual to the state, the meaning of evil, and the place of the psychological in our understanding of reality.

In many of the readings on religion and theology in this Reading Plan, we see religion as directly experienced reality rather than as indirect reflection and system. For Abraham, Moses, and the Jesus of the Sermon, the heart of this immediacy is the God who is met in the fullness of the concrete present. For St. Augustine it is the Eternal Being whose Present contains the whole of time. For Dante it is the "Light Eternal" apprehended in the mystic vision.

"Religion is the covenant of the Absolute with the concrete," says Martin Buber, "philosophy of the Absolute with the universal." In practice, however, the universal and the concrete are always mixed. The relationship between the immediacy of religious experience and the universal forms, such as theology and metaphysics, in which that experience is expressed is a central problem in our understanding of religion. Philosophy is supplanted by revelation as Dante's guide to Paradise, but at the highest reaches revealed knowledge is itself supplanted by the immediate vision of the mystic. To Biblical man revelation is itself immediate, but it is hearing and responding rather than seeing. The Ten Commandments are the direct address of an I that speaks to a Thou that hears. Jesus calls for a direct personal relation with God—an unconditional trust that "takes no thought for the morrow." Aquinas, in contrast, sees faith as having to do not with God but with propositions about God; the God of whom he speaks is no longer the I who commands but "He Who Is"—Eternal Being rather than the Eternal Thou.

For Aquinas it was possible for natural reason to give true knowledge of God. For Pascal, the modern man who is terrified by "the silence of the infinite spaces," human reason can neither know the infinite God nor understand man's own place in an infinite world. Pascal rejects "the God of the Philosophers" who can be proved and demonstrated in favor of the "God of Abraham, Isaac, and Jacob" in whom one can have faith only through personal commitment and risk. To Hobbes, Locke, and Hume the dichotomy which Pascal makes between the reasons of the mind and the "reasons of the heart" is inadmissible, while Freud dismisses both philosophy of religion and immediate religious experience as "unscientific."

Religion has always meant primarily a way of life rather than a method of knowing, a way of life which places a demand. Is the source of ethics the direct dialogue between God and man, as in the Biblical command, "Love thy neighbor. I am the Lord."? Or is ethics impersonal law deriving from an impersonal Absolute, as in Plato? Is religion a pragmatic means of bolstering the ethical, as in Hobbes? Or is it an illusion that stands in the way of the ethical, as in Freud? Religion is concerned with the whole of human life, and in the Covenant between God and Israel that stands at the center of the Old Testament this means not only one's individual actions but the life of the community and the relations of the community with its neighbors. This demand for integrity, justice, righteousness, and loving kindness is present in the Ten Commandments, in the Biblical injunction to become "a kingdom of priests and a holy nation," in the command to love God with one's whole being *and* to love one's neighbor as oneself. In ancient Israel there was no distinction between religion and society, "church" and "state." The Biblical Covenant was between God and the people. If this Covenant still holds, on what is its demand placed?—the individual? the church? the state? the people as a whole? the people of Israel? all mankind? Should we, like Hobbes, identify the organic state and the kingship of God so that religion becomes a function of the state? Or should we, as Locke insists and as the Biblical prophets, Socrates, and the modern conscientious objector all did, oppose the state where its demands conflict with the commands of religion?

At the heart of many of these selections stand man's attempts to reconcile the reality of evil with his trust in God. Abraham and Job obey God in contrast to Prometheus who defies the arbitrary Zeus; yet the trust of Abraham and Job includes contending with God, for their God is a God of mercy as well as of power, and the evil and suffering that they experience become meaningful to them in their dialogue with Him. Milton's Satan is a Promethean figure, but Milton's God is a benevolent deity who gives man freedom of will which he will not abridge even when men use it to do evil. For Augustine evil is imperfect participation in the Good; for Zossima it is the self that cuts man off from God; for Freud it is the reality of a "dark, unfeeling, and unloving" universe that only wishful thinking sees as sympathetic to human needs and values.

Freud extends Hume's empiricism to include Zossima's vitalistic sense of life as "an ocean flowing and blending," but he does so in such a way as to reduce Zossima's religious ecstasy to dependence on the father. Even when we do not follow Freud in doubting the truth of religious doctrines as illusions that minister to our psychological need, we are apt to transfer their truth from the meeting *between* man and what transcends him to the psychological sphere *within* man. To many in our day God is no longer really "Thou," "He," or even "It," but "I"—a function of one's "self-realization." True existence is no longer, as for Biblical man, the dialogue with God.

In our day the issues of religion and theology are joined more basically than ever before. Through making these issues our own we may enter into dialogue with many whose views differ widely from ours but who share with us seriousness and concern.

WILHELM PAUCK

Charles A. Briggs Graduate Professor of Church History,
Union Theological Seminary, New York City, New York

A person of culture is one who is enlightened concerning the things of the mind and able to make competent judgments about them. Most men yearn to become such persons. Therefore, they seek education, *i.e.*, they desire that one should lead them to the sources of knowledge. Sooner or later, they learn that they can reach these sources only by entering upon the whole cultural legacy which has been left to them by their fathers and predecessors.

They thus become cultured as they appropriate this heritage for themselves and make it their own and then try to fit it to their own lives by relating it to the values which they wish to see cultivated and which they hope will be embodied in civilization.

In other words, men share in the life and upbuilding of civilization insofar as they relate themselves responsibly to the heritage of the past (*i.e.*, the cultural achievements of the generations that have gone before them), first by appropriating it for themselves, and then by weighing and evaluating it according to their needs and insights, and thus transforming it in order, finally, to transmit it to their children. Cultural knowledge is always historical knowledge, and historical knowledge is not merely an acquaintance with past human achievements, but it is primarily the exercise of cultural responsibility by way of a critical assessment of such achievements, a judgment that will mean either their arrestment or their preservation and development in new situations.

Would'st thou possess thy heritage, essay
By use to render it thine own!
What we employ not, but impedes our way;
That which the hour creates, that can it use alone.[1]

This admonition must be heard and followed also by all those who are concerned for Christianity. For the Christian religion is a faith with a historical legacy. This consists of the Biblical testimony of the apostles and prophets about Jesus Christ and of the interpretation which this testimony has been given throughout the ages. It was transmitted to the succeeding generations of Christians through liturgies and forms of worship, through the symbolical expressions of the several arts, through ecclesiastical institutions and their social disciplines, but particularly through doctrines and dogmatic teachings. All

---

[1] From Goethe's *Faust*, as translated by Anna Swanwick (Boston, 1884).

Was Du ererbt von deinen Vätern hast,
Erwirb es, um es zu besitzen.
Was man nicht nützt, ist eine schwere Last,
Nur was der Augenblick erschafft, das kann er nützen.

It is instructive to compare the various translations of these lines, for such a comparison illustrates exactly what I am trying to state about the nature of historical and cultural knowledge: The translations of one and

these forms, but especially the dogmas and doctrines, reflect the way by which Christians of different times and places were related to various civilizations. Indeed, these teachings represent not only interpretations of the Christians' communion with God but also the ways by which they tried to exercise a responsibility for the preservation of human civilization. Everyone who calls himself a Christian must by some way or other come to terms with this legacy in his own thinking.

Most especially, Protestant Christians must render this heritage their own if they want to possess it, for (in accordance with the Reformers' interpretation of the nature of faith) every Christian believer is personally responsible to God for what he thinks and does: Everyone, so Luther taught, must do his own believing, just as he will have to die his own death.

Such a faith cannot be actualized, unless each believer thinks for himself and judges and decides by himself in all things of religion. But he can do this responsibly only if he learns to shape and develop his thinking in relation to the

---

the same text are different, because each translator has his own understanding of it. He then expresses this understanding in his own words, thus giving his own meaning to the ideas of the poet.

Bayard Taylor's translation (Boston, 1870) reads as follows:

> What from your father's heritage is lent,
> Earn it anew, to really possess it.
> What serves not, is a sore impediment;
> The Moment's need creates the things to serve and bless it.

William P. Andrews (his translation was edited and published by George M. Priest and Karl E. Weston, Princeton, 1929) renders Goethe's lines in the following fashion:

> Whate'er you have, bequeathed you by your father,
> Earn it in order to possess it.
> Things a man uses not, a heavy load beget,
> But what the hour brings forth, that he can use and bless it.

Dr. Abraham Hayward (Boston, 1892), whose translation is the most literal of all, gives the text an entirely different meaning:

> What thou hast inherited from thy sires, enjoy it, in order to possess it. What one does not make use of, is an oppressive burden. What the moment brings forth, that one can profit by.

forms in which the Christian religion has found expression, especially the basic theological doctrines.

Therefore it cannot but be of great benefit to anyone who as a Christian desires to believe, think, and judge for himself concerning the truths of religion and theology, if in disciplined dialogue with the authors of the *Great Books of the Western World*, in which the cultural heritage of the West is embodied, he endeavors to come to terms with the ways in which they dealt with these truths—directly and indirectly, as friends or as foes, as defenders of the faith or as its critics.

FOREWORD

T his Reading Plan is an aid to the study of religion and theology. You need not have done the readings in previous Reading Plans to undertake these readings. We do occasionally refer to previous readings for the interest of those readers who have already done them. For instance, in the Guide to the First Reading, *Prometheus Bound,* we refer to the Book of Job, one of the readings in the Introductory Plan. Such references are merely suggestions for further study.

How to Use the Reading Plan. This Plan contains three parts: a list of readings, guides to each of the readings, and suggestions for additional readings.

1. *The Reading List.* There are fifteen readings. You should take about two weeks for each reading. The length of each reading is designed for that period.

2. *The Guides.* These should prove most helpful to the reader of the *Great Books of the Western World* who is going it alone, without teacher, discussion leader, or other study aids. The purpose of the guide is to help you get started on an assignment by providing you with background material and by stimulating your thinking about the reading. Background material may include information about the particular historical setting—tradition, culture, and contemporary conditions—in which the book was written. It may also include remarks on the form and style of the readings, which range

from a Platonic dialogue to a modern Russian novel. A major portion of each guide describes the content and analyzes the meaning of the reading. Significant and difficult passages are cited and discussed. Where a whole work is being studied, we try to show how the parts fit together in the whole. Above all, we consider the principal religious ideas and attitudes in the reading and try to relate them to perennial and contemporary religious concerns. We want to help you to associate the meanings you discover in the reading with meanings to be found in your own life and faith.

The final section of each guide raises thoughtful questions that are suggested by the reading. You cannot answer such questions merely by repeating what the text says, or by an unqualified "yes" or "no," or by a flat "true" or "false." Hence, a brief discussion follows the statement of a problem, in order to indicate its significance and suggest some of the possible answers. You may be satisfied simply to read the questions and give them a little thought. Or you may want to delve more deeply into them and write out considered answers. The discussions following the questions are intended to stimulate your own inquiry and thought. They are not meant to provide the final or "right" answers. Try to answer the questions yourself.

Each guide concludes with a section entitled SELF-TEST-ING QUESTIONS. These are quite distinct from the discussion questions. They are factual questions about the reading that can be answered by citing a particular part of the text. They give you an opportunity to check how thoroughly you have read and how much you have remembered of what you have read. You can mark your score by referring to the list of answers at the end of Part II of the Reading Plan, immediately after the Guide to the Fifteenth Reading.

3. *Additional Readings.* This is a carefully selected list of readings intended to help the reader of this guide to pursue further his study of religion and theology. They are designed to provide him with a sound introductory knowledge of: (1) the history of Judaism and Christianity, (2) Biblical literature and interpretation, (3) the essential teachings of Judaism and

Christianity, (4) religious experience and worship, and (5) philosophical discussion of basic religious themes.

Before we start out on our readings, let us get some broad, general notions of religion and theology, and of their relation to philosophy.

What is Religion? The word *religion* comes from the Latin. Its original meaning may have been "rigorous care" (the opposite of "negligence"), or "bond" (from the same root as "obligation"). Both meanings apply to religion as we know it. Religious people act with rigorous care—"conscientiously"— in ritual and other special observances, in ethical conduct, or in the attainment of certain inner states. But this rigorous care in devotion, services, and observances aims at a bond or relation with an ultimate being or power.

Men have had different ideas of the nature of that ultimate reality. Sometimes the religious absolute is considered to be an impersonal, abstract principle; sometimes it is regarded as a personal God with attributes analogous to human intelligence and will; sometimes it includes both the impersonal and personal aspects. In the West, it is the personal or "theistic" element that is emphasized, though speculation about the impersonal element is not uncommon.

In any case, our basic view of the nature of God has theoretical and practical consequences. It determines the meaning and value we ascribe to man and the world, to nature and history, to matter and mind. And it also governs the characteristics of our religious acts and religious life.

Religion enlists the whole of man's being and activity. It is both contemplative and active, personal and communal, spiritual and material. The key religious term "holy" means not only "separate" but also "whole." Evelyn Underhill puts it thus: "Man, incited by God . . . responds to Him best not by a simple movement of the mind; but by a rich and complex action, in which his whole nature is concerned." Hence the religious man prays or meditates, performs ritual or ethical acts, finds holiness in solitude or in society.

Religious leaders and the persons regarded as especially religious comprise a rich variety of human types. They include the founders of religion, their apostles or disciples, the teachers of religious doctrine or a way of life, priests administering holy sacraments, reformers striving to purify religious life, prophets "called" to proclaim a new message from God to the people, saints who are the concrete epitomes of holiness, and various types of seers and diviners. These types of religious leaders and personalities appear in almost all religions the world over. The great religious writings are an expression and interpretation of their life and work and of the religious communities which they belong to and inspire.

What is Theology? Religion has various modes of expression. It may be expressed in action—in ritual, communal prayer, the dance, or other overt behavior. It may also be expressed in thought—through myths, which are the imaginative expression of basic religious truths, and through doctrine and dogma, which are their intellectual expression. The first chapters of the Book of Genesis, for instance, express in story form basic notions about the relation of God to the world and to man. Talmudic and later Jewish commentators and Christian theologians—such as Augustine, Aquinas, Luther, and Calvin—spell out what these ancient stories mean. Out of such interpretations come the basic religious doctrines, dogmas, and creeds—statements of the essentials of faith accepted by a religious community as authoritative.

Literally, *theology* means the knowledge of God or of divine things. Actually, the term covers a good deal more than this. Theologians usually try to provide a total view of God, man, and the world. Hence theology usually includes an *anthropology; i.e.,* a doctrine about man. It also considers the order and meaning of the physical world, and so may include a *cosmology:* a doctrine about the world. Man and the world are considered religiously, in relation to God.

The term "theology" may refer to systematic thought about God *within a particular religious tradition*—thought which starts from a specific faith or revelation that is accepted as authoritative. The term "theology" may also refer to rational reflection about God and about man's relation to Him, independent of religious tradition. The first type is usually called "sacred" or "dogmatic" theology. Aquinas' *Summa Theologica* (Vol. 19-20) is a good example of this. The second type is usually called "natural" or "philosophical" theology. Aristotle's *Metaphysics* (Vol. 8) and Spinoza's *Ethics* (Vol. 31) provide classic examples of this type.

We should note that not all faiths aim at an explicit systematic theology. Certain faiths and denominations look upon such attempts as impossible or even impious undertakings. Even in faiths with authoritatively pronounced, explicit articles of faith and highly developed theological formulations, leading religious personalities or groups may stress piety, devotion, or inner experience, as against the intellectual expressions of religion.

Religion and Philosophy. Wherein do religion and philosophy differ? It is difficult to answer this question with a hard and fast answer unless we accept oversimplified versions of religion and philosophy. If philosophy is only rational inquiry into the nature of things, restricted to the attainment of theoretical knowledge through rigorous conceptual thought, then obviously it has little in common with religion. For religion claims to offer communion with God through worship, conduct, and all of life's activities, as well as knowledge of God's nature and His purpose for the world. If we accepted the theoretical view of philosophy, we could then say that the aim of religion is essentially practical and the aim of philosophy essentially contemplative.

But the trouble is that philosophy, too (at least in some of its forms), propounds a theology, a way of life, and even a mode of access to God. Philosophy has long been interested in teaching a way of life in conformity with the purpose and meaning of things, as well as theoretical knowledge. Moreover, the attainment of philosophical knowledge requires an inner purification and an absolute conscientiousness that is deeply religious in character. And philosophy has long pointed to contemplation as a way to union with or participation in the divine. Here it accords with the stress on contemplation to be found in certain types of religion. Moreover, many philosophers, both ancient and modern, have expressed their thought in the mythical, symbolical, imaginative forms that we usually associate with religious expression. And we can find expressions of will and emotion, as well as of pure reason, in Western philosophy.

A more decisive distinction may be the fact that religion is usually tied to a particular historical tradition. It perpetuates a basic teaching that has been promulgated in the past by a human founder or by divine revelation, and is handed down through the religious community. It follows one particular "furrow" in human history as authoritative and binding. It takes particular events, persons, or symbols as the rule for thought and action. Philosophy appears to offer no parallel to this. Does it not strive to arrive at universal truths that cannot be measured by any single event, person, or experience, and that can be attained by universal human reason alone? But perhaps philosophy, too, is committed to particular traditions, schools, and masters, as unique and binding as anything to be found in religion. Perhaps it, too, follows certain "furrows" to the truth. And perhaps Western philosophy is just as distinct from Eastern philosophy as Western religion is from Eastern religion.

Finally, we may seek for the distinction between philosophy and religion in the motivations or sanctions for adherence to various beliefs, attitudes, and practices: in the communal aspect of religion (belonging to a religious fellowship or a church); in the material, sensible actions that mark religious life, with all its specific observances; or in the basic traditional distinction between what follows from revelation, the Word of God, and what follows from reason, the word of man.

In any case, there is a difference which is more easily sensed than expressed between religion and philosophy. In some ages religion and philosophy are friends, in others they are enemies, and in still others they are indifferent to one another. The mutual attitude depends on the particular type of religion and the particular school of philosophy involved.

The Purpose of This Plan. This Reading Plan is intended to provide an introduction to the major themes of religious thought in the Western world. Admittedly, only a few of the classics of Western religious thought and literature are included in the *Great Books* set. We have no works from the Talmud, the Jewish and Christian mystics, or the Protestant reformers, and only one of the great Church Fathers is represented. Hence we do not pretend to furnish a guide to all the significant religious writings of the West.

Our basic aim is to single out the main ideas and attitudes about man's relation to God that are to be found in this set. We assume that these religious views are worthy of careful thought and study, and we have striven to present them without fear or favor. We leave judgments about the truth of particular beliefs, religious systems, or religion itself to you, the individual reader.

Despite the unavoidable limitations mentioned above, we offer you a rich array of readings. We consider a selection from the father of Western philosophy on religious questions that have been discussed throughout our tradition. We also include selections from the Bible that are basic for the Jewish and Christian faiths. Following these are an interpretation of the doctrine of creation by the greatest of the Church Fathers, a discussion of theology and faith by the foremost medieval Christian theologian, a vigorous debate on the question of church and state by two English philosophers, a famous defense of Christian faith from one of the classic devotional writings, and strong attacks on the rational grounds of religious faith by an 18th-century philosopher and a 20th-century psychoanalyst. We have also included imaginative expressions of religious thought from drama, poetry, and the novel.

CONTENTS

A NOTE ON

REFERENCE STYLE

In referring to *Great Books of the Western World,* the same style is used as in the *Syntopicon.* Pages are cited by number and section. In books that are printed in single column, "a" and "b" refer to the upper and lower half of the page. In books that are printed in double column, "a" and "b" refer to the upper and lower half of the left column, "c" and "d" to the upper and lower half of the right column. For example, "Vol. 53, p. 210b" refers to the lower half of page 210, since Vol. 53, James's *Principles of Psychology,* is printed in single column. But "Vol. 7, p. 202b" refers to the lower left quarter of page 202, since Vol. 7, Plato's *Dialogues,* is printed in double column.

In Bible references, if there is a difference between the King James and the Douay version, the King James reference is given first, followed by (D) and the Douay reference.

THE READING LIST

1 AESCHYLUS, *Prometheus Bound.* Vol. 5, pp. 40-51.

2 PLATO, *Euthyphro* and *Laws*, Book X. Vol. 7, pp. 191-199, 757-771.

3 OLD TESTAMENT, *Book of Genesis*, 12:1-9; 13:14-18; 15; 17; 18:17-33; 22:1-19. *Book of Exodus*, 3-4; 6:1-8; 14-15; 19-20; 24.

4 NEW TESTAMENT, *The Gospel According to St. Matthew.*

5 ST. AUGUSTINE, *The Confessions*, Book XI, Sections I-XIII; Book XII. Vol. 18, pp. 89-93, 99-110.

6 AQUINAS, *Summa Theologica*, Part I, Q. 1 and Part II-II, QQ. 1-3. Vol. 19, pp. 3-10; Vol. 20, pp. 380-401.

7 DANTE, *The Divine Comedy*, "Paradise." Vol. 21, pp. 106-175.

8 HOBBES, *Leviathan*, Part I, Ch. 12; Part II, Ch. 31; Part III. Vol. 23, pp. 79-84, 159-246.

9 MONTAIGNE, *The Essays*, in Vol. 25. "That a Man Is Soberly to Judge of the Divine Ordinances," pp. 98-99; "Of Prayers," pp. 152-156; "Of Liberty of Conscience," pp. 324-326.

10 MILTON, *Paradise Lost*, Books I-III. Vol. 32, pp. 93-151.

11 PASCAL, *Pensées*, Sections III-IV. Vol. 33, pp. 205-225.

AESCHYLUS

Prometheus Bound

Vol. 5, pp. 40-51

Divine power has not always been regarded as just and beneficent. The tension between the divine and the human is a perennial problem. Aeschylus, the Greek tragedian, has dramatized this tension by staging the myth of Prometheus, the Greek hero, or demigod, who was cruelly punished by Zeus for bringing culture to mankind. This myth of the benefactor of mankind, chained to a rock and tortured for countless ages but always maintaining his defiance of the supreme power, has stirred the imagination of readers for thousands of years.

The myth, as presented through the powerful dramatic genius of Aeschylus, raises basic and disturbing religious problems. Can the ultimate power in the universe consist merely in absolute might? "Shall not the Judge of all the earth do right?" Is it right or wrong to stand up against the divine power over the universe? Shall man rely on his own cultural powers alone and judge the universe by his own ethical standards? Which is right: revolt or obedience? Can human autonomy and divine rule be reconciled?

1

First Reading

Sören Kierkegaard, the 19th-century Danish religious philosopher, remarked that in modern times the theater was becoming more and more like a church, while the church was becoming more like a theater. This was intended as an ironic commentary on the preachiness of the modern stage and the entertainingness of the modern pulpit. In ancient Greece the criticism would have been out of place. The Greek theater originated in religious festivals. (Note the derivation of the word *tragedy* from a Greek term meaning "goat-song," the choral lyric for the god Dionysus.)

Poets, sculptors, and painters played a remarkable role in shaping the religious consciousness of ancient Greece. They assumed the functions usually performed in other cultures by priests, prophets, and theologians. Homer and Hesiod brought into order the vague and chaotic multitude of popular divinities and gave them distinct identities and personalities. Philosophers, such as Plato, found some of the poets' stories very unedifying. (See *The Republic*, the *Laws*, and the *Euthyphro*.) However, these stories were the basis for new interpretations of the gods by serious and profound tragedians, such as Aeschylus.

Aeschylus is regarded as the true founder of Greek tragedy, because he made dialogue and stage action possible by adding a second actor to the single actor and chorus previously employed, and he originated many other dramatic devices. He is noted for the lofty religious spirit and themes that characterize his dramas. He transformed the traditional, popular beliefs and stories into powerful tragedies which proclaimed divine justice and providence, and portrayed the suffering and joy involved in man's relation to God. Scholars regard Aeschylus as a great Greek theologian as well as a great dramatist. Many have likened him to the Hebrew prophets.

The mythical background out of which Aeschylus created *Prometheus Bound* is one of tyranny and violent revolt from beginning to end. The primal couple, as in many ancient myths, were Heaven and Earth (Uranus and Gaea). Their children were the twelve Titans—gods and goddesses representing natural forces and abstractions. One of them, Cronus, led a revolt against the tyranny of their father, Uranus, castrated him, and took over supreme power. Cronus' son, Zeus, in turn led a successful revolt against Cronus and his fellow Titans, and became the supreme ruler of the gods. The losers were banished to Tartarus, save for Atlas, who was condemned to support the heavens on his shoulders. One Titan, Oceanus, and Prometheus, the son of another, had supported Zeus. (The term Titan is also accorded to descendants of the Titans, such as Prometheus and his brothers Atlas and Epimetheus.) Zeus in his turn became tyrannical: His rule was absolute and he brooked no opposition from the other gods. His punishment of Prometheus for bringing culture to mankind is an example of this.

Prometheus (whose name means "forethought") stole fire from heaven and brought it down to men in a hollow tube. He taught men all the useful arts which helped to maintain them on earth. He tricked Zeus into choosing the worst parts of animal sacrifices for the gods, leaving the best parts to men. In revenge for this favoring of mankind, Zeus had Pandora created by Hephaestus and sent her down to Prometheus' brother Epimetheus (or "afterthought"), to bring all kinds of woes to man. Zeus also had Prometheus chained to a rock on Mt. Caucasus, where an eagle ate his liver every day and it was restored every night. This torture continued for many aeons, until finally Hercules killed the eagle and released Prometheus.

This is the material out of which Aeschylus wrought his great drama. We have here only a fragment of what was probably a trilogy of plays. The other two were probably called *Prometheus Unbound,* dealing with the Titan's release, and *Prometheus the Fire-Bearer,* perhaps dealing with the reconciliation of the opposing forces or connecting the myth with some religious festival. In reading this play, you must keep in mind that we have here only a part of the whole. This is by no means all that Aeschylus has to say on the nature of Zeus. Zeus is viewed here from Prometheus' side. We do not have Zeus's side nor the final reconciliation of opposing forces, as we have in the trilogy made up of *Agamemnon,* the *Choephoroe,* and the *Eumenides* (see Vol. 5, pp. 52-91). You will find a lofty view of Zeus in these plays and in *The Suppliant Maidens* (see Vol. 5, pp. 1-14).

In Greek religion Zeus, originally a god of the sky and weather—a storm god armed with thunder and lightning—became the supreme ruler and father of gods and men. He was associated with law and justice and the good and evil that are allotted to men. Prometheus was one of the culture-bringers or culture-heroes that are found in the myths of ancient and primitive peoples. They bring fire, writing, agriculture, and other useful and liberal arts to men. Can you think of any other culture-bringers in Greek mythology?

II

Dramatically this play is odd, for the main character is stationary. Hence we cannot have dramatic action (a series of events progressing to a climax and conclusion). Instead, we have one situation revealed in various aspects, through a succession of solos and duets by the characters.

As the play opens, Kratos and Bia (Power and Force) bring in Prometheus and hold him while Hephaestus, the divine smith, shackles him to the rock. During the process Hephaestus laments his sad duty, but Kratos and Bia exult at Prometheus' fate as just punishment for his treacherous favoring of mortals over the gods. After they depart, the chained Prometheus, previously silent, bursts out in lament at his anguish, but expresses determination to bear whatever Necessity brings, all of which he foresees.

After this prologue (pp. 40a-41c), the chorus of the Oceanides, the daughters of Oceanus (the god of the water which surrounds the earth), enter and express their compassion for Prometheus' plight and their resentment at Zeus's tyranny. Prometheus replies that he knows a secret vital to Zeus's safety but that he will not reveal it until he is released. He tells the Oceanides how he helped Zeus to gain power, and how Zeus turned against him when he, Prometheus, prevented the destruction of mankind and bestowed fire and the arts on them. He laments that freeing mankind from its brutish condition has resulted in imprisonment for himself.

At this point (p. 43a) the Titan Oceanus enters. He expresses his grief at seeing a brother Titan thus abused and begs Prometheus to be prudent—to adjust himself to the new and absolute rule of Zeus. He offers to intercede with Zeus on Prometheus' behalf, but Prometheus will have none of it. He maintains his defiance, and Oceanus leaves.

The chorus breaks into lament over the fate of Prometheus and Atlas (see p. 44a-c). Prometheus then tells of the arts and sciences he has bestowed on mankind, raising them from barbaric stupidity to civilization. The chorus utters a song of reverence for Zeus and his holy power and contrasts it with the weak and finite condition of men (see pp. 45b-c).

At this point the most poignant character in the play enters: Io, the king's daughter, with whom Zeus had fallen in love and whom he had turned into a heifer to protect her from the wrath of his jealous wife Hera. This poor girl—driven by a gadfly sent by Hera to wander over the face of the earth—is distracted to the point of madness. Io, one of the most touching characters in literature, contrasts sharply with the implacable Prometheus. She narrates all that has happened to her, and Prometheus foretells her future woes. He also prophesies Zeus's future fall through a fateful marriage and his own release by a descendant of Io's (Hercules, who is not named directly). Io departs in a raving frenzy (see pp. 45c-49c).

The chorus, moved by Io's fate, draws the moral that marriage should be only between equals: no good comes of mating between gods and humans. Prometheus continues to

utter his defiance of Zeus and to predict his fall from power.
At this point, Hermes, the envoy of Zeus, enters and tries to
draw the secret about Zeus's future marriage from Prometheus.
The latter berates Hermes as the servile lackey of an upstart,
while Hermes calls Prometheus a renegade and a thief, and
threatens him with horrible punishment unless he talks.
Prometheus stands firm, and Hermes leaves without the secret.
As the play ends, we hear earthquakes and thunder, and
Prometheus and the Oceanides—loyal to him to the end—fall
into the abyss (see pp. 49c-51d).

Thus ends the fragment of the Prometheus trilogy which has
come down to us.

III

What does *Prometheus Bound* have to say about the nature
of the ultimate power in the universe and of man's relation to
that power? Of course, the hero of this piece is a Titan or the
son of a Titan, and thus a demigod and not a human being.
But there is no doubt that the main attributes that are given
to him—forethought, cunning, and technical power—are specifically human traits.

Alfred North Whitehead, the distinguished modern philosopher, said that God appears to man in three stages: as
God the Void, God the Enemy, and God the Friend. In this
play we certainly encounter God the Enemy. Prometheus says
that "suffering is the due a foe must pay his foes" (p. 51b).
Zeus, here, is overpowering force, not only omnipotent, but
tyrannical, merciless, and unjust. Those under his sway suffer
without recourse. No plea or entreaty influences him.

Ah, they are wise

Who do obeisance, prostrate in the dust,
To the implacable, eternal Will. (p. 50a)

. . . for none is free but Zeus. (p. 40c)

For not by prayer to Zeus is access won;
An unpersuadable heart hath Cronos' son. (p. 42a)

He hath a heart

Of iron, hewn out of unfeeling rock. (p. 42c)

Is not the only ruler of the Gods
A complete tyrant, violent to all,
Respecting none? (p. 47d)

. . . an arch-despot who no audit dreads
Rules by his own rough will. (p. 43c)

In the whole play, not one benevolent trait or kind deed
is ascribed to Zeus, save for the prophesied cure of Io (see
p. 49a).

But is Zeus the ultimate power? The fate of Io and her
eventual release show us that a hierarchy of divine powers
is assumed in this play. Hera is able to hound Io down all
the paths and roads of this world, but in the end Zeus's protection provides safety and fruition. Zeus himself, however, is
not the ultimate power, for he, too, is bound by overarching
Fate, or Necessity, which apportions lots to men and gods
and decrees all things.

Ch. Who is the pilot of Necessity?
Pr. The Fates triform, and the unforgetting Furies.
Ch. So then Zeus is of lesser might than these?
Pr. Surely he shall not shun the lot apportioned.
Ch. What lot for Zeus save world-without-end reign? (p. 45b)

It is Fate that the characters and the chorus cry out against.
Fate allots to Io her dreadful plight (see p. 47b). And it is
Necessity, not Zeus, that Prometheus finds unconquerable.

. . . . what's determined
Bear, as I can, I must, knowing the might
Of strong Necessity is unconquerable. (p. 41b)

Moreover, the power of Zeus is not eternal. Just as he supplanted a ruler of the gods, so his rule can be overturned.

For now new steersmen take the helm
Olympian; now with little thought
Of right, on strange, new laws Zeus stablisheth his realm,
Bringing the mighty ones of old to naught . . .
Nor shall he cease until his heart be satiate,
Or one a way devise
To hurl him from the throne where he doth monarchize. (pp. 41d-42a)

Apparently Zeus is not omniscient, for Prometheus warns that he will fall unless he learns from Prometheus the secret source of his ruin (see p. 42a).

Prometheus tells Io of the fated fall.

Pr. But now of suffering there is
    No end in sight till Zeus shall fall.
Io.   And shall
    Zeus fall? His power be taken from him? . . .
                    And shall he quit
    The throne of all the worlds . . . ?
                    And he will find
    No way to parry this strong stroke of fate?
Pr. None save my own self—when these bonds are loosed. (p. 48a-b)

Prometheus refuses scornfully to bow down to the reputedly eternal will of Zeus who, like his predecessors, will be deposed from power.

Nothing care I for Zeus; yea, less than naught!
Let him do what he will, and sway the world
His little hour; he has not long to lord it
Among the Gods . . .

Ye are young! New come to power! And ye suppose
Your towered citadel Calamity
Can never enter! Ah, and have not I
Seen from those pinnacles a two-fold fall
Of tyrants? And the third, who his brief "now"
Of lordship arrogates, I shall see yet
By lapse most swift, most ignominious,
Sink to perdition. And dost thou suppose
I crouch and cower in reverence and awe
To Gods of yesterday? I fail of that
So much, the total all of space and time
Bulks in between. (p. 50a-b)

So much for the picture of Zeus and of ultimate power. What of the figure who protests against the divine power? What are his characteristics and why does he protest? He protests because he is being persecuted by Zeus after having helped him to gain power. Prometheus and Oceanus were the only Titans who supported Zeus in his revolt against Cronus.

The friend of Zeus, co-stablisher of his rule,
See, by this sentence with what pains I am bowed! (p. 43b)

> I hate all the Gods,
> Because, having received good at my hands,
> They have rewarded me with evil. (p. 50c)

He protests because friendship and co-operation with the gods have brought him only suffering and shame.

But we must stop and ask ourselves why Zeus turned against him. Was it not because of Prometheus' disobedience and deceit in stealing the divine fire from heaven and giving it to men? We learn this at the very beginning of the play.

> For thine own blossom of all forging fire
> He stole and gave to mortals; trespass grave
> For which the Gods have called him to account,
> That he may learn to bear Zeus' tyranny
> And cease to play the lover of mankind. (p. 40a)

Only once does Prometheus admit that he has done wrong and deserves some punishment.

> Of my free will, my own free will, I erred,
> And freely do I here acknowledge it.
> Freeing mankind myself have durance found.
> Natheless, I looked not for sentence so dread. (p. 42d)

Throughout the rest of the play he refuses to admit Zeus's right to punish him. He maintains his attitude of stubborn defiance and seeks to pit his resourcefulness and foresight against the sheer power of the ruler of the gods. More than once he is admonished, both by friends and foes, about his recalcitrance and imprudence. The chorus chants:

> High is the heart of thee,
> Thy will no whit by bitter woes unstrung,
> And all too free
> The licence of thy bold, unshackled tongue. (p. 42a)

And his friend warns him:

> Nevertheless, of a too haughty tongue
> Such punishment, Prometheus, is the wage . . .
>   Keep a quiet mind
> And use not over-vehemence of speech—
> Knowest thou not, being exceeding wise,
> A wanton, idle tongue brings chastisement? (p. 43b-c)

And Zeus's henchman Hermes blames Prometheus' stubbornness and impatience for his fall.

This is that former stubbornness of thine
That brought thee hither to foul anchorage ...
                              Time
Hath not yet taught thy rash, imperious will
Over wild impulse to win mastery ...
                    Patience! patience! thou rash fool!
Have so much patience as to school thy mind
To a right judgment in thy present troubles ...
For stubbornness, if one be in the wrong,
Is in itself weaker than naught at all ...
And do not in thy folly think self-will
Better than prudent counsel. (pp. 50c-51b)

How, then, are we to interpret this play? Are we to take Prometheus as the benevolent enlightener of mankind and the defiant protagonist of spiritual liberty against a divine tyrant? That is what the English poet Shelley does in *Prometheus Unbound.* He has the culture-bringer triumph over the divine despot.

Or is Prometheus a tragic hero of noble character who falls through the defect of self-willed pride? Is he like Milton's Lucifer, a heavenly being who tries to usurp the supreme power, in this case for the good of mankind?

Perhaps none of these interpretations is quite true. In the absence of the remainder of Aeschylus' trilogy, we cannot tell how Aeschylus resolved the conflict between Prometheus and Zeus. Our safest guess may be that Aeschylus reveals here only one aspect of the man-God relation, the aspect of God as Enemy. We know from the ending of the *Eumenides* that Aeschylus had a fuller and loftier view of divine power.

IV

Before we ask some further questions about this play, let us turn briefly to a comparison of *Prometheus Bound* with the Book of Job, which was discussed in the *General Introduction.*

The Book of Job deals with the problem of the suffering of the righteous and the prosperity of the wicked in a world ruled by a God of righteousness. Job is a man of perfect faith and piety who suffers the worst kind of calamities. They have been visited upon him by God as a test of faith. Job maintains his faith in a righteous God, but he cries out his bewilderment at his fate, which seems to contradict his belief. He stoutly maintains his innocence under the vexing admonitions of tradition-minded friends, who are sure he must have sinned since he suffers so.

Job disputes with God. He wants to know why he, a friend of God, is treated like an enemy. He acknowledges the omnipotence—the sheer, overpowering might—of God. But he questions the justice of the divine acts. Why do the innocent suffer and the wicked prosper? He rejects the traditional notion of suffering as the retribution for sin. Do not natural calamities, like the rain from heaven, fall on good and bad alike? Do not the wicked prosper? A merely omnipotent God of absolute power, who acts unjustly and does not distinguish between the righteous and the wicked, would not be God for Job. Such a God would be like the Zeus of *Prometheus Bound*, with his two henchmen Power and Force. Job faces an agonizing religious problem—that his experience seems to belie his faith.

The answer of the Book of Job to the question about the suffering of the righteous is that the ways of God are inscrutable, in the ethical as in the physical sphere. We must accept such suffering in faithful trust as trials sent by God to "test" our faith and lead us ultimately to holiness and joy. The book ends in a burst of divine glory, as God enters the scene in person to answer Job. God reminds Job of his human limitations—of his unworthiness as compared with God's majesty and holiness—and Job accepts his lot in a spirit of trust and humility.

In the end, all that Job has lost, and more, is restored to him. He has triumphed in the trial of faith; and Satan, who demanded this contest, is discomfited.

There is one basic similarity between Prometheus and Job. Both stand up and doggedly maintain their case against overwhelming divine power. Both question the sufferings they are forced to undergo. But each stands in a different relation to the divine ruler. Each expresses a different attitude toward his lot.

The magnificent resistance of Prometheus is a matter of Titanic will and pride. Zeus is the Enemy, and nothing but Enemy. Prometheus complains about the injustice of his punishment, but he does not expect justice from Zeus. On the other hand, Job's resistance is that of a man of faith, for whom God is the Friend, and wholly Friend. God is perfect righteousness. Why, then, should a man who walks in the path of justice and holiness suffer so? Job's suffering is a contradiction for him. He knows that he is innocent, and we know that suffering is God's way of testing him. Prometheus knows, and we know, that there is some justification for his punishment.

In the end Job accepts: "I abhor myself, and repent in dust and ashes." (Job 42:6) Prometheus, in the fragment we have, goes down into the abyss, cursing his divine persecutor. Job is rewarded with earthly happiness, and Prometheus is punished with endless torment. (Note that Aeschylus probably ended his trilogy with a reconciliation between Zeus and Prometheus.)

The Prometheans among us (or the Promethean in each of us) may applaud the Titan's intransigence. The Jobians among us (or the Jobian in each of us) may venerate the pious man's humility and acceptance. Which attitude would you advocate for the righteous man who suffers?

V

Is it right or wrong to rebel against divine power?

Traditionalists (like Job's friends) believe it is always wrong to question the divine decrees, while Prometheans believe one must resist them unceasingly. Is either of these views satisfactory? Would an unquestioning attitude reduce us to a subhuman state, like atoms and stones? Would a rebellious attitude lead inevitably to a centerless nihilism? The orthodox religious view is that man achieves fulfillment in affirming and carrying out the divine commands. But what about the case of Prometheus? Was it wrong for him to defy Zeus in order to benefit man? Of course, there is always the question of just *who* and *what* God is, and *which* are his decrees.

Perhaps the Public Press are merely saying to the traditional-ists: "These things are not from God, and we shall resist them. What you call God is a devil or an idol of your own imagina-tion." What about the Zeus of this play? Is he truly God? What of the God of Job?

What is the religious evaluation of man's acquisition of the arts and sciences?

From Prometheus' eloquent description of his benefactions (see pp. 44c-45a), which include the gift of spiritual insight as well as technical powers, it is plain that the arts and sci- ences are regarded as something very wonderful; indeed, of divine origin. The gods regard men—"the creatures of a passing day"—as unworthy to receive such heavenly gifts. Yet the gifts bestowed by Prometheus do not give men the strength to oppose the gods and aid their benefactor. Prometheus complains that Art is much weaker than Necessity, since man, with all his new-found inventions, cannot devise a single one to save the beneficent Titan.

Does this complaint of Prometheus indicate a view that human culture has limited power? As against what? Natural necessity? The divine power over things? After first showing how man is lifted above the brutes by the possession of the arts and sciences, does Aeschylus leave us with an impression of the puniness of human powers?

Let us turn to the Book of Genesis for a comparison with Aeschylus' drama. You remember the story of Adam and Eve eating the fruit of the tree of knowledge of good and evil and being driven out of Eden lest they attain eternal life. God complains that already "man is become as one of us." He sends man out into the world to till the soil.

What attitude toward knowledge and the useful arts is implied in this story? Is there a higher knowledge that befits only the divine? Does man become like God through attain- ing such knowledge? Are agriculture and other arts fit only for a state of sin and separation from God? Or are they divinely ordained to help man make his way on earth?

How do you interpret the story of the Tower of Babel in

Genesis 11? Does it show divine jealously of human creativity, or merely righteous punishment for blasphemous pride? Some modern theologians take Babel to be the symbol for man's attempt to create a culture that is independent of God. Is there any justification for this interpretation?

How would you compare the attitude implied in Aeschylus with that expressed in the Bible stories: (1) As regards the power of men to become like God, or the gods, through knowledge and culture? (2) As regards the attitude of God, or the gods, toward man's attaining knowledge and culture?

Is there a nonrational, nonethical element in the divine?

Is there some depth in the divine nature and power which is not measurable in terms of human reason and human ethics? Both Prometheus and Job convey the sense of a divine omnipotence beyond good and evil, as humans measure it. Prometheus is powerless and without justification before "the implacable, eternal Will" of Zeus or the "unconquerable might of strong Necessity." In the Book of Job, both the regularities of nature and the mysteries of creation are summoned up to evoke awe and submission from a mere man who confronts God with questions of right and wrong? Must we desist from such questioning when we meet with certain aspects of existence that seem to contradict the divine reality? Or would shutting off such questions subvert man's ethical nature?

Let us suppose that there is an apparent conflict or disharmony between divine justice and human justice. In such a situation, should a man give up all claim to righteousness and bow down before what seem to be the divine decrees? Or should he shake his fist at heaven and maintain an absolute defiance of the divine will? Or should he maintain his own integrity and righteousness, while accepting the transcendent righteousness that seems to contradict it? What do *Prometheus Bound* and the Book of Job have to say about these alternatives?

The following questions are designed to help you test the thoroughness of your reading. Each question is to be answered by giving a page or pages of the reading assignment. Answers will be found on page 269 of this Reading Plan.

1 Why must Prometheus be bound so securely?

2 What did Zeus intend to do to mankind?

3 What arts and sciences did Prometheus bestow on man?

4 How does Io's father find out what is in store for her?

5 What bodies of water are named after Io?

6 What will a god have to do to release Prometheus?

PLATO

Euthyphro and *Laws*

Book X

Vol. 7, pp. 191-199, 757-771

The relation between the good and the holy, between the ethical and the religious, has perplexed men for thousands of years. Is holiness or piety a matter mainly of ceremonial correctness and ritual purity, or is it above all a righteous life? Does the ultimate power over things care what men do or do not do on this earth? Why do the wicked prosper if there is a righteous divinity overseeing all things?

Plato takes up these and other questions in the *Euthyphro* and in the famous Book X of *Laws*. In the *Euthyphro*, he pits a cocksure and literal ceremonialist against the astute ethical philosopher Socrates. They discuss the question, "What is piety?" The dialogue delights and instructs us as it shows the inconsistencies that may underlie a rigidly ceremonialist attitude. In the *Laws*, Plato raises major theological problems about God's existence, providence, and the divine response to sacrifices and prayers.

17

Plato raises one more disturbing problem: Shall the state decree right religious belief and punish disbelief? Plato takes the affirmative position on this question. That is why this book has shocked many generations of philosophers. But Plato's view, shocking or not, raises the issue of religious liberty for our consideration.

Second Reading

Our first selection is the *Euthyphro*. It is usually associated with the *Apology* and *Crito*, which make up the First Reading in *A General Introduction to the Great Books and to a Liberal Education*. These are all short dialogues connected with Socrates' trial and condemnation for allegedly teaching impious doctrines to the youth of Athens. They belong to a group of dialogues called "Socratic" because they deal mainly with Socrates' teachings rather than with Plato's own doctrines. The Socratic dialogues try to show what Socrates was like as a person and what he really thought. (For a discussion of the style and content of these dialogues, see the *General Introduction*.)

The *Euthyphro* deals with the question of piety or holiness —man's relation to the divine. It is the only one of Plato's dialogues that is devoted completely to religion. Many readers find the piece unsatisfactory because it explores the issues without coming to any definite conclusions. However, this is characteristic of the Socratic dialogues. Plato does this on purpose, to raise the questions and leave them open rather than set up hard and fast answers.

We may get a better notion of what Plato is doing here if we note how he stages the dialogue. The scene is the porch of the King Archon, one of the nine archons, or chief magistrates, of Athens. The King Archon was in charge of religious affairs. Socrates has to appear before him for preliminary hearings on the charge of impiety. "And now I have to go to the porch of the King Archon, where I am to meet Meletus and his indictment," Socrates says at the end of the *Theaetetus*. (See Vol. 7, p. 550c; for the details of the indictment, see the

First Reading in the *General Introduction*.) Euthyphro, the other character in the dialogue, has come to the King Archon's porch to bring a charge of murder against his father. This is the situation chosen by Plato for the discussion of piety.

It seems odd that a charge of murder should be brought before the official in charge of religious affairs. But in Athens at that time murder was a crime against the state only if it involved religious pollution. Otherwise it was a private matter, a wrong only to the family or master of the slain person. Socrates says to Euthyphro:

I suppose that the man whom your father murdered was one of your relatives—clearly he was; for if he had been a stranger you would never have thought of prosecuting him. (p. 192b)

Euthyphro makes it clear that he has taken this unusual step to clear himself of the implication that he is involved in "pollution." This corporate sense of guilt and stain is prevalent in ancient and primitive cultures. Sin is a communal as well as a personal matter. In Biblical terms, the slain man's blood cries out from the ground.

In this case, a field laborer on the estate of Euthyphro's father has died of neglect while being held for the murder of a domestic servant. Euthyphro takes the matter literally; a man is responsible for the laborer's death; hence, he, Euthyphro, must prosecute that man even if it be his father. The greater piety and ritual correctness ordained by the gods must override the claims of filial piety, of honoring father and mother. Euthyphro claims to be an expert on divine things as well as a prophet. Socrates calls him, perhaps ironically, a "soothsayer" and a "theologian."

The stage is set for the discussion of piety. The parties are a philosopher charged with impiety and a theologian charging impiety. Plato does not let the irony escape us. He has Socrates say, in effect: "If I'm a subversive blasphemer, and you're a sacred theologian, I'd sure like to know what piety is." (See p. 192d.)

II

Socrates' main effort in the discussion is to arrive at a general concept of piety, to be used as a measure or a standard of what is essentially pious in all cases of piety. Euthyphro suggests as his first real definition:

Piety, then, is that which is dear to the gods, and impiety is that which is not dear to them. (p. 193d)

With Socrates' amendment that this should read, "dear to *all* the gods," this definition becomes the starting point for one of the major questions of the dialogue. Socrates says:

The point which I should first wish to understand is whether the pious or holy is beloved by the gods because it is holy, or holy because it is beloved of the gods. (p. 195b-c)

Socrates' point is that we do not explain *what the holy is* by saying that it is *what is loved* by the gods. We still have not found out what the *essence* or *nature* of the holy is, even if we agree that it is loved by the gods. *What* is it that they love? *Why* do they love it? Being loved by the gods is an "attribute" of the "substance" of holiness.

From here on, Socrates comes closer to the point. If piety is right action or duty to the gods, it must be an aspect or part of right action generally, that is, of justice. "What part of justice is piety?" he asks Euthyphro. The latter then advances a second definition of piety:

Piety or holiness, Socrates, appears to me to be that part of justice which attends to the gods, as there is the other part of justice which attends to men. (p. 197a)

What kind of service can man render to the gods? What noble end or purpose does piety serve, as medicine serves the end of health? Euthyphro is unable to think of a single purpose (he says it is much too complicated to explain) and falls into a third definition:

. . . piety or holiness is learning how to please the gods in word and deed, by prayers and sacrifices. (p. 198a)

Socrates interprets this to mean that piety is a practical art, or science of prayer and sacrifice: asking the gods for things and giving them things. Thus it is a kind of barter or exchange— tit for tat. But this trade must be one-sided, for the gods have all good things to give to men while men have nothing to give to the gods. Euthyphro falls back again on his previous definition that piety is what is pleasing to the gods. He cuts the discussion short and runs off on some pretext to avoid his importunate questioner, leaving the question unresolved.

III

Our second passage from Plato is from one of his later writings, the *Laws*. This dialogue is concerned with the political, social, and religious institutions that could be established in a state of Plato's time, rather than with the ideal community portrayed in *The Republic*. The chief person of the dialogue is an unnamed Athenian, with scientific, philosophic, and political experience somewhat like Plato's. The other two characters are a Spartan named Megillus and a Cretan named Cleinias. Book X deals with religion and theology. It is the only systematic presentation of Plato's views on religion.

The striking thing about these views for modern readers is that they are to be decreed and enforced as right belief by the state. Obdurate refusal is to be punished by imprisonment or death. Plato's reason seems to be that intentional immorality or unlawfulness results from religious disbelief or impiety (see p. 758a). But even an unbeliever who leads a righteous life is to be punished by imprisonment for a first offense and by death for a second offense (see p. 770a-c). That such views should come from a man who started his philosophical career by defending his teacher Socrates, who was put to death by the state for impiety, has shocked and puzzled many students of philosophy. Did Plato change his views as he grew older, or did he earlier oppose putting a pious man to death on false charges while not questioning the right of the state to punish impiety?

The shock caused by Plato's punitive proposals has often prevented a careful consideration of the religious views presented in the *Laws*. Let us concentrate here on the content of Plato's religious philosophy. We shall not examine the detailed steps of the Athenian's argument, but just try to understand Plato's views. Actually Book X of the *Laws* is a monologue, and the dialogue form is a mere literary device.

The Athenian argues against three irreligious positions: (1) that God does not exist; (2) that if he does, he does not care for man; and (3) that he may be swayed by sacrifice and prayer. Let us take these up in order.

1. *God's Existence.* Plato's attack here is directed against: (a) the materialists, who make the physical prior to the mental and see all things as caused by nature or by chance; and (b) the Sophists, who say that religion and morality are human inventions having no basis in the order of things (see p. 760a-c). As against both of these sources of atheism, the Athenian argues that mind and purpose rule the physical and human order.

[the soul] is among the first of things, and before all bodies, and is the chief author of their changes and transpositions . . . Then thought and attention and mind and art and law will be prior to that which is hard and soft and heavy and light. (p. 761c-d)

The Athenian attempts to demonstrate this priority of the mental over the physical by examining various types of causes and by distinguishing between the type of cause that moves other things and the type that both moves itself and initiates all other movements. This second type of mover we call the "soul" or "animating principle." (Look in your dictionary for the origin of the word "animate.") We ascribe the first type of movement, which can move other things—*but only after it has been started by something else*—to inanimate bodies, to the merely physical.

Then characters and manners, and wishes and reasonings, and true opinions, and reflections, and recollections are prior to length and breadth and depth and strength of bodies, if the soul is prior to the body . . . the soul is the cause of good and evil, base and honourable, just and unjust, and of all other opposites . . . the soul orders and inhabits all things that move . . . (p. 764a-b)

Thus soul, or mind, is the source or cause of both the ethical order and the physical order. What about evil, negative and ugly emotions and physical irregularities, which Plato equates with evil (the regular and harmonious being good)?

Is soul or mind responsible for these, too? Yes, says Plato: an evil type of soul. There are at least two souls, "one the author of good, and the other of evil." The good world soul controls the whole universe and guides it on the good path. It is responsible for the movement of the heavenly bodies and other regular movements.

. . . those souls are Gods, whether they are living beings and reside in bodies, and in this way order the whole heaven, or whatever be the place and mode of their existence;—and will any one who admits all this venture to deny that all things are full of Gods? (p. 765c)

You will note that Plato calls the good souls gods, but does not give a name to the evil souls. Does he have some notion of diabolical forces, devils, or demons?

2. *God's Providence.* Plato raises here a question astonishingly similar to the one raised in the Book of Job: "Why do the evil prosper?" (See the Seventh Reading in the *General Introduction.*) This question is asked by pious men who believe that there are gods and feel an affinity with them, but who are caused by experience to believe that the gods "take no heed of human affairs" (p. 765d).

If we grant that the world must be ruled by a good and wise soul or principle, which knows all things and can do all things, then the prosperity of the wicked evokes the thought that perhaps human affairs are too trivial for the gods to bother with. But this would be to accuse the gods of the unholy sins of carelessness and indolence, says the Athenian. The best physicians and artists are scrupulously careful about the minutest details. And is not man especially dear to the gods, since he is "the most religious of all animals," and since "all mortal creatures are the property of the Gods"? (p. 767a) The gods do care and they arrange all things for the good of the whole. "The ruler of the universe" handles each part of the whole through "ministers" (agents or principles serving the divine power and purpose), so that good wins out and evil is defeated.

Do not be misled by appearances in this life, warns the Athenian. The individual has free will; his soul has the power to choose a course of life that will either bring him into communion with the gods or condemn him to Hades. No one can escape divine justice. Do not take account only of what happens in this life. There may be an endless succession of lives, and the soul, good or bad, ends up where it belongs. Do not try to judge the ways of the divine ruler of the universe, who has all things in mind and brings all things to work for the good of the whole (see pp. 767c-768c).

3. *Propitiation: Sacrifice and Prayer.* Plato deals here with a familiar religious problem: Can a man do evil and avert divine wrath through ritual actions, such as sacrifice, adoration, and prayer? Plato rejects this indignantly. He likens good men to a flock, the gods to shepherds, and the evil men to wolves. What kind of shepherds would accept part of the loot torn away by the wolves—"libations of wine and the savour of fat"? Even sheep dogs are not that vile. How can we attribute such corruption to the gods! Be assured that our divine guardians will not betray us, nor will the sly flatterers succeed. Injustice and evil will ultimately be punished (see pp. 768a-769c).

The rest of the dialogue deals with the various penalties to be meted out to those who refuse to accept these three basic points of doctrine. Plato reserves his most intense ire for the profiteering leaders of private cults or mysteries—those who indulge in prophecies, witchcraft, necromancy, and similar practices. He also shows special opposition to private or family worship. The laws should forbid family shrines, says Plato, and command that rites be performed only in public temples.

IV

Should filial piety outweigh all other religious and ethical considerations?

The *Euthyphro* begins with a concrete ethical situation and always returns to it. Socrates never lets Euthyphro escape the imputation that charging his father with murder is an immoral or impious act. Socrates' point is that filial impiety is worse than ceremonial impurity, for piety is not a materialistic matter of the correct practice of ritual acts. But why this emphasis on filial piety? Is Socrates, too, being a formalist? Why is the precept, "Honor thy father and mother," so important that it is placed in the Ten Commandments? What about the laborer who died of neglect? Socrates does not seem to worry about him. It is implied that he was himself a sottish murderer and so did not deserve much consideration. Is Socrates' attitude unfeeling, lacking in compassion, irreligious? Is it immoral and irreligious for a son to testify against his father in a murder case?

What kind of service should men render the gods?

Euthyphro evaded this question and Socrates, keeping to his role as questioner, let it slide by unanswered. But note that Socrates managed to slip in the idea of justice, as the larger concept of which piety is a part. In *The Republic,* Plato makes justice the supreme virtue. In the *Apology,* Socrates says that he serves God by becoming perfect in mind and virtue and by helping other men to become perfect. In the *Theaetetus,* he sets the imitation of God, becoming like God, as the end of human life:

> Wherefore we ought to fly away from earth to heaven as quickly as we can; and to fly away is to become like God, as far as this is possible; and to become like him, is to become holy, just, and wise. . . . God is never in any way unrighteous—he is perfect righteousness; and he of us who is the most righteous is most like him. (p. 530c)

Is this the service of God hinted at by Socrates—holiness, justice, wisdom, righteousness?

Are the mental aspects of reality primary, rather than the physical?

Plato, in the *Laws,* considers these aspects primary: "will, consideration, attention, deliberation, opinion true and false, joy and sorrow, confidence, fear, hatred, love, and other primary motions akin to these" (p. 764b). The modern tendency, fostered by the natural sciences and some schools of philosophy, is to view physical properties and forces—especially those that can be weighed and measured—as primary, and to view mental qualities as derivative or comparatively unreal. Is it plausible that will and wish and purpose may produce the physical world? Or is such a view a naïve form of animism? The primacy of the mental is stressed in all types of religions: primitive and civilized, Eastern and Western, ancient and modern. Is such a viewpoint consonant with modern scientific method and knowledge? But does science, including psychology, have anything to say about whether the mental or physical aspect of reality is primary? Where should we turn for an answer, or at least a proper statement of the question?

Is the world ruled by a supreme will?

Plato thinks that things occur according to some basic will and purpose which work for order and right, and that they do not occur purely by chance. According to the opposite view, things have come about through chance combinations, first of inanimate, then of animate material. To this, thinkers like Plato say that the world would then be without an ultimate meaning or purpose. But why must the world have an ultimate meaning and purpose? Can we not lead pleasant and useful lives without acknowledging a *basic, ultimate* meaning in things? Those who agree with Plato say that human reason and morality would then not have any cosmic source or ground. But why is this necessary? Why can man not be satisfied with the reason and good he discovers or constructs for himself? Must he ask the question of how reason and morality are possible in a universe ruled by chance or natural necessity? Is man creating a divine spirit to fit his own needs, as the Sophists suggests, or is he created and governed by it?

Does God care about human affairs?

"Why do the wicked prosper, and the innocent suffer?"—note that Plato does not mention the latter—is a question that can become acute only for those who believe in a God of righteousness. Plato assumes that "the divine ruler of the universe" is absolutely righteous, just as Abraham says, "Shall not the Judge of all the earth do right?" (Genesis 18:25) Hence he understands that the prosperity of the wicked makes divine providence questionable.

What are the possible answers to the man who in the face of the actual facts of worldly experience, doubts the watchful care of God or the gods over human affairs? Plato suggests one answer: that things are evened out in an afterlife—actually, a series of afterlives. This idea of retribution or recompense for the deeds of this life in a series of future existences pervaded the ancient world and formed the basis of whole religious systems.

Can you think of any other answers? You may recall that Socrates says in another of Plato's dialogues that the good man cannot come to harm either in this life or the next. Does this mean that prosperity or failure in the worldly sense are not important, not essential? Is good, then, its own reward; and evil, its own punishment? Do you agree with Socrates that it is worse to do harm to others than to have harm done to you?

This takes care of the individual sinner or good man. But what of the whole world order, and especially of its human sector? Does God watch over the world, bringing all things to good fruition? How, then, can we explain the fact of evil and the triumphs of the wicked? What is the ultimate effect of the evil that men do or suffer? Can the divine ruler of the universe transform evil into good and make it serve the final good that is the goal of all things?

Do sacrifice and prayer have any ethical and religious value?

In both the *Euthyphro* and the *Laws*, ritual acts are attacked from an ethical viewpoint. In the *Euthyphro*, Socrates holds up to scorn a rigid ritualist who is more interested in performing ceremonial acts according to protocol than in seeing that justice is done. In the *Laws*, the Athenian attacks the use of sacrifice and prayer by evildoers to escape just punishment, and he also attacks the mystery cults with their communion rites and ritual purifications.

Are ritual and prayer of any use, or are they mere wasted motion? Do they accomplish anything? Can human acts and words affect the divine will? Do they have any moral influence on human character?

Most religions assume that ritual establishes an actual relation with the divine and that ceremonial observance has a moral value. Protest movements arise within religions to condemn ritual observance when it becomes mere externality, uninspired by holy intention and righteousness of life. Sometimes the protest is a rejection of all formal ritual as an impediment to the direct relation between man and God. Sometimes the protest is a criticism of the moral iniquity and religious corruption that may accompany a ritual that is nevertheless regarded as holy and proper. The place of ritual in religion varies with the basic idea of God and of man's relation to God. It varies within different forms of the same religion, from being the very life of faith to having little or no role at all.

Which Christian denominations or churches make sacraments central and which do not? What is the relation of the attitude on sacraments to the basic belief in each case? Is there anything in human nature that would account for the existence of sacraments in religion?

What about prayer? Plato, in these dialogues, sees it merely as a petition for material gifts or as an attempt to avoid righteous judgment. But is this all there is to prayer? Is prayer a selfish attempt to get something material from the divine power or is it a spiritual effort to commune with the divine?

What about sacrifice, whether actual or symbolic? Socrates says that sacrifice can only be an empty gesture, for God gives everything to man and man can give nothing to God, since God is absolutely perfect. Is there a real mutuality between God and man, or is the relation between God and man a one-sided affair? Does God need man's offerings? What does man have to offer God?

Plato apparently assumes that there is no moral value in religious observances. Does the conscientious observance of ritual requirements, dietary laws, fasting, etc., work as a discipline to form character, as well as perform a service to God? Proponents of observances point out that they help men to restrain their natural appetites and to submit their lives to a regular order and rhythm. Opponents of observances claim that such discipline may result in an obsessive attention to details, inflexible rigidity of action, and a terrible anxiety about deviating from a fixed pattern. They also assert that it makes a mechanical routine out of what should be spiritual spontaneity.

What do you think? Do traditional observances and inner sincerity necessarily exclude one another?

The following questions are designed to help you test the thoroughness of your reading. Each question is to be answered by giving a page or pages of the reading assignment. Answers will be found on page 269 of this Reading Plan.

1 How does Euthyphro justify his action by the tales of the gods?

2 What relation does Socrates see between fear and reverence?

3 Why does Cleinias accept the existence of the gods?

4 What are the three possible relations between the world soul and the physical world?

5 What is the punishment for a first offense by an unbeliever of good moral character?

6 Why does "the Athenian" want to forbid private shrines?

OLD TESTAMENT

Book of Genesis

12:1-9; 13:14-18; 15; 17; 18:17-33; 22:1-19

Book of Exodus

3-4; 6:1-8; 14-15; 19-20; 24

The world of the Bible is ever near and ever strange to us.

A group of wandering tribes, comparatively uncivilized, creates the foundations of the religious faith of the Western world. Their racial memories and their sagas go back to a patriarchal ancestor who comes out of Mesopotamia, leaving all worldly security behind him, and travels toward a land that God has promised him and his seed. This amazing patriarch is holy man, warrior, family head, and crafty bargainer, all in one.

The Bible tells, too, of the founder of a people and a religion who is a man of violent rages and self-doubts and, at the same time, the chosen spokesman of the Lord, the human vessel of divine revelation and redemption. Yet this human, all too human, figure— this reluctant aide of God—is the supreme model of

Old Testament faith and the greatest of the prophets. And the people themselves, also chosen as a vehicle of divine action in the world, struggle in a constant tension between faith and unfaith, between loyalty and backsliding, between trust and doubt.

The Bible deals with the whole of human life as imbued with religion: mating and begetting, war and work, historical events and communal acts. In the Bible, domestic, ethical, and political activity—as well as religious worship—express and embody the service and imitation of God. These early books of the Old Testament help us to realize the full scope of the religious life.

Third Reading

I

The Old Testament is the Christian name for the Jewish sacred scriptures. It constitutes the complete Jewish Bible and the first part of the Christian Bible. The early Christian Church distinguished between the old covenant, or testament, made through Moses, and the new covenant, or testament, made through Christ. Hence came the names Old Testament, for the ancient scriptures, and New Testament, for the Gospels and other Christian scriptures.

The original Old Testament, written almost entirely in Hebrew, consisted of thirty-nine books, divided into *Torah* ("Law" or "Teaching"), *Prophets,* and *Writings. Torah* consists of the five books of Moses, usually called the Pentateuch (Genesis, Exodus, Leviticus, Numbers, and Deuteronomy). *Prophets* includes the books of Joshua, Judges, I and II Samuel, I and II Kings, Isaiah, Jeremiah, Ezekiel, and the Twelve Minor Prophets. *Writings* comprises Psalms, Proverbs, Job, Ecclesiastes, and the remaining books of the Old Testament.

Other books were included in the Greek translation but were not recognized as sacred scriptures in the official Hebrew text. These writings were accepted as sacred by the early Christian Church. Protestant Bibles follow the Hebrew canon and do not include this section, which comprises fourteen writings, including I and II Esdras, I and II Maccabees, Wisdom of Solomon (Book of Wisdom), and other works. Protestants call these works "apocryphal," or spurious; Roman Catholics consider them as "deuterocanonical" (a secondary canon) and include them in the Bible.

In the present reading we are going to consider selected passages from the Five Books of Moses. These books contain the basic elements of Old Testament faith and are referred to by later Biblical writers. For the most part, we will not concern ourselves with scholarly or historical questions about these texts. We will take them as they have come down to us, seeking in them the special Old Testament version of the relation between God and man.

To that end, we have chosen key passages from the books of Genesis and Exodus; they center on the ancient saga of Abraham, the "father of the faithful," and on the narrative of Moses, the "spokesman of the Lord" and the founder of Israel. The traditional date for Abraham's career is the 20th century B.C. Scholars place the exploits of Moses in the 13th century B.C. Thus the Biblical narratives go back to an era long before that recorded, or even known, by the Greek historians. It was the era of the great empires in Egypt and Mesopotamia, and of forgotten peoples, such as the Hittites and the Chaldeans.

II

Our first text, Genesis 12:1-9, deals with the mission of Abraham. The Bible calls Abraham the father of the faithful (see Romans 4:11-12; Galatians 3:7), and the friend of God (see Isaiah 41:8; II Chronicles 20:7, [D] II Paralipomenon 20:7; James 2:23). If we go back a few verses, to Genesis 11:27-32, we learn that Abraham (originally called Abram) came from Ur of the Chaldees in ancient Babylonia, stopping at Haran on his way west to Canaan. Ur and Haran were important towns politically and commercially, as well as centers of the moon-god cult.

Chapter 12 begins suddenly with the call and promise of God to Abram:

Get thee out of thy country, and from thy kindred, and from thy father's house, unto a land that I will shew thee: And I will make of thee a great nation, and I will bless thee, and make thy name great; and thou shalt be a blessing. (12: 1-2)

Abram does not hesitate. He heeds the divine voice and sets out on his quest, abandoning all worldly security and ties. He is sustained during his sojournings only by the divine call and promise. When he arrives in Canaan, God promises the land

to Abram and to his seed. Abram celebrates this event by setting up an altar to the Lord.

The promise made in Chapter 12 and repeated in 13:14-18,
becomes in Chapters 15 and 17, a formal *covenant,* or partner-
ship, between man and God. This notion is one of the unique
contributions of Biblical faith. Man and God enter into a personal relationship or agreement, sealed with a solemn pledge
on both sides. In 15:9-10 and in Chapter 17, the ancient Semitic rite of cutting an animal in half and having the two
covenanting parties pass between the pieces to be united by
blood, is applied symbolically to the covenant between God
and Abram. The childless Abram, without apparent chance for
direct heirs, trusts utterly and wholly in God and His promise.
God ascribes Abram's faith to his righteousness (see 15:1-6).

In Chapter 17 appears the sacramental token of the covenant: *circumcision.* This ritual act is not original with the Hebrews, but they endowed it with a special meaning. The
spiritual covenant with God is concretely expressed in the
external sign of circumcision. Among religious Jews, this ritual
act still goes by the name of Covenant (*Berith*). They have
adhered to it so loyally that they have endured martyrdom
rather than abandon it (see I Maccabees 1:63-64).

Notice, in Genesis 17:5, the change of Abram's name to
Abraham, the "father of many nations." The Old Testament
frequently reads a religious meaning into names of places and
persons, whether etymologically justified or not. The name
takes on a peculiar significance in the religious community and
tradition.

Chapter 18:17-33 furnishes an astonishing interlude in this
saga of Abraham, the hero of righteousness. An ordinary man
of flesh and blood—mere "dust and ashes"—stands up to God
and argues with Him for mercy to the wicked city of Sodom.
This is an extraordinary thing in the light of Abraham's belief
in an almighty God and the prevailing social context of tribal-
ism and clannishness. Abraham pleads not for his own clan, but
for the alien and corrupt folk of Sodom. He argues from the
viewpoint of strict justice that the righteous must not be punished for the sins of the wicked. He shrewdly bargains with

"the Judge of all the earth," demanding that He "do right" (18:25), and driving down the price of Sodom's deliverance from fifty to ten righteous men. (Perhaps he would have driven the price down to one righteous man if the Lord had not concluded the palaver.) Notice that Abraham argues that the whole city be saved for the sake of the few righteous (see 18:24). He wants to save human beings from destruction. His motivation is mercy, and he ascribes that quality, as well as justice, to God.

Our texts on this extraordinary figure conclude with the famous passage dealing with the sacrifice of Isaac (see 22:1-19). This story has long furnished rich material for religious interpretation. The sacrifice of Isaac is the supreme test, or trial, of Abraham's faith. The traditional rendering of verse 1 (that God "tempts" Abraham) is archaic and misleading. The verse is more accurately rendered: "And it came to pass after these things, that God did *prove* [or *test*] Abraham." The proof of Abraham's trust is his willingness to sacrifice his son, the miraculous offspring of his old age and the one chosen to carry on his inheritance ("thy son, thine only son Isaac, whom thou lovest").

What takes place is conveyed to us through a sparing but effective use of words and details. Abraham shows complete and prompt obedience. He is up early in the morning making the necessary preparations. He and his son and his helpers ride to the place to which God directs him. Abraham goes up the mountain with his son, the former carrying the fire and knife, the latter the wood. When Isaac asks where the sacrificial lamb is, Abraham answers that God will provide the lamb. Arrived at the spot, Abraham binds Isaac, lays him on the altar, and prepares to slay him. His hand is held back by a voice from heaven, forbidding him to harm his son and praising his faith.

Lay not thine hand upon the lad, neither do thou any thing unto him: for now I know that thou fearest God, seeing thou hast not withheld thy son, thine only *son* from me. (22:12)

Abraham substitutes a ram, providentially caught in a thicket. The voice from heaven promises him fulfillment of the promise and the covenant. Man's steadfastness is confirmed by God's.

III

Our second set of texts opens with the call of Moses in Chapter 3 of the Book of Exodus. If you will refer to Chapter 2, you will find an account of Moses' background, his violent reaction against Egyptian oppression, and his flight to Midian. The closing verses (2:23-25) give us the prelude to Moses' call. They tell us that God is aware of the suffering of Israel and that He remembers His covenant with His people. The implication is that somehow He will act to redeem them.

As Chapter 3 opens, Moses—cut off from his people—is tending the flock of his father-in-law, a Midianite priest, when suddenly the divine will and call are revealed to him. In the Biblical account of this experience, God speaks to Moses not directly, but through an angel (literally, a "messenger") and a burning bush—apparently a thornbush, a common and lowly plant. The bush burns with a fire that does not consume it. Moses hears the announcement of the divine presence and covers his face in dreadful awe.

God identifies Himself as both the God of the ancient patriarchs and the God of their present-day children—one and the same God. God knows the sufferings of His people and will deliver them through Moses. There follows an extraordinary passage in which Moses voices doubt of his own capacity for such a mission, and then asks just who it is that is speaking to him. God first assures Moses: "I will be with thee." As to His name,

And God said unto Moses, I AM THAT I AM: and he said, Thus shalt thou say unto the children of Israel, I AM hath sent me unto you . . . The LORD God of your fathers, the God of Abraham, the God of Isaac, and the God of Jacob, hath sent me unto you: this *is* my name for ever, and this *is* my memorial unto all generations. (3:14-15)

God here declares Himself as Eternal Being, or Presence, and in this light instructs Moses to inform the elders of Israel of God's revelation and of His support in the coming liberation of Israel from Egypt. Nevertheless, Moses keeps on expressing doubt about the success of his mission.

But, behold, they will not believe me, nor hearken unto my voice: for they will say, The LORD hath not appeared unto thee. (4:1)

Whereupon the Lord endows Moses with all kinds of magical powers, enabling him to perform signs and wonders to make this incredulous folk believe.

Moses is still uncertain. Now it is his inadequate power of speech (perhaps a physical defect) that bothers him. He tries vainly to beg off from the mission in another remarkable passage:

And Moses said unto the LORD, O my Lord, I *am* not eloquent, neither heretofore, nor since thou hast spoken unto thy servant: but I *am* slow of speech, and of a slow tongue. And the LORD said unto him, Who hath made man's mouth? or who maketh the dumb, or deaf, or the seeing, or the blind? have not I the LORD? Now therefore go, and I will be with thy mouth, and teach thee what thou shalt say. And he said, O my Lord, send, I pray thee, by the hand *of him whom* thou wilt send. And the anger of the LORD was kindled against Moses. . . . (4:10-14)

He proposes that Moses' brother Aaron, an eloquent man, speak for Moses, as Moses speaks for God. God's message shall come to Israel through Moses and Aaron.

And thou shalt speak unto him, and put words in his mouth: and I will be with thy mouth, and with his mouth, and will teach you what ye shall do. (4:15)

Throughout this dialogue God repeats His initial assurance: "I will be with thee." This assurance is a constant element in Biblical faith.

We learn much about the essential characteristics of the Biblical prophets from this account of Moses' call. It tells of the intimacy between the overwhelming and awful God and a mere man, who, whatever his great capacities, is obviously a weak, finite, and uncertain mortal. These human limitations are characteristic of the great prophets in the Old Testament. They are not superhuman beings, but quite human figures doing the work of the Lord at certain stages in the history of Israel.

Note also the uncertainty and reluctance of Moses in the face of the divine call. Such hesitance is a marked trait of many great Biblical figures. Jeremiah, too, responds to God's call with the protest that he is utterly inadequate. But God's mission and power are upon him, and he must do and say what he is appointed to. God is with him—that is all he needs to know (see Jeremiah 1:4-10; see also Jonah 1-2).

IV

So far we have dealt with two extraordinary moments of personal religious experience. Now, in this saga of the religious pilgrimage of Israel, we come to public events—to the story of a people as the bearer of faith and the witness to the presence of the divine power in actual history.

And I will take you to me for a people, and I will be to you a God: and ye shall know that I *am* the LORD your God, which bringeth you out from under the burdens of the Egyptians. (6:7)

The experience of Moses at the burning bush is not a self-contained spiritual experience. It sends him on a mission to and for a people—the liberation of the Israelites from Egypt. This is the primal event in the history of Israel as a religious community, and it is referred to continually in the Biblical writings, all the way down through the later prophets. It is the "sign," or "wonder," which prepares the way for the Covenant on Mount Sinai, and it is the basis for the observance of the Decalogue and other divine ordinances.

The Biblical narrative describes and celebrates Israel's liberation from bondage as an act of God, done through His presence and power. The God Who revealed Himself in the burning bush is the Redeemer of Israel. The text by no means paints the Israelites as simon-pure believers, however; they are shown as full of doubt and misgiving (see 5:21-23; 14:11-12). The doubt and misgiving continue all the way to Canaan.

All kinds of natural calamities occur in the course of the conflict between Pharaoh, the ruler of Egypt, and Moses, the spokesman of the Lord. Both the Israelites and the Egyptian court, especially Pharaoh, accept the interpretation which Moses gives of them—that they are messages from God saying, "Let my people go." Pharaoh finally agrees to the Exodus.

And he called for Moses and Aaron by night, and said, Rise up, *and* get you forth from among my people, both ye and the children of Israel; and go, serve the LORD, as ye have said. (12:31)

So the children of Israel go forth from Egypt, bearing the bones of their patriarch Joseph and led by visible symbols of the Lord's presence (see 13:17-22).

The Biblical account of Israel's exodus from Egypt comes to a resounding climax with the song celebrating the crossing of the Red Sea. It memorializes not Israel's victory, but God's saving power and deed.

> I will sing unto the LORD, for he hath
>   triumphed gloriously:
>   the horse and his rider hath he
>   thrown into the sea.
> The LORD *is* my strength and song, and
>   he is become my salvation . . .
>
> Thou didst blow with thy wind,
>   the sea covered them:
>   they sank as lead in the mighty
>   waters.
> Who is like unto thee, O LORD, among
>   the gods?
>   who *is* like thee, glorious in
>   holiness,
>   fearful *in* praises, doing wonders?
> Thou stretchedst out thy right hand,
>   the earth swallowed them.
> Thou in thy mercy hast led forth
>   the people *which* thou hast redeemed:
>   thou hast guided *them* in thy strength
>   unto thy holy habitation. (15:1-2; 10-13)

All these events culminate in the Covenant on Mount Sinai. This covenant is a personal bond between God and a whole people, not between God and an individual. The people is appointed to be holy, to be the priest of God. Here, too, we have the primal notion of the Judaeo-Christian religious community—of the holy people, or the Church.

Ye have seen what I did unto the Egyptians, and *how* I bare you on eagles' wings, and brought you unto myself. Now therefore, if ye will obey my voice indeed, and keep my covenant, then ye shall be a peculiar treasure unto me above all people: for all the earth *is* mine: And ye shall be unto me a kingdom of priests, and an holy nation. (19:4-6)

This is repeated in Moses' discourse in Deuteronomy 7:6-11, and in the famous verse 26 in Chapter 20 of Leviticus:

And ye shall be holy unto me: for I the LORD *am* holy, and have severed you from *other* people, that ye should be mine. (Leviticus 20:26)

Here, of course, we have the idea of the *imitation,* as well as of the *service,* of God.

What the people must do to become holy and to fulfill the Covenant is made concrete in the Ten Words, or Commandments (the Decalogue), proclaimed on Mount Sinai. The Decalogue is traditionally divided into two "tables." One contains man's duties toward God; the other, man's duties toward man. The first "word" identifies the source of these precepts:

I *am* the LORD thy God, which have brought thee out of the land of Egypt, out of the house of bondage. (Exodus 20:2)

Notice the person-to-person mode of address ("I," "thy," and "thee") and the reference to the liberation from Egypt.

The second commandment forbids idolatry, either as the worship of false gods or the veneration of images. The third commandment forbids using the name of God frivolously or falsely (note that the name of God—Yahweh—was held holy, and could not even be pronounced except on rare occasions); many people interpret this commandment as an injunction against profanity or perjury. The fourth commandment enjoins the observance of the Sabbath, a unique religious celebration, unconnected with seasonal cycles; it commemorates the creation of the world (and embodies an imitation of the Creator) in a day of rest and peace, separated from the workday week. The fifth commandment enjoins respect for parents. It seems odd to see this precept in the table dedicated to man's duties toward God, but for many ancient peoples filial piety was connected with piety toward God.

The second table consists of five *thou shalt not's:* against murder, adultery, theft, false witness, and covetousness.

The so-called religious and the so-called moral commandments are united in the Decalogue and sanctioned by the God who brought Israel out of Egypt. They are all taken as divine law. The promulgation of the Decalogue constitutes a central event in the making of a people that is both a religious and political community under the supreme leadership of God.

Observe that no ritual acts are enjoined in the Decalogue. But a dramatic ritual event solemnizes the Covenant at Mount Sinai. As narrated in Exodus 24, the people vocally accept the covenant: "All the words which the LORD hath said will we do." (v. 3) Then Moses builds an altar, before which the young men make sacrifices of oxen. Moses takes half of the blood and throws it against the altar; he throws the other half on the people. Thus the two parties to the covenant, the people and God, are united symbolically in "the blood of the covenant." Then Moses and the elders go up on the mountain and eat a sacred sacrificial meal. The elders have a vision of God; and Moses, separated from them, has a vision of the divine glory. What is begun with the deliverance of religious and moral precepts, and sealed by a material sacrament, culminates in a moment of deep religious experience.

V

Here are some questions which the texts raise.

What, exactly, is a covenant, in the Biblical sense?

How can there be a contractual agreement between parties on such different levels as God and man? Is this really a contract in the usual sense? Let us look at a few other covenants in the Bible. In Genesis 9:8-17, God makes a covenant with Noah—representing the human race—and with all living things, promising that they will never be destroyed. In I Samuel ([D] I Kings) 18:3, Jonathan and David make a covenant of brotherhood. In II Samuel ([D] II Kings) 5:3, King David makes a covenant with the elders of Israel. These covenants are all unconditional pledges of loyalty, protection, or service. They are not "contracts" with precise requirements and guarantees. God's Eternal Being or man's whole life is pledged.

The covenant between Jonathan and David is between equals. The other covenants are between a higher party (God or king) and a lower party (man or subjects). The Covenant at Mount Sinai (like that between David and the elders) is a binding relationship with a people, bestowed by the higher power. The higher party rules and guides; the lower serves and obeys.

Are covenants always two-sided? What about the covenant with Noah? Does man promise God anything in this case?

What is the religious meaning of Abraham's willingness to sacrifice Isaac?

There have been two main interpretations of this episode. Some interpreters see it in the light of the sacrifice of first-born sons to the gods, a common practice in the ancient Middle East (see Deuteronomy 12:13). For them, the episode signifies a major ethical advance in religion from human sacrifice to animal sacrifice, and then to spiritual sacrifice—a major step in the progress toward ethical and rational monotheism.

Other interpreters stress the utter obedience and trust of Abraham, his willingness to carry out the transcendent command, although it was in conflict with all human and ethical instincts. Abraham, in this view, obeyed a particular and unique command coming from a realm beyond nature and cutting through all common systems of thought. Abraham's willingness to sacrifice the beloved son of his old age is, then, typical of Biblical faith, which holds that for God all things are possible. Abraham believes that ultimately all will be made right by God. What other "Isaacs" can you think of that a man of faith might have to sacrifice in order to serve God?

Is Old Testament religion essentially personal or communal?

The typical form of address in the Old Testament is "Thou." Even the Decalogue of Mount Sinai, the Law pronounced to the whole people, is put in the second person singular, the intimate form of address to the individual. The call to Abraham and his response are portrayed as deeply personal, and so is Moses' experience at the burning bush. But this is all within the context of a people—a community of faith—extending into the future.

Abraham receives the call and the promise in utter aloneness, but he does so as a trustee for his seed and for all nations. Moses alone undergoes the overwhelming directive experience of the burning bush, but he does so in order to bring a message and leadership to a people. The people are the ultimate recipients of the revelation at Mount Sinai. Spiritual events in their own lives start the later prophets, such as Jeremiah, on their careers, but they act as transmitters of a message from God to the people.

According to the philosopher Alfred North Whitehead, "religion is what the individual does with his own solitariness . . . religion is solitariness." Do you find such "solitariness" in the religion of Abraham and Moses? Do you find the combination of personal and communal elements in Old Testament religion confusing or natural? Does the communal, corporate element fade out at a later, more developed stage of religion, or is authenic religion always both personal and communal?

In your opinion, what religion or denomination most emphasizes the personal element? Which one stresses the communal element most?

What does the name I AM THAT I AM mean?

Names, as we have seen, are very important in the Old Testament. They inform us of the nature and character of the person named. Abraham, for instance, means "father of many nations," and Israel means "one who struggles with God." Obviously, Moses is not seeking merely the proper name of God; strictly speaking, that has already appeared in the text in the term Yahweh, which we translate as "the LORD" (Exodus 3:2, 4, 7). "Who are you?" here means "What are you?" "What is your name?" means "What does your name mean?"

What, then, is the meaning of God's answer to this question? There have been two main interpretations of the text. One holds that God announces Himself as eternal being, the absolute reality that is the source and end of all things: I AM. The other says that God announces His continual and effective presence, His being-*with* Israel. Thus, he is merely repeating in an absolute form the constant reassurance, "I will be with you," that runs through this text.

Read through Chapters 3-4, then reread especially the verses in which God tells his "name" (see 3:13-14). Does either of the interpretations given above make sense to you or help you to understand the passage we are examining? The literal sense of the "name" will not help us here, because the term

I AM is itself the translators' interpretation of a term which elsewhere in the text they translate literally as "I will be." Are the two main interpretations contradictory? Could we interpret the "name" to mean both eternal being and effective presence, both absolute being and constant being-with, both God in Himself and God in relation to His people and His world?

How does the addition THAT I AM (or "that I will be") affect the meaning of the "name"? Does it leave indeterminate just what God is or will do? Or does it intensify God's assurance and determination? Compare this passage with Exodus 33:19, where God says He will show mercy on whom He will show mercy.

There is a discussion of this text in Aquinas' *Summa Theologica*, First Part, Question 13, Article 11 (Vol. 19, pp. 73c-74b). Aquinas adopts the first interpretation (that the name means eternal being). He notes the indeterminateness of the name and its connotation of eternal presence. He renders the name as HE WHO IS. Does the change from the first to the third person affect the meaning of the name?

How can the God of one people be the God of the whole world?

Put in others words, this question asks whether the idea of a special revelation of the Eternal Being to a particular people at a particular place and time is not offensive to reason—especially when the claim is made that this revelation discloses God's nature, will, and purpose for all men at all times and places. How can universal truth be transmitted in one historical event or series of events?

The particular covenants with Abraham and Israel are proclaimed as a legacy and rule for all the families and nations of the earth. All mankind is to share in Abraham's blessing, and the Law is to go forth from Zion to all the peoples. The later prophets are sure that the God of Israel is the God of all nations and that His judgment and mercy fall on all alike.

Those who find this notion of special revelation a "scandal," that is, an offense, believe that ultimate truths are available generally to the human race, or to gifted individuals, through natural reason or a general revelation. Of course, it may be questioned whether there is anything special about the revelation in Exodus which distinguishes it from what natural reason may attain or general revelation disclose.

Does Exodus reveal or proclaim anything that is not to be found elsewhere in human thought or experience? Where would you look for the uniqueness of the Old Testament revelation? In God's "name"? In His action and proclamation in historical events? In the working out of the revelation in the destiny of a people?

Assuming that this revelation is special, does it follow that it should be final and authoritative for all peoples and faiths? Are not all revelations special and final for those who believe in them? What of the revelations in the New Testament and in the Koran, which claim to complete the revelation in the Old Testament? Are all three revelations true, or do they contradict one another?

Does the covenant with Noah in Chapter 9 of Genesis imply a general revelation to mankind? If so, would it include moral precepts, such as those included in the Decalogue?

The following questions are designed to help you test the thoroughness of your reading. Each question is to be answered by giving a page or pages of the reading assignment. Answers will be found on page 269 of this Reading Plan.

1 Who went with Abram from Haran?

2 Why did Abraham fall on his face and laugh?

3 What magical signs did God have Moses perform to re-assure him?

4 What did the Israelites say to Moses when they saw Pharaoh's forces overtaking them?

5 What preparations did the people have to make before receiving the revelation at Mount Sinai?

6 What instructions on worship are given after the proclamation of the Decalogue?

NEW TESTAMENT

The Gospel According to St. Matthew

No religious writings in the history of religion have ever had the universal appeal of the New Testament Gospels. They possess a unique simplicity, clarity, and wholeness. Historical narrative and religious vision are fused in writings of noble plainness and deep sensitivity. The essentials of the ministry and destiny of Jesus of Nazareth are told with an elemental directness and force. These writings have made the "news" about Jesus known to the whole world.

But the Gospels are not merely historical documents or literary masterpieces. They express the faith of the early Christian Church that God had directly revealed Himself in the life, teaching, and death of Jesus of Nazareth, that God was uniquely incarnate in this man. The fusion of history and eternity, of the earthly and the heavenly, of the human and the divine that we find in these writings comes from this faith in the incarnate God.

The idea of a suffering God is a contradiction for many schools of philosophy—"unto the Greeks foolishness." But the New Testament proclaims that God

49

took on human form, suffered gross indignities, and died an ignominious death. In this humiliation and this death, as well as in the subsequent resurrection, lie the meaning and the glory of the Gospel story for the Christian faith.

Fourth Reading

I

Christianity arose out of Hellenistic Judaism, which began about 300 B.C, after Alexander the Great had occupied Palestine. He and his successors spread Greek culture peaceably, through education and example. Alexandria in Egypt, as well as the model Greek colonies set up in Palestine, were persuasive examples of the Greek way. Many Jews, both at home and in the cities of the eastern Mediterranean, adopted Greek culture. Many "Greeks" (then the general term for Gentiles) were converted to Judaism. Thus the Greek and Jewish spiritual worlds came into contact and opened the way for the spread of Christianity.

The initial era of peaceful persuasion, however, was followed by a period of oppression and revolt, or frustrated resentment. A Syrian dynasty tried to prevent the Jews from practicing their religion. The result was the Maccabean revolt and an independent Jewish state that lasted a century (see I and II Maccabees). Internal conflict brought intervention by the Romans, who ruled partly through procurators and partly through the local Herodian dynasty.

Heavy taxation and the unsympathetic rule of pagan Roman governors aroused the resentment of the populace. The people looked forward to the day when they would be freed from Roman rule by heavenly intervention or political revolt. Good examples of the "apocalyptic" or "eschatological" hope for divine intervention can be found in the books of Daniel and Revelation. This hope involved the expectation of a Messiah (or "anointed one") accompanied by hosts of angels, whom God would send to redeem the faithful and usher in a new world order, the "end of the age." There would be a resurrection of the dead, a Last Judgment, and a Kingdom of Heaven on earth. Some scholars believe that many of these notions came from Persian Zoroastrianism, and were not typically Judaistic. However, they were in the air at the time.

Let us glance briefly at the land, people, religion, and politics of Palestine in Jesus' time. The land consisted of three main sections: Galilee in the north (Jesus' home province), Samaria in the middle (the land of the Samaritans), and Judaea in the south (where Jerusalem was located). The Samaritans, of mixed Israelite and Gentile stock, had their own temple and accepted only the Five Books of Moses as scripture. The Israelites lived mainly in Judaea and Galilee.

The national center of religious worship, except for the Samaritans, was the temple in Jerusalem. A vast number of priests carried on the animal sacrifices. The country people would come up to Jerusalem for the major festivals, usually on the Passover. The local centers of worship were the synagogues, where the Scriptures were read and prayers were offered. These were lay organizations run by "rulers," or elders, who also oversaw local law and justice. The synagogues often had specially qualified "rabbis," or teachers, to preach and comment on the readings.

Religion and government were intertwined in the Jewish community. The high priest was civil as well as religious leader of the people; as head of the Sanhedrin, the high council of Jewish elders, he was also supreme judge. The priesthood was in charge of domestic and foreign affairs, so far as possible under Rome. Their tendency was to be culturally liberal, tolerant of Hellenistic ways, and adaptable to Roman rule, while remaining religiously conservative and formalistic. Of the political and religious parties, the Sadducees were closest to the priestly way of thinking. Composed mostly of priests and some "scribes," or scholars, they were the spokesmen of the higher, conservative, worldly classes. They rejected the apocalyptic notions of angels, resurrection, and imminent world redemption. They insisted on literal fulfillment of the written law in religious matters, but they were friendly to Greek culture and philosophy, and they accepted Roman rule.

Opposed to the priests and the Sadducees were the Hasidim (*i.e.*, the "pious ones") and the Pharisees. The Hasidim were interested mainly in retaining the purity of Judaistic religion, both inwardly and outwardly. They were nonpolitical and unworldly, and resisted assimilation to Greek ways. Their spokesmen were the Pharisees, composed of most of the scribes and rabbis and some of the lower priests. The Pharisees preached the new apocalyptic doctrines of the imminent advent of the Messianic redemption and judgment, and the resurrection of the dead. But they insisted on living in accord with the traditional law, adapting it to the conditions of the time. They emphasized the oral, unwritten law, and insisted on moral, ceremonial, and spiritual purity in inner and outward fulfillment of the law. They were an important cultural force, with great schools and famous teachers. They created the Talmud, a systematization of the oral law and the form of Judaism which survived the destruction of Jerusalem in A.D. 70. They accepted Roman rule as an abominable necessity, imposed by God and to be removed by His intervention.

The Zealots were a militant party who advocated armed resistance to Roman rule. Their motto was: "No God but Yahweh, no tax but to the Temple, no friend but the Zealot." They seized the town and the armory of Sepphoris, near Nazareth, in A.D. 6. Although the Romans crushed the revolt and crucified thousands of Zealots, the movement remained strong well into Jesus' lifetime. Simon the Zealot was one of his disciples, and many references to the Zealots occur in the Gospels.

The Essenes, at the opposite extreme, were a nonviolent sect. They lived apart from the world in monastic communities, practicing celibacy and communism, working in the fields, praying, and undergoing purifying baths. The communities uncovered by the recent archaeological discoveries on the Dead Sea were probably of the same type.

In Galilee, the political and religious situation was somewhat different from that in Judaea. There were many Gentiles in Galilee, and across the Jordan River were model Hellenistic settlements. Galilee was ruled by one of Herod's sons, Herod Antipas, instead of by a Roman procurator, as was Judaea.

The attempt by Herod Antipas to build up his power and influence resulted in a crushing burden of taxation and an oppressive network of government officials. We hear overtones of this in the New Testament. The "people of the land" were pious and faithful Jews, who steadfastly kept up the traditional observances and attended the synagogues. Some of them listened to the folk preacher, John the Baptist, who urged immediate repentance and proclaimed the imminent coming of the Kingdom of God. Herod Antipas had him beheaded. John was soon followed by another and more important preacher from the folk of Galilee.

II

Before we take up the story of that folk preacher, let us see how the New Testament came into being.

Worship in the early Church at first followed the model of the Jewish synagogues, with readings from the Torah and the Prophets. Gradually a body of specifically Christian writings developed, which was introduced into the worship service. The twenty-seven writings included in the New Testament were selected as sacred canon in the 4th century. They consist of the Four Gospels (or "good news" about the ministry and Passion of Jesus) letters from Paul, Peter, and other apostles, the Acts of the Apostles, the Letter to the Hebrews, and Revelation.

The Gospels were probably based on oral traditions, or documents preserving them. The books of Matthew, Mark, and Luke are commonly called the Synoptic Gospels, because they apparently used a common source material. John has a different tone and stress, as well as much unique material. It is a beautiful and unified piece of religious narrative and interpretation.

We have selected Matthew for our Gospel readings because it contains essential elements of Jesus' life and ministry, includes some of the best-known passages in the New Testament, and fits in with our previous readings from the Old Testament. Matthew consistently emphasizes Jesus' role as the successor of Moses—the new Torah or Revelation through Christ—and the Church as the new Israel. Some interpreters, finding that the book may be divided into five groups of sayings, hazard the guess that Matthew may have intended to write a new Pentateuch.

III

From the viewpoint of the historian of religions, Christianity begins with the baptism of Jesus in the Jordan River. Mark actually begins his narrative with this event. But just as John signals the religious meaning of these events by his prologue about the Word made flesh (see John 1:1-18), so Matthew heralds the early Christian conviction that Jesus was the Christ by a genealogy that traces Jesus back to David and Abraham, an account of the Virgin Birth, and stories of marvelous events in Jesus' infancy (see Matthew 1-2).

Texts are summoned up from the Old Testament as prophecies of what has come to pass. As with the etymologies in the Pentateuch, the meaning may sometimes be forced; but the use of such Old Testament texts as proofs indicates how the early Christian community viewed Jesus and how it argued for its faith. The story of the flight of Jesus' family to Egypt has overtones of the story of Moses and the Exodus—"Out of Egypt have I called my son" (Matthew 2:13-15). The key sentence in Matthew's prologue is verse 21 of Chapter 1.

> And she shall bring forth a son, and thou shalt call his name JESUS: for he shall save his people from their sins.

Yeshua (Jesus' name in his native Aramaic tongue) was a common Jewish name, the same as Joshua. It means "Yahweh saves." Thus the redemptive power of the God of Exodus is proclaimed again in the Gospel According to Matthew.

The Gospel accounts of Jesus' baptism in the Jordan River (Chap. 3) tell us of the "call" of a religious personage, a familiar event in the Old Testament and in other religions. Here is the setting: John the Baptist comes out of the Judaean wilderness, preaching immediate repentance, or "turning," and warning that the Kingdom of Heaven is "at hand." The sign of repentance is baptism by immersion in the Jordan River. (Baptism was a symbol of conversion in Judaism and a regular ceremonial act among the Essenes and the Dead Sea sects.) But John the Baptist is merely the forerunner of a much loftier person, who will baptize with the Holy Spirit and with fire instead of with water (see 3:11-12). Jesus, a man in his late twenties, comes down from Nazareth to the Jordan River and undergoes baptism. Thereupon he has the experience of being filled with the Spirit of God and of being appointed—not merely as prophet, but as Son.

After the call and appointment comes the period of retirement and meditation in the wilderness (see 4:1-11). There Jesus meets temptation and successfully resists it. Men have been fascinated for thousands of years by this image of the Devil tempting Jesus and have tried to interpret its meaning. (See Dostoevsky's dramatic treatment of this episode in Vol. 52, pp. 127-137.) One thing is certain: an utter adherence to God is advocated as a bulwark against the powers of evil within and without us. Jesus responds to the taunts of the Devil, rejecting, in turn, the idolatries of belly filling, wonder working, and worldly power. Jesus prefaces each answer with the words "It is written that . . . ," referring to Deuteronomy 8:3; 6:16; 6:13.

After the temptation, Jesus begins his ministry (at the age of thirty, according to Luke 3:23). He goes out to the people, as John the Baptist had, preaching, "Repent [turn ye]: for the kingdom of heaven is at hand." (Matthew 4:17). He gathers disciples in Galilee and engages in *teaching, preaching, and healing,* in which consists his ministry. Crowds listen to him and follow after him.

At this point occurs the celebrated Sermon on the Mount (see Chap. 5-7). The constant stress of this remarkable religious utterance is on absolute adherence to God, rightness of inner disposition, and purity of heart. Jesus distinguishes between what is basic, or ultimate, and what is secondary, or instrumental. The Sermon says, in brief: Concentrate your spirit on Life and the Giver of Life, rather than be anxiously obsessed with its sustenance. We need to eat and be clothed, but do not dissipate your spiritual powers on mere means. First, seek the Kingdom of Heaven and righteousness; then all the rest will follow (see 6:19-34).

God alone is to be served. You can serve *either* God *or* an idol (mammon), but not both at once. Serve God in spirit and in truth, without hypocrisy and outward show. If you truly seek God, He will be there; He will be with you.

Ask, and it shall be given you; seek, and ye shall find; knock, and it shall be opened unto you: For every one that asketh receiveth; and he that seeketh findeth; and to him that knocketh it shall be opened. (7:7-8)

The criterion of salvation is doing God's will, not giving lip service to Jesus' lordship.

Not every one that saith unto me, Lord, Lord, shall enter into the kingdom of heaven; but he that doeth the will of my Father which is in heaven. Many will say to me in that day, Lord, Lord, have we not prophesied in thy name? and in thy name have cast out devils? and in thy name done many wonderful works? And then will I profess unto them, I never knew you: depart from me, ye that work iniquity. Therefore whosoever heareth these sayings of mine, and doeth them, I will liken him unto a wise man, which built his house upon a rock: And the rain descended, and the floods came, and the winds blew, and beat upon that house; and it fell not: for it was founded upon a rock. And every one that heareth these sayings of mine, and doeth them not, shall be likened unto a foolish man, which built his house upon the sand: And the rain descended, and the floods came, and the winds blew, and beat upon that house; and it fell: and great was the fall of it. (7:21-27)

The sermon opens with the famous beatitudes proclaiming blessedness for the meek and pure of heart, and offering solace to Jesus' followers in the coming time of persecution. Jesus next takes up the question of whether he is subverting the Law (the Torah, or Pentateuch) and the Prophets. He says that, on the contrary, he has come to fulfill them, and that entry into the Kingdom of Heaven depends on doing and teaching what the Law commands.

Think not that I am come to destroy the law, or the prophets: I am not come to destroy, but to fulfil. For verily I say unto you, Till heaven and earth pass, one jot or one tittle shall in no wise pass from the law, till all be fulfilled. Whosoever therefore shall break one of these least commandments, and shall teach men so, he shall be called the least in the kingdom of heaven: but whosoever shall do and teach *them,* the same shall be called great in the kingdom of heaven. For I say unto you, That except your righteousness shall exceed *the righteousness* of the scribes and Pharisees, ye shall in no case enter into the kingdom of heaven. (5:17-20)

Later he says that the Law and the Prophets may be summed up in the golden rule: Do unto others as you would have them do unto you (see 7:12).

The disavowal of an intent to annul the Law and the Prophets is followed immediately by the proclamation of six new precepts (see 5:21-48). Each addition is announced with the formula of personal authority: "Ye have heard that it was said by them of old time, . . . But I say unto you, . . ." Five of the precepts forbid baseless anger against one's fellow man, lust, divorce (unless one's wife has been unfaithful), oaths, and revenge or retribution for evil. The sixth commands love of enemies and oppressors. (Compare the six precepts in Matthew with the six commandments in Mark 10:19.)

The sermon ends with the crowd's wonder at Jesus' assumption of lawgiving authority.

And it came to pass, when Jesus had ended these sayings, the people were astonished at his doctrine: For he taught them as *one* having authority, and not as the scribes. (7:28-29)

Healing, a part of Jesus' ministry, is described in Chapters 8-9. The healing miracles are intended to demonstrate Jesus' authority and the power of faith. Sometimes the faith or will is that of Jesus, sometimes that of the other person involved. Note how "sin" and "sickness" are tied together and are cured by faith. Jesus compares himself to a physician, the sinners to the sick, and the righteous to the healthy (see 9:9-13). He orders the disciples to go to the "lost sheep" of Israel, who need teaching, preaching, and healing: "Heal the sick, cleanse the lepers, raise the dead, cast out devils" (10:6-8).

In a remarkable passage, Jesus asks from his followers the same kind of absolute devotion that God demanded from Abraham. The obligation to adhere to him transcends all ties of kinship. His followers must endure suffering and give up their lives in order to save them.

Think not that I am come to send peace on earth: I came not to send peace, but a sword. For I am come to set a man at variance against his father, and the daughter against her mother, and the daughter in law against her mother in law. And a man's foes *shall be* they of his own household. He that loveth father or mother more than me is not worthy of me: and he that loveth son or daughter more than me is not worthy of me. And he that taketh not his cross, and followeth after me is not worthy of me. He that findeth his life shall lose it: and he that loseth his life for my sake shall find it. (10:34-39; see also 12:46-50)

Jesus' proclamation of a new Law, or a new version of the Law, and his claim to divine power to heal the sick and remit sins arouse opposition. He is accused of blasphemy, of being possessed by the Devil, and of teaching apostasy from the Mosaic law and revelation. Such acts as the plucking of corn and the healing of the man with the withered hand on the Sabbath bring suspicion and enmity (see 12:1-14). So does laxness among the disciples in regard to washing hands before meals, and perhaps also in regard to the dietary laws (see 15:1-20).

Jesus and his disciples withdraw across the Jordan River into southern Syria. There, at Caesarea Philippi, occurs the famous recognition scene—the "confession" of Peter, acknowledging Jesus as the Messiah, or Christ (see 16:13-17). Jesus enjoins silence on the disciples and prophesies his imminent suffering, death, and resurrection. After the recognition scene comes the "transfiguration" scene, signaling the divine confirmation of Jesus' messiahship and his glorification as the Son of God. Again silence is enjoined on the three intimate disciples who have witnessed it (see 17:1-13).

These events are as decisive for Jesus as his baptism in the Jordan. Next he heads for Jerusalem, where the country folk are coming to celebrate the Passover festival. On the way, there are arguments with opponents, parables to seekers, and prophecies of the Passion and the coming Kingdom of God. Jesus makes a triumphal entry into Jerusalem, applauded by the country folk, who spread clothes and palm branches on his path. The city people ask what the fuss is all about, and are told: "This is Jesus the prophet of Nazareth of Galilee" (21:1-11).

Events mount to their tragic climax as Jesus wrathfully over-
turns the tables of the money-changers, performs healing acts,
and teaches in the temple. The religious leaders are disturbed
by these acts and by the popular response to Jesus. They question his authority and engage him in disputation. He emerges
spiritually victorious. He sums up the essence of the Torah in
two incisive sentences, uniting the love of God and the love of
man:

> But when the Pharisees had heard that he had put the Sadducees
> to silence, they were gathered together. Then one of them, *which
> was* a lawyer, asked *him a question,* tempting him, and saying,
> Master, which *is* the great commandment in the law? Jesus said
> unto him, Thou shalt love the Lord thy God with all thy heart, and
> with all thy soul, and with all thy mind. This is the first and great
> commandment. And the second *is* like unto it, Thou shalt love thy
> neighbour as thyself. On these two commandments hang all the law
> and the prophets. (22:34-40)

Jesus cites these two commandments "in the law" from Deuteronomy 6:5, and Leviticus 19:18.

The tension mounts between Jesus and his opponents. He
utters harsh and bitter words against the scribes and Pharisees,
and laments the tragic fate of the prophets of Israel: "O
Jerusalem, Jerusalem, *thou* that killest the prophets, and stonest
them which are sent unto thee." (Matthew 23:37)

Jesus prophesies his crucifixion to the disciples and he predicts that one of the disciples will betray him at the Last Supper.
He institutes the rite that is later called the Eucharist, or Holy
Communion. Through it, the disciples participate in the
Passion and the New Covenant. Possibly based on the sanctification of bread and wine occurring on the Jewish Sabbath Eve
or Passover Eve, the practice is transformed into a new and
unique rite. Through it, Christians re-enact and participate in
the redemptive sacrifice of Christ. They are with him and he
is with them, now and forever.

> And as they were eating, Jesus took bread, and blessed *it,* and brake
> *it,* and gave *it* to the disciples, and said, Take, eat; this is my body.
> And he took the cup, and gave thanks, and gave *it* to them, saying,
> Drink ye all of it; For this is my blood of the new testament, which
> is shed for many for the remission of sins. But I say unto you, I

will not drink henceforth of this fruit of the vine, until that day
when I drink it new with you in my Father's kingdom. (26:26-29)

The rest follows quickly. There is Jesus' moment of agony
in the Garden of Gethsemane at the prospect of his imminent
suffering, and his prayer to be spared, ending "nevertheless
not as I will, but as thou *wilt*." He is arrested, brought before
the high priest and the council of elders, and condemned to
death for blasphemy. The next day he is brought before
Pontius Pilate, the Roman procurator of Judaea, in order that
the sentence may be executed. Just as he has refused to say
directly to the council that he is the Son of God, so he refuses
to say directly to Pilate that he is the King of the Jews. Since
it is the custom on the eve of Passover for the procurator to
release one prisoner, whom the people choose, Pilate asks the
crowd to choose between Jesus and Barabbas, who was probably a Zealot revolutionary. The crowd chooses Barabbas for
life and Jesus for death. Pilate washes his hands of the responsibility.

The Roman soldiery mock Jesus' claim to messiahship by
dressing him up as King of the Jews—with a scarlet robe, a
crown of thorns, and a reed as a scepter. They hail him, then
spit on him and mock him, and take him away to be crucified.
The crucifixion takes place at Golgotha, or Calvary, an open
place north of Jerusalem. Jesus is crucified between two
thieves, and mocked again about being the Messiah and the
Son of God. At one point occurs the famous cry of dereliction:
"My God, my God, why hast thou forsaken me?" (28:46)
Finally, Jesus cries again with a loud voice and gives up the
ghost.

The cross, the Roman instrument of death for common criminals, became for Jesus' followers the symbol of their faith in
redemption from sin through divine love and suffering.

After the Passion comes the Resurrection—the starting point
for the primitive Christian Church and the symbol, or pledge,
of ultimate redemption for the Christian faith. The disciples—
dispersed and fearful—return from hiding and reunite in the
firm conviction that their Lord has risen from the dead and
will soon return. Inspired by their profound experience, the

disciples are emboldened to carry the "good tidings" and bear witness to their faith in him whom they believed to be Messiah, Lord, and Son of God. The rest is history.

The Resurrection was, for the primitive Christian Church, what the Exodus was for ancient Israel—a crucial demonstration of divine power, the basis and proof of faith.

IV

Why does Jesus put together the two commandments—to love God and to love one's neighbor? (Matthew 22:34-40)

Why does Jesus pick out these two widely separated verses of the Law to sum up the teaching of the whole Bible? Need they go together? Many men have thought otherwise. Men of ascetic, mystical, and solitary disposition have insisted that the religious man should concentrate on his soul's relation to God, avoiding as much as possible entangling love-relations with other creatures. On the other hand, there have been those who have accented the human bond (the love and service of others) without bringing in a personal relation between man and God.

In what sense does Jesus liken the love of other men to the love of God? Does the use of the word "all" in the phrase "with all thy heart, and with all thy soul, and with all thy mind" indicate any difference in the two kinds of love? Can a man love God without loving his neighbors? Can he love his fellow men without loving God? Or does he express his love of God in his love and service of fellow creatures? What is the connection between Jesus' ethical precepts and the "double commandment?" (See I John 4:20-21, for one view of the "double commandment" of Jesus.)

Is Jesus' commandment to leave one's family destructive of human relations and hence contradictory to the law of love? (Matthew 10:34-39)

There are many possible interpretations of Jesus' injunction. You will have to seek them out and think them over. Is he, perhaps, repeating the divine injunction to Abraham (Genesis 12:1)—to leave his father's house in the land of idolatry and to go to a new land of faith? Perhaps this is an absolute imperative to transcend all finite bonds in order to concentrate on the one essential—doing God's will. But then, what about the love of one's fellow men, enjoined by the "double commandment"?

Perhaps there is a suggestion that natural familial ties are to be transferred to the religious community. Is this the meaning of the passage in Matthew 12:46-50, in which Jesus says that the disciples—or anyone who does God's will—are his mother and brothers? Would a literal application of Jesus' injunctions in these two passages from Matthew divide a Christian from his family? Is Christianity an ascetic religion which, when fully and purely practiced, removes a man from his family and society? Or does Christianity add newer and richer meaning to a man's relation with his kin and kind? Reread these passages in Matthew, in association with the rest of the text, and venture your own interpretation of their meaning.

Was Jesus' ethical teaching influenced by his expectation of the imminent advent of the Kingdom of God?

It is undeniable that the chief figures in the Gospel narratives expected the early advent of the Kingdom. It is "at hand," say John the Baptist and Jesus of Nazareth. Hence the urgency of the message to change one's life: "Repent ye."

Many thinkers, notably Albert Schweitzer, have interpreted the pure and absolute ethics taught by Jesus, as well as his lack of interest in social and political matters, as a direct consequence of this belief. Such interpreters believe that Jesus taught an "interim ethics" that was intended only for the interval before the Kingdom was established—an event which was to occur shortly after his death and resurrection.

Other interpreters think that Jesus' ethical teaching is addressed to ordinary earthly existence, but is couched in supernatural terms in order to emphasize the unique and special nature of the time that has *already* come. According to this view, the central point is Jesus' remark that "the Kingdom of Heaven is *among you.*" He urged men to change their lives so as to be fit to live in the Kingdom which had become present.

The pertinent question for us is whether the teachings of Jesus are relevant to our lives in the present day. Are the ethics taught by Jesus applicable to private and public life today? Is the Gospel morality a norm for our religious institutions too? Can Jesus' rule of life provide an absolute measure for all of man's works?

What does the term "Son of Man" mean?

The term "Son of Man" in Jesus' native Aramaic meant simply mankind, the human race. It had, however, a special meaning in apocalyptic literature. It signified the Messianic figure who would herald the final redemption and judgment (see Daniel 7:13-14).

This phrase is used eighty-one times in the Gospels, and is especially prominent in Matthew. What it means there is often hard to determine. Sometimes Jesus is simply referring to "man" as such. Very often he used it for the heaven-sent redeemer who will usher in the end of days. Sometimes he seems to be speaking of the Son of Man in the third person, as a general type, like the Messiah. At other times he seems to be referring to himself as the Son of Man.

Notice how sometimes the term "Son of Man" is substituted for the word "I," as in Jesus' question to the disciples at Caesarea Philippi. In Mark 8:27, Jesus says: "Whom do men say that I am?" In Matthew 16:13, Jesus says: "Whom do men say that I the Son of man am?" Usually the term signifies the Messianic redeemer, but you will have to decide from the context what it means in each case.

What does the term "Christ" mean in Matthew? Does it have the same meaning as the Jewish concept of the Messiah, described above on page 51? Does the meaning of the term "Christ" include the meanings of the terms "Son of Man" and "Son of God"? Does it add an additional meaning?

The following questions are designed to help you test the thoroughness of your reading. Each question is to be answered by giving a page or pages of the reading assignment. Answers will be found on page 269 of this Reading Plan.

1 What two great Old Testament figures is Jesus the "son" of?

2 Who were Jesus' first disciples?

3 Did Jesus preach asceticism?

4 What sign did Jesus draw from the story of Jonah?

5 What was Jesus' attitude toward the Canaanite woman who wanted him to cure her daughter?

6 Who does Jesus say is Elijah returned?

7 What did the rich young man lack to enter eternal life?

ST. AUGUSTINE

The Confessions

Book XI, Sections I-XIII; Book XII

Vol. 18, pp. 89-93, 99-110

In all our serious reading we are concerned with the meaning of what we read. "What did the author intend to say?" "What does this writing say to us?" These questions and the search for the answers become especially acute with Sacred Scriptures for those who accept them as authoritative.

What, for instance, does the Bible mean by its opening words: "In the beginning God created the heaven and the earth"? Here and in the following verses the Bible deals with one of the great questions which man has asked down the ages: How did the world originate? Are we to take the Biblical answer literally, according to the simplest dictionary meanings of the words used? Or should we read into these simple words a rich message as to the spiritual meaning and purpose of the world? How are we to go about finding the meaning, or meanings, of Scripture?

In this text St. Augustine, one of the greatest thinkers of the early Christian Church, gives us a profound and impressive example of Biblical interpretation. We witness a unique combination of personal piety and spiritual vision fused with literary and philosophical judgment. We see a man with an impassioned soul, wrestling for the truth, using all the highly developed faculties of his mind, and at the same time relying on divine grace to get at the supremely important meaning of Genesis. The words almost steam from the page in the heat of his ardor, but they bring us light and depth as well as heat.

Their speaker is no mere archaeological specimen in the history of thought. Augustine has had a remarkable, continuing influence on religious thought in the Western world from the 4th century to the present day. Texts like this one have earned him that perennial, vivifying influence.

Fifth Reading

(See the Eighth Reading in the *General Introduction to the Great Books*, as well as the Biographical Note in Vol. 18, for information about Augustine and *The Confessions*.)

You may remember that in the Foreword we said that our basic idea of the nature of God determines our evaluation of this world. We pointed out there that the great Jewish and Christian commentators try to clarify the basic notion of God's relation to man and the world which is expressed in the first chapters of Genesis. Chapters XI and XII of Augustine's *Confessions* comprise a classic text in Biblical exegesis (that is, the interpretation or explanation of the meaning of Scripture). It deals with the divine creation of the world, proclaimed in the opening words of the Bible.

Augustine was not only a Christian theologian with a deep knowledge of Sacred Scripture. He was also a philosopher, deeply versed in Greek thought. He wrote with a knowledge of classical pagan views about the origin of the world. Let us glance at some of these alternatives to the Biblical doctrine of creation in order to understand better some of the points in his interpretation, which was addressed to the Greco-Roman world of his day.

The Biblical faith that divine power brought the world into being out of nothing, merely by an act of divine will, is alien to the Greek mind. "Nothing comes from nothing," said the Greeks. Aristotle proclaimed: "It is impossible that anything should be produced if there were nothing existing before" (Vol. 8, p. 555d). Lucretius said: "Nothing is ever gotten out of nothing by divine power" (Vol. 12, p. 3a). Hippocrates said: "Everything has its natural cause, and nothing occurs without a natural cause." And Galen, who wrote with knowledge of Biblical doctrine, said:

Moses' opinion greatly differs from our own and from that of Plato and of all the others who among the Greeks have rightly handled the investigation into nature. To Moses, it seems enough that God willed to create a cosmos, and presently it was created; for he believes that for God everything is possible, even if out of ashes He wanted to make a horse or an ox. We, however, do not hold such an opinion; for we maintain, on the contrary, that certain things are impossible by nature, and these God would not even attempt to do; rather would His reason choose the best among those things for which it is possible to come into being.

The early Greek philosophers believed that the world had developed or emanated from an original substance. They regarded nature as divine and animated by a universal soul or reason. The most developed and systematic form of this basic Greek idea is Aristotle's doctrine that the world is eternal—a doctrine with which medieval Islamic, Jewish, and Christian philosophers had to contend. There is one great exception to the typical Greek idea of the origin of the universe, and that is the cosmology of Plato—the founder of the school of philosophy to which Augustine adhered.

In the *Timaeus,* Plato constructed a speculative myth of divine creation (see Vol. 7, pp. 447b-448a). He saw God as a "demiurge," or artificer, who fashions the world out of pre-existing formless stuff, bringing original chaos into form in conformity with an eternal Idea of the Good. The first and highest creature is the world soul, which becomes the divine agent for the further creation of things. There is a striking similarity between Plato's notion of creation and the Biblical notion of creation as interpreted by Augustine. The differences as well as the similarities between Augustine's and Plato's ideas of creation will become apparent below. It will also become apparent how Augustine was able to make creative and constructive use of his philosophic heritage in order to express an essentially Christian point of view.

Augustine was a follower of the Neoplatonic school of philosophy, which flourished during the first centuries of the Christian era. The main exponent of this school was Plotinus, whose writings Augustine knew well, and whose *Six Enneads* comprise Volume 17 of the *Great Books*. God, in Neoplatonism, is the ultimate, eternal, perfect reality from which all existence is derived. The world is an emanation (a flowing out) from the divine substance. It is made up of graded levels of reality, which participate in the divine perfection in decreasing measure as they are farther away from the source. The highest level is that of the eternal ideas, which are agents in the formation of activities on the next level (that of soul, mind, or intelligence). The lowest level is that of unformed matter, which is a void, nothingness (the realm of evil, which, however, has no real existence). There is a conflict in the human soul between its aspiration toward the purely spiritual and unchangeable realm (the good and the real) and that toward the merely sensual and material realm of space and time (the evil and unreal).

It is this system of thought, based on the notion of an impersonal godhead as the absolute source and end of all things, that is fused by Augustine with the Biblical message of a personal God who creates the world by an act of will. Augustine constructed an amazing synthesis of what appear to be two irreconcilable views. Here is Augustine's own view of Neoplatonism as expressed in his work *Against the Academics*:

> After many centuries and many disputes at length a system of philosophy was discovered, which, in my opinion, is most true. It is not, what our sacred religion so rightly abhors, a philosophy of the material world, but reveals another and intelligible world.

II

Augustine's interpretation of the Biblical doctrine of creation rests on the opening words of two texts: Genesis, and the Gospel According to John—an Old Testament and a New Testament reading. The words of Genesis are the direct object of interpretation, and the words of John are Augustine's guide to the meaning of the text in Genesis. These are the words that Augustine interprets:

In the beginning God created the heaven and the earth. And the earth was without form, and void; and darkness *was* upon the face of the deep. (Genesis 1:1-2)

And these are the words that offer him an orientation:

> In the beginning was the Word, and the Word was with God, and the Word was God. The same was in the beginning with God. All things were made by him; and without him was not any thing made that was made. (John 1:1-3)

The latter passage expresses the Christian doctrine that Christ is the creative Word of God, which initiates, orders, and sustains the universe.

Book XI opens with an invocation imploring God's assistance in the author's quest, for this text is a "confession" (an address to God). Next, Augustine states the question that disturbs him: "I would hear and understand how in the beginning Thou madest the heaven and earth" (p. 90b). Augustine does not question that the world has been derived *somehow* from something else. He concludes from the change and variation of existing things—from their coming into being and their passing away—that they must come from an unchanging and absolute source.

> Behold, the heavens and the earth are; they proclaim that they were created; for they change and vary. Whereas whatsoever hath not been made, and yet is, hath nothing in it which before it had not; and that it is, to change and vary. They proclaim also, that they made not themselves; 'therefore we are, because we have been made; we were not therefor, before we were, so as to make ourselves.' Now the evidence of the thing is the voice of the speakers. Thou, therefore, Lord, madest them; (p. 90c-d)

For Augustine, the existence, beauty, and good of the finite and changing world clearly depend on an absolute and eternal being, beauty, and good. His question concerns only the way in which the world was brought into being—the mechanism ("engine") of creation. God might have made the world out of some already-existing primal substance, as did Plato's divine artificer; or the world could have flowed forth from the divine substance, as in the emanationist doctrines. But then the world would be coeternal, or of the same substance with God—equal instead of secondary—in contradiction with Augustine's view and with Biblical doctrine. Augustine seeks a transcendent realm—beyond nature, space and time, and even mind—from which the divine "Word" issued to bring this world into being.

How, O God, didst Thou make heaven and earth? Verily, neither in the heaven, nor in the earth, didst Thou make heaven and earth; nor in the air, or waters, seeing these also belong to the heaven and the earth; nor in the whole world didst Thou make the whole world; because there was no place where to make it, before it was made, that it might be. Nor didst Thou hold anything in Thy hand, whereof to make heaven and earth. For whence shouldest Thou have this, which Thou hadst not made, thereof to make anything? For what is, but because Thou art? Therefore Thou spakest, and they were made, and in Thy Word Thou madest them. (p. 91a; see also pp. 91c, 100d)

There we have Augustine's answer to the "how" of creation— "Thou spakest, and they were made, and in Thy Word Thou madest them"—a fusing of Genesis and John. From God's "speech," says Augustine, followed light, firmament, and gathering of the waters. This, of course, is not speech in the ordinary sense—not audible sounds, spoken and heard in temporal succession. This is the eternal Word, expressed from the realm beyond time, although fulfilled in time. This is the "beginning" of the world, the foundation and principle of all things.

In this Beginning, O God, hast Thou made heaven and earth, in Thy Word, in Thy Son, in Thy Power, in Thy Wisdom, in Thy Truth; wondrously speaking, and wondrously making. (p. 92a)

Augustine does not look to Genesis for a description of the natural processes and the sequence of physical causes whereby the material universe came into existence. Augustine pushes far beyond that—to a Beginning, or Principle, beyond the natural order. He is concerned with the mystery of being, with why there is anything at all, instead of nothing. He regards the existence of this finite, temporal world as an absolute miracle. (See *The City of God,* Vol. 18, pp. 306d-307a.) The world did not ultimately *originate* from a physical beginning in time, but from an act of divine wisdom and goodness—outside of time—that created both time and the world.

That is why Augustine finds irrelevant the question put by the Manicheans and other philosophers: "What was God doing before He made heaven and earth?" There is no "before" or "after" in Eternity. "Wake up!" Augustine tells the nodding student of this passage (see p. 92d). There are no times when God did nothing or did something, for there are no times for God—God is beyond time. Whereas we creatures have the constant succession and perpetual perishing of time, God has the Eternal Present, in which all things are present to Him at once. Our passing world depends on the Eternal Being that is always present, whose "today" is Eternity (see pp. 92a-93a).

III

Thus far Augustine has interpreted the first five words of Genesis—"In the beginning God created. . ." He has told us what he thinks the "beginning" and the *mode* of creation are—God's Word or "speech." And he has emphasized the eternal character of the Word, of the origin of creation.

Next he proceeds to deal with the *content* of creation, expressed in the next five words of Genesis: ". . . the heaven and the earth." We can take this literally and simply, as referring to the visible world of land and sky. But Augustine finds richer significance in the two key words, "heaven" and "earth," attributing to them the symbolic meanings of that which is highest and that which is lowest in the hierarchy of created being. What is above, he calls the "heaven of heavens"; this is the spiritual aspect of things, the divine abode of spirit and light, "wisdom" (in the created sphere), "mind," or intellect. This is the highest level of creation and the first of God's creatures—the "house" or "city" of God, which is almost eternal.

The lowliness of my tongue confesseth unto Thy Highness that Thou madest heaven and earth; this heaven which I see, and this earth that I tread upon, whence is this earth that I bear about me; Thou madest it. But where is that heaven of heavens, O Lord, which we hear of in the words of the Psalm, The heaven of heavens are the Lord's; but the earth hath He given to the children of men? Where is that heaven which we see not, to which all this which we see is earth? For this corporeal whole, not being wholly everywhere, hath in such wise received its portion of beauty in these lower parts, whereof the lowest is this our earth; but to that heaven of heavens, even the heaven of our earth is but earth; yea, both these great bodies may not absurdly be called earth, to that unknown heaven, which is the Lord's, not the sons' of men. (p. 99c-d; see also p. 103d)

We must note that this wisdom or light, though the highest
level of created being, is below the divine wisdom or Word,
by whom all things are made. This is not the Logos, the second
person of the Christian Trinity, who is coeternal with God the
Father. It is rather the sphere of the angels—purely spiritual
creatures—which, though made before time, is not eternal,
but quasi-eternal.

For although we find no time before it, for wisdom was created before
all things; not that Wisdom which is altogether equal and coeternal unto
Thee, our God, His Father, and by Whom all things were created, and
in Whom, as the Beginning, Thou createdst heaven and earth; but that
wisdom which is created, that is, the intellectual nature which, by con-
templating the light, is light. For this, though created, is also called
wisdom. . . . Therefore since a certain created wisdom was created
before all things, the rational and intellectual mind of that chaste city of
Thine, our mother which is above, and is free and 'eternal in the heavens'
(in what heavens, if not in those that praise Thee, the 'Heaven of
heavens'? Because this is also the 'Heaven of heavens' for the Lord);
though we find no time before it (because that which hath been created
before all things, precedeth also the creature of time), yet is the Eternity
of the Creator Himself before it, from Whom, being created it took the
beginning, not indeed of time (for time itself was not yet), but of its creation. (p. 103c-d; see also p. 104a)

This is the "heaven" that God created. What, then, is the
"earth" that God created? It is not the earth we walk upon,
says Augustine; it is not even the terrestrial globe, nor the
physical universe. It is the basic material substance—the shapeless, primordial stuff—out of which the definite material world
of our experience was made. Augustine takes his cue from the
second sentence of the Bible: "And the earth was without
form, and void; and darkness *was* upon the face of the deep."
The Biblical writer, he says, chose these common, concrete
terms to evoke what is almost impossible to conceive and express. Augustine proceeds to interpret this sentence.

The Biblical writer, he says, wanted to express the original,
absolute formlessness which is the substratum from which
sensible things were made. It is not mere nothing, for out of
it came formed things, and change of forms. It is the very root
and matrix of change. Augustine grasps vainly for the right
words to express this primal formlessness, somewhere between

the formed and the nothing. He tries the terms "nothing some-thing," "is, is not," and "almost nothing." These seemingly non-sensical phrases are, Augustine says, the conceptual equiva-lents of the simple Biblical words: "earth," "void," "deep," and "darkness."

Again we must note an important distinction. This formless stuff—this "void"—is not the same as the eternal chaotic sub-stance of which Plato's divine artificer made the world. Nor is it absolute nothing. This "earth," or formlessness, is the lowest of creatures and the farthest from God, as "heaven," or the angelic world, is the highest and closest to God.

But whence had it this degree of being, but from Thee, from Whom are all things, so far forth as they are? But so much the further from Thee, as the unliker Thee; for it is not farness of place. Thou therefore, Lord, Who are not one in one place, and otherwise in another, but the Self-same, and the Self-same, and the Self-same, Holy, Holy, Holy, Lord God Almighty, didst in the Beginning, which is of Thee, in Thy Wisdom, which was born of Thine own Substance, create something, and that out of nothing. For thou createdst heaven and earth; not out of Thyself; for so should they have been equal to Thine Only Begotten Son, and thereby to Thee also; whereas no way were it right that aught should be equal to Thee, which was not of Thee. And aught else besides Thee was there not, whereof Thou mightest create them, O God, One Trinity, and, Trine Unity; and therefore out of nothing didst Thou create heaven and earth; a great thing, and a small thing; for Thou art Almighty and Good, to make all things good, even the great heaven, and the petty earth. Thou wert, and nothing was there besides, out of which Thou createdst heaven and earth; things of two sorts: one near Thee, the other near to nothing; one, to which Thou alone shouldest be superior; the other, to which nothing should be inferior. (pp. 100d-101a)

It is between these two levels of creation—between the high-est and the lowest—that the sensible, formed, and changing world of our experience comes. Our world is an in-between world of material form, related to—though distinct from—both the ideal forms above and the formless substance below. Be-fore there can be distinct forms and species of things there must be "a primitive formed and a primitive formless"—the original "heaven and earth." Then, and only then,

another Heaven might be created, together with a visible and well-formed earth: and the waters diversely ordered, and whatsoever further is in the formation of the world, recorded to have been, not without days, created; and that, as being of such nature, the successive changes of times may take place in them, as being subject to appointed alterations of motions and of forms. (p. 102c-d)

The foregoing is Augustine's interpretation of Genesis 1:1-2. The absolute and eternal origin is God and his Word. He created the world out of nothing by his act of creation alone. First he created the two primal aspects, or levels, of the world —the intellectual and the material. Then he created the sensible world of space and time—the formed world of our actual experience. But we are confusing things when we say "first" and "then"; for there is no time, no "earlier" and "later," until the sensible world is formed. Priority here is a qualitative matter of levels of being—or grades of reality with respect to God—not a chronological matter of earlier and later. Note, in this connection, that Augustine does not mean that formlessness was created chronologically before formed things; indeed, he emphasizes in another writing that they were "concreated," or created at the same time. The chronological stages of creation, or "days," do not start until the formation of the visible heaven and earth.

Augustine presents a detailed and neat argument about the types of priority, in Book XII, 40 (pp. 109b-110a). He distinguishes between

what precedes by eternity, what by time, what by choice, and what in original. By eternity, as God is before all things; by time, as the flower before the fruit; by choice, as the fruit before the flower; by original, as the sound before the tune. (p. 109c)

He gives an extended analysis of the latter type of priority, which corresponds to the way in which formless substance is prior to formed things. A tune is a formed sound. The sound exists "before" it is formed into a tune, but not "before" in being, in time, or in choice (value). The sound is not prior in being, for it does not make the tune. It is the mind of the composer or singer that makes the tune out of the sound, as the Creator forms the world out of formlessness. The sound does not precede the tune in time, for it is expressed at the same time—in, and with, and by the tune. And the sound is not

"first" in choice, for the formed tune is better than the unformed sound. The sound is only first "in origin," that is, as the
material substance out of which the formed thing is made.
Without the unformed sound, the formed tune cannot be; similarly, without the priority of original formlessness, the formed
world cannot be.

IV

Augustine is aware that this interpretation of the first verses
of the Bible will seem rather farfetched to most readers. For
one thing, there are the simple folk who will understand the
words in their literal, surface meaning. Augustine does not
want to disturb these people in what he regards as their
simple, but precious faith. For another thing, there are those
who, like Augustine, look for a deeper meaning in the Bible,
but who arrive at a different interpretation. Augustine's attitude is one of tolerance toward other interpretations, so long
as they are made in a spirit of piety toward the Scriptures.
There are many different possible meanings of Scripture, all of
which may be true, and none of which need be the one that
was consciously intended by the author.

Hence, Augustine is not disturbed by critics who say:
"Moses did not mean what you say, he means what we say."
He points out that there can be two types of disagreement
about the meaning of a writing: first, in regard to the truth of
what is said; and, second, in regard to the meaning intended
by the author. Augustine feels much more certain about the
first than the second. He is sure from what his own mind tells
him, from the inner voice of his spirit, that Moses' doctrine of
divine creation is true. But he cannot be certain that Moses
meant exactly what Augustine interprets him to mean.

Augustine is not disturbed by this possibility. He feels that
Scripture, which is the Word of God, is more likely to be rich
in all possible meanings and truths than just to intend one particular meaning and truth. Perhaps Moses himself intended
many truths and meanings. The truths intended by Moses,
Augustine, and Augustine's critics are not their private truths;
they contribute to the common store of truth for all men who

seek it. The terse, simple language of Scripture must communicate the truth of divine creation to the unsophisticated and at the same time convey the meanings discernible by persons of deeper understanding.

Augustine is aware, for instance, that various interpretations of the phrase "heaven and earth" are possible. Some say it simply means the whole visible world; others, that it means the original formless stuff; still others, that it is a distinction between the visible and invisible realms; and so on. So, too, there may be varying interpretations of the phrase "in the beginning." Augustine holds to his own interpretation of these phrases, while admitting that other interpretations may be true. But the main thing, for him, is that they all agree on one single, essential truth: that the world is created by God out of nothing, through His transcendent act alone.

V

Does Genesis say that the world was made out of nothing, or out of formlessness?

The explicit idea of creation out of nothing first appeared in the 2nd century B.C. in the apocryphal, or deuterocanonical, Second Book of Maccabees (see II Maccabees 7:28; see also Romans 4:17). The key phrase, "God made them of things that were not" (or "out of nothing"), first appears in the Greek rendering of II Maccabees and was probably an intentional contrast with the Greek notion that "nothing comes out of nothing." It is the basic expression used by protagonists of the Biblical view of creation to emphasize its distinction and uniqueness.

But is it not possible to read the first words of Genesis as pointing to a pre-existing chaos or formlessness which is brought into form and ordered by the creative power of God, as is done in the *Timaeus* by Plato's Demiurge? Indeed, there is a Talmudic dialogue between a philosopher and Rabbi Gamaliel in which the philosopher twits the Rabbi: "Your God is a great Craftsman, but He found good materials which were of assistance to Him in the work of Creation, viz. formlessness, void, darkness, spirit, water, and the deeps." The Rabbi answers, like Augustine, that the Bible says that these things also were created by God.

If we assume the philosopher's interpretation to be correct, what, then, would be the first thing to be created, according to Genesis? Would it necessarily follow that the pre-existence of the formless stuff derogated from the supreme perfection of God? Or would we have to assume, as did the Greek emanationists, that the formless stuff flowed forth from God, and thus have to adopt the pantheistic view that the world and God are of the same substance? If we assume the coeternality of God and formless stuff, then must we go back to some prior being to reach the "beginning" or "principle" which Augustine is concerned with? If one absolute, eternal being is assumed as the source of all things, are (1) emanation and (2) creation from nothing the only logical possibilities? Which of the two alternatives is more in accord with Neoplatonism?

If God is omnipotent and perfectly good, why did He create an imperfect world?

For Augustine, *to be* is itself a good; even imperfect being is good; and God's act of bringing the world into being is a pure act of absolute goodness. Evil, for Augustine, is an imperfect participation in,—or a willful alienation from—the absolute being and goodness of God. But why did not God create a perfect world, and one without any capacity for falling away from the divine perfection?

Does Augustine have the same idea as Plato, in our Second Reading: namely that a greater good is intended to result ultimately from the relative evil of particular times and places? Is this imperfect universe straining toward perfection? Is this world more dramatic, more humanly interesting and edifying, more character-building than a perfect one would have been? Would a perfect universe have been equal to God, and hence destructive of the idea of a qualitatively transcendent creator?

Are graded levels of being necessary for an interpretation of Genesis?

A man once objected to the notion of hierarchy held by the late neo-Humanist philosopher Irving Babbitt, by quoting the words of Jesus: "In my Father's house are many mansions [apartments]." To this Babbitt replied, "Yes, but they are not all on the same floor." The latter is Augustine's view, and also that of all other Neoplatonic interpretations of Genesis, notably in medieval Jewish mysticism.

Does the Biblical passage admit or require any other interpretation? If the world—including mind as well as matter—is created out of absolute nothing and sustained in being only by an act of divine power, does this mean that all things are equally distant, or equally close, to God? Is that also the implication of Augustine's doctrine that God exists in an eternal "now" in which all things are present to him at once? Are all times the same distance from God? Or, granted the original gulf between the eternal reality of God and the derived being of creation, must we assume qualitative distinctions in the various aspects of created being, *i. e.*, lesser and greater worth in relation to the absolute reality and good of God?

Are we to assume a special, privileged status in the universe for man, as made in the image and likeness of God and having dominion over the natural world? This would accord with the story of the creation of Adam, which some interpreters consider a second creation story. Are there special moments in history, such as the Exodus and the Passion, in which the divine power is particularly present?

Wherein is Augustine a Neoplatonist and wherein is he a Christian?

The Neoplatonic view of the world's origin includes the notions of an absolute being and goodness as the source of all things, of the emanation of the world from this absolute source, of levels of emanation from the realm of eternal ideas down to pure formlessness, and of the more or less adequate participation of the various levels in the absolute perfection of the source.

The Christian doctrine of creation includes the notion of a divine person (a "Thou," not an "It") who creates the world by an act of will (purposely and benevolently) and sustains it continually with watchful care; the Christian view also emphasizes ethical action, the state of the will, and the active service of man to God, and recognizes, in some sense, the reality of evil.

Are all of these notions—Neoplatonic and Christian—present in Augustine's view of creation? Are they a confusing and contradictory jumble, or are they harmonized into a meaningful synthesis? Where, if at all, does Augustine make a decisive break with Neoplatonism? Where should a Christian thinker break with Neoplatonism in discussing the origin and nature of the world?

The following questions are designed to help you test the thoroughness of your reading. Each question is to be answered by giving a page or pages of the reading assignment. Answers will be found on page 269 of this Reading Plan.

1 Are the things of this world beautiful and good?

2 How did God speak the creating Word?

3 Why doesn't Genesis mention the number of days required to create heaven and earth?

4 What thing alone is not from God?

5 What is God's "city," or "house"?

6 Should we believe God made anything not mentioned in Genesis?

7 How do ordinary folk interpret the creation story?

AQUINAS

Summa Theologica

Part I, Q. 1; Part II-II, QQ. 1-3

Vol. 19, pp. 3-10; Vol. 20, pp. 380-401

W hen men face an apparent conflict between faith and reason—between the teachings of religion or theology and the teachings of philosophy or science—they react in various typical ways. Some of them reject sacred doctrine entirely, some of them reject secular teachings entirely, and some of them try to reconcile the sacred and the secular. When Christian Europe came into contact with previously unknown writings of Aristotle, such as the *Physics, Metaphysics,* and *Ethics,* in the 12th and 13th centuries, the persons entrusted with the exposition and defense of the Christian faith faced just such alternatives.

Alarmed Church authorities forbade the teaching of Aristotle's metaphysical and natural philosophy at the University of Paris. Some Christian thinkers elected to attack or ignore the new-found writings as a threat to the faith. Others chose to expound Aristotelian philosophy as natural truth distinct from the supernatural truth of revelation, valid in its own sphere even when it appeared to conflict with Christian doctrine.

A third group tried to synthesize or reconcile the truths of Aristotelian philosophy with the dogmas of the Christian faith. They attempted to fit the conclusions of natural reason into the framework of supernatural truth. They were convinced that the findings of reason and the teachings of revelation could and must be reconciled. Otherwise the human spirit would be split up into two separate and irreconcilable realms, and the Christian mind would become hopelessly schizophrenic.

The greatest of these medieval synthesizers of Greek thought and Christian faith was the Italian Dominican scholar, Thomas Aquinas. He had many great predecessors and many illustrious contemporaries, but his construction of an intellectual edifice to house both faith and reason is unique. This solid and elegant structure, comprising all the forms of being from prime matter to God, has been compared to a 13th-century cathedral. Questioned in its own day, and attacked as heretical in some of its doctrines, this synthesis of reason and revelation has become in modern times the accepted intellectual structure of the Roman Catholic Church.

Sixth Reading

I

The *Summa Theologica*, from which our readings are taken, is designed to sum up in systematic form all theological knowledge attained at the time the work was written. The term "theological knowledge" here includes knowledge about man and the world as related to God. You will remember that in our Foreword we said that systematic theology includes doctrines about the world and about man, as well as about God. The First Part of the *Summa* includes treatises not only on God, but also on the creation, on man, and on the government of the world. The same inclusiveness is characteristic of the Second Part.

The *Summa Theologica* refers to classical Greek and medieval Jewish and Islamic philosophers, as well as to Christian thinkers. Jewish philosophers, such as Maimonides, shared with Christian thinkers a common revelation in the Old Testament. Greek philosophers, such as Aristotle, and the Arabic Aristotelian philosophers, shared with them a common starting point in human reason. Natural theology based on reason is joined in the *Summa* with sacred theology based on revelation.

Very often, in answering a question of theological doctrine, Aquinas cites both Sacred Scriptures and pagan philosophy in support of his contentions. And he refers to non-Christian thinkers, such as Plato, Aristotle, Avicenna, Averroës, or Maimonides, almost as often as to Christian thinkers, such as Augustine, Dionysius the Areopagite, Gregory the Great, John of Damascus, or Peter Lombard. The *Summa Theologica* is a systematic exposition of theological knowledge, compiled from all available sources with the master purpose, of course, of setting forth and defending Christian doctrine.

The form of exposition employed in the *Summa*, a style typical of the day, may be annoying to you at first. The subjects treated are not set forth in direct exposition; instead, each treatise is broken up into questions, which are further divided into subquestions, called "articles." The title of each article puts the question in affirmative form, as in Question 1, Article 1 (Vol. 19, p. 3): "*Whether, besides Philosophy, any further Doctrine is required?*" Next comes a general negative answer, which is introduced by the words: "*We proceed thus to the First Article.*" In this case, the answer is as follows: "It seems that, besides philosophical doctrine we have no need of any further knowledge." Then specific negative points, called "objections," are listed numerically, thus: "*Obj.* 1. For man should not seek to know what is above reason . . . *Obj.* 2. Further, knowledge can be concerned only with being. . . ."

After all the objections have been advanced, Aquinas summarizes the view opposite to that taken by the objectors and then goes on to judge between the two views, conceding the truth which he finds in each view and rejecting what he considers false. The summary is introduced by the words "*On the contrary*" and is usually accompanied by a citation from authorities—Scriptures, Church Fathers, philosophers. The body of the article, presenting Aquinas' judgment on the various views, is prefaced by the words "*I answer that . . .*" Finally, Aquinas replies to the numbered objections in order: thus, "*Reply Obj.* 1 . . . *Reply Obj.* 2," and so on.

We suggest that, at first, you read each article exactly as it is written, starting with the objections and ending with the replies. It is usually easier to understand Aquinas' own argument, as well as his replies to the objections, if the latter have been read first. As you get used to Aquinas' thought and style, you may find it desirable to go immediately from the question in the title of the article to Aquinas' answer and arguments, and then take up the *Objections* and *Replies*. In any case, do not neglect what Aquinas says in his *Replies*. They often contain, in a sentence or a phrase, some of his most important insights.

The *Summa Theologica* comprises three parts. Each part is

divided into treatises. For this reading, we have chosen selections from the "Treatise on God" in the First Part, and from the "Treatise on Faith, Hope, and Charity" in the Second Part. The Second Part is itself divided into two parts: our second selection is from Part II of the Second Part.

I I

Our first selection is from the very beginning of the *Summa Theologica*—Part I, Question 1: "The Nature and Extent of Sacred Doctrine." It comprises these ten subquestions or Articles:

1   On the necessity of this doctrine?
2   Whether it is a science?
3   Whether it is one or many?
4   Whether it is speculative or practical?
5   How it is compared with other sciences?
6   Whether it is a wisdom?
7   What is its subject matter?
8   Whether it is a matter of argument?
9   Whether it rightly employs metaphors and similes?
10 Whether the Sacred Scripture of this doctrine may be expounded in different senses?

The subject of Question 1 is the nature, aim, and content of sacred theology. Is sacred theology a science? If so, what kind of science is it? Is it possible to have a scientific discipline which deals with matters handed down by divine revelation and believed on faith? What are the relations of sacred theology to other sciences, especially to philosophy, which claims to deal with all things, including God, in the light of reason alone? Such are the kinds of questions which Aquinas answers in Question 1 of the "Treatise on God" in Part I.

Article 1, "Whether, besides Philosophy, any further Doctrine is required?" answers the objection that a philosophical theology already exists which treats of God as the highest being, as far as rational inquiry may do so. Since no other scientific discipline can do more than this and since anything further is a matter of faith, what need is there for sacred theology? Aquinas replies that sacred theology is absolutely necessary because it is based on divinely revealed truths—

accepted on faith—which direct human thought and action toward ultimate salvation.

No other science deals systematically with such truths, or guides man toward eternal happiness. The Scriptures furnish sacred theology with truths about God that are not available to any other science. Furthermore, even those truths which are knowable through reason alone are known more certainly and more accurately through divine revelation. Even more important, they are made known by divine proclamation to all men who will hear, rather than to a few philosophers.

But why do we need scientific study and reasoning in such matters? Since man has been granted divine revelation, should not faith and inspiration be all that he needs to attain these unique, special truths? Aquinas answers this question in his Reply to Objection 3 of Article 6, and also in Article 8.

Article 6 discusses the question whether sacred theology is wisdom. Objection 3 cites the scriptural notion that wisdom is acquired through divine inspiration, and notes that sacred theology is learned through study. Aquinas answers that there is a twofold wisdom in religion, just as there is in ethics. The first kind of wisdom is that of the habitually virtuous man, who makes intuitively right judgments about moral actions. The second type is that of the man who is not virtuous by habit, but who has learned to make accurate judgments about right and wrong. Similarly, in religion, holy and inspired men have the first kind of wisdom about divine things; while men who are not themselves holy, who have not personally experienced divine revelation and inspiration, have the second kind of wisdom. They have learned to make correct judgments about divine things by systematic thought and study. Only if Aquinas' argument is correct, is theology possible as an academic discipline which can be taught and studied by men of spiritual gifts less than those of the prophets, apostles, saints, and mystics. Aquinas' answer deserves close reading. Here it is in full:

Since judgment pertains to wisdom, according to a twofold manner of judging there is a twofold wisdom. A man may judge in one way by inclination, as whoever has the habit of a virtue judges rightly of what concerns that virtue by his very inclination towards it. Hence the virtuous man, as we read in the *Ethics,* is the measure and rule of human acts. In another way, by knowledge, just as a man learned in moral science might be able to judge rightly about virtuous acts, though he had not the virtue. The first manner of judging divine things belongs to that wisdom which is set down among the gifts of the Holy Ghost: *The spiritual man judgeth all things* (I Cor. 2:15). And Dionysius says (*Div. Nom.* ii): "Hierotheus is taught not by mere learning, but by experience of divine things." The second manner of judging belongs to this doctrine, since it is acquired by study, though its principles are obtained by revelation. (Vol. 19, pp. 6d-7a)

Aquinas develops this argument further in his answer to Article 8, "Whether Sacred Doctrine Is a Matter of Argument?" Is not belief in revealed truths reached through faith, rather than by rational argument? Yes, answers Aquinas, but rational argument can develop and illuminate the conclusions that follow from the revealed truths; it can set forth systematically the connection between the various articles of faith (as, for example, between belief in the Resurrection of Christ and belief in the general resurrection of the flesh).

. . . sacred doctrine makes use even of human reason, not, indeed, to prove faith . . . but to make clear other things that are put forward in this doctrine. (Vol. 19, p. 8b-c)

Such reasoning can, of course, be addressed only to those who accept the Christian revelation in principle, to those who are adherents of the Christian faith.

Thus we can argue with heretics from texts in Holy Writ, and against those who deny one article of faith we can argue from another. But if our opponent believes nothing of divine revelation, there is no longer any means of proving the articles of faith by reasoning, but only of answering his objections—if he has any—against faith. (Vol. 19, p. 8b)

Aquinas deals similarly with the question of the relation of sacred theology to the philosophical sciences. Just as he sees sacred theology as an auxiliary of revelation, so he sees the philosophical sciences as "handmaidens" to sacred theology. Men can more easily understand the things of faith, which are *above* reason but not *against* reason, if they are first translated into terms that reason can grasp. In his Reply to Objection 2 in Article 5, which maintains that sacred theology is dependent on the philosophical sciences and, hence, inferior to them, Aquinas says:

This science can in a sense take from the philosophical sciences, not as though it stood in need of them, but only in order to make its teaching clearer. For it takes its principles not from other sciences, but immediately from God, by revelation. Therefore it does not take from the other sciences as from the higher, but makes use of them as of the lesser, and as handmaidens; just as the master sciences make use of the sciences that supply their materials, as political of military science. That it thus uses them is not due to its own defect or insufficiency, but to the defect of our intellect, which is more easily led by what is known through natural reason (from which proceed the other sciences), to that which is above reason, such as are the teachings of this science. (Vol. 19, p. 6a)

Note that Aquinas considers the philosophical sciences as auxiliary, ministerial, not self-sufficient for the knowledge of divine things. Knowledge of God as the origin and end of all things can be known only through divine revelation, which enables man to share in God's knowledge of Himself and of the world. In his answer to Article 6, Aquinas says:

But sacred doctrine most especially treats of God viewed as the highest cause—not just in so far as He can be known through creatures, which the philosophers knew—*That which is known of God is manifest in them* (Rom. 1:19)—but also in so far as He is known to Himself alone and revealed to others. (Vol. 19, p. 6c)

Aquinas sets forth directly in Articles 5 and 6 his belief that sacred theology is the highest of the sciences. His reasons are that sacred theology rests on divinely revealed principles and deals with the highest possible object of knowledge. Hence, sacred theology may judge and order all the other sciences; it is the "queen" of the sciences.

But the objection is made that sacred theology deals with many other things besides God. It deals with men and angels and natural objects, too. It does not seem to be a unified science with a single subject. Aquinas answers these objections in Article 3, "Whether Sacred Doctrine Is One Science?" and Article 7, "Whether God Is the Subject of This Science?"

He compares sacred theology to a natural faculty, such as sight. With this faculty we may perceive color in men, animals, and things. Color is the "formal aspect" under which we view these things. It is the *formal* object of sight, which is single, although we perceive it in a variety of *material* aspects or things; hence, sight is a unified faculty. So it is with sacred theology, which deals with all things in their relation to God or "under the aspect of God"; that is, with God Himself, or with God as the origin and end of all things. Whatever sacred theology teaches about man and other creatures has to do essentially with God. Here is Aquinas' own statement in the answer to Article 7:

God is the subject of this science. The relation between a science and its subject is the same as that between a habit or power and its object. Now properly speaking the object of a power or habit is the thing under the aspect of which all things are referred to that power or habit, as man and stone are referred to the power of sight in that they are coloured. Hence coloured things are the proper objects of sight. But in sacred science all things are treated of under the aspect of God, either because they are God Himself, or because they are ordered to God as their beginning and end. Hence it follows that God is truly the subject of this science. This is clear also from the principles of this science, namely, the articles of faith, for faith is about God. The subject of the principles and of the whole science must be the same, since the whole science is contained virtually in its principles.

Some, however, looking to what is treated of in this science, and not to the aspect under which it is treated, have asserted the subject of this science to be something other than God—that is, either things and signs, or the works of salvation, or the whole Christ, that is, the head and members. For we treat of all these things, in this science, but only so far as they are ordered to God. (Vol. 19, p. 7b-c)

III

Aquinas says that sacred theology deals with revealed truths known through faith. But what is faith, and how is it a form of knowledge? Aquinas deals with these questions in our second selection, Questions 1-3 of the *Treatise on Faith, Hope, and Charity*. Question 1, "Of Faith," devotes an article to each of these topics:

1 Whether the object of faith is the First Truth?
2 Whether the object of faith is something complex or incomplex, that is, whether it is a thing or a proposition?
3 Whether anything false can come under faith?
4 Whether the object of faith can be anything seen?

Let us start with Articles 4 and 5 to discover what faith is, according to Aquinas. These articles distinguish between faith and science in terms of the "seen" and the "unseen." According to Aquinas, the intellect affirms that something is true either (1) because the intellect is compelled to do so by the *evidence* (first principles, conclusions, sense experience), or (2) because it is moved to do so by an act of the will, an act of free choice. *Knowledge* consists in affirmations of the first type; *opinion*, in affirmations of the second type.

According to Aquinas, faith is like opinion in one respect, and like knowledge in another. It has the certitude of science or knowledge, but it always involves an act of the will—a voluntary decision to assent to something that is in itself not evident to the intellect. In the case of faith, this act of the will is itself of supernatural origin, for faith is a gift of God's grace. It is this fact about faith which, according to Aquinas, distinguishes it from merely human beliefs or opinions, and gives faith a certitude greater than that of science, even though it deals with matters beyond the ken of reason.

It is instructive to see how Aquinas handles the story of Doubting Thomas in John 20:24-29 (cited in Obj. 1 of Art. 4) to show us that we can both *see* and *believe* in the same thing. In the Gospel story, Thomas refuses to believe that Jesus has been resurrected until he has seen and felt the nail holes in Jesus' body. Jesus rebukes Thomas for not believing without seeing. However, Aquinas insists that what Thomas saw and what he believed were two different things:

Thomas saw one thing, and believed another. He saw the Man, and believing Him to be God, he made profession of his faith, saying: "My Lord and my God." (Vol. 20, p. 383a)

Indeed, faith makes us see what should be believed; belief gives us sight. "The light of faith makes us see what we be-

lieve." Sense experience and rational insight alone—what is
seen— do not produce faith, but science.

Aquinas establishes a clear dichotomy between science
(knowledge of the manifest, the evident or self-evident, the
seen) and faith (belief in the unseen). Hence nothing can be
both an object of faith and an object of science *for the same
person, in the same respect, at the same time*. Aquinas insists
on this exact, qualified distinction in his answer to Article 5.

If philosophical knowledge of the existence and unity of
God is granted, it would seem that the objects of faith can be
seen by reason. Aquinas maintains that this is not so. In the
first place, what is believed on faith by one person may be seen
through reason by another person, but it is not both seen and
believed *by the same person at the same time*. In the second
place, something may be an object of science (seen) *in one
respect*, and an object of faith (believed) *in another respect*.
For instance, a man may know by rational demonstration that
God exists, but believe in the triune nature of God through
faith. In the third place, there are certain things, such as the
Trinity and the Incarnation, which are absolutely matters of
faith for all.

Most of the other articles in Question 1 deal with the articu-
lation of Christian faith in the specific propositions comprised
in the formal creeds. In Article 2, Aquinas deals with the objection that faith has to do with God, not with propositions
about God. He answers that faith, like science and opinion,
must deal with propositions because the human intellect is so
made that it can attain truth only through propositions. Only
in the beatific vision may man know God immediately and as
He is. Faith is "a virtue that perfects the intellect," but it must
do so in conformity with the nature of the intellect.

Article 2 furnishes the basic concept underlying Articles
6-10, which deal with the articles of faith and formal creeds.

Isidore says: "An article is a glimpse of Divine truth, tending thereto."
Now we can only get a glimpse of Divine truth by way of distinguishing,
since things which in God are one, are many in our intellect. Therefore
matters of faith should be divided into articles. (Vol. 20, p. 384d)

The articles are so called because they are parts that fit together as the parts of the body are "articulated." The articles of faith are put together properly in the creeds, which are "rules" of faith (that is, the objective norm of faith for all Christians). Aquinas denies that a creed is an arbitrary addition to Scripture. He regards it instead as a necessary explication of the implicit meaning of Scripture, so that all believers may know the content of faith.

As the Apostle says (Heb. 2:6), *he that cometh to God, must believe that He is.* Now a man cannot believe, unless the truth be proposed to him that he may believe it. Hence the need for the truth of faith to be collected together, so that it might the more easily be proposed to all, lest anyone might stray from the truth through ignorance of the faith. (Vol. 20, p. 389a-b)

It is this need to make the content of faith explicit and to protect the common believer from heresy that makes new versions of the creed necessary. The later versions contain essentially the same substance as the earlier versions, but are more explicit about certain aspects, as the times require. Aquinas, following Paul, admits a progressive illumination in man's knowledge of the substance of faith during the period before Christ. According to this view, the Incarnation, Passion, and Resurrection of Christ were contained implicitly in the Old Testament faith in God's existence, providence, and salvation; but only with the coming of Christ, "in the fullness of time," was the implicit made fully known (see Art. 7).

Aquinas sets forth the content of this fully revealed faith in Article 8. The articles of faith deal with two mysteries: the majesty of God and the human nature of Christ.

Now with regard to the majesty of the Godhead, three things are proposed to our belief. First the unity of the Godhead, to which the first article refers. Secondly, the trinity of the Persons, to which three articles refer, corresponding to the three Persons. And thirdly the works proper to the Godhead: the first of which refers to the order (*esse*) of nature, in relation to which the article about the creation is proposed to us; the second refers to the order (*esse*) of grace, in relation to which all matters concerning the sanctification of man are included in one article; while the third refers to the order (*esse*) of glory, and in relation to this another article is proposed to us concerning the resurrection of the dead and life everlasting. Thus there are seven articles referring to the Godhead.

In like manner, with regard to Christ's human nature, there are seven articles, the first of which refers to Christ's incarnation or conception; the second, to His virginal birth; the third, to His Passion, death and burial; the fourth, to His descent into hell; the fifth, to His resurrection; the sixth, to His ascension; the seventh, to His coming for the judgment, so that in all there are fourteen articles. (Vol. 20, pp. 387d-388a)

Remember that these articles express the objective content of faith for the Church as a whole, whether all individual members inwardly believe in the creed or not. Since "there should be but one faith of the whole Church," the pope may, directly or through Church councils called by him, draw up a new version of the creed. (See Reply Obj. 3 of Art. 9, and Art. 10.)

IV

In Questions 2 and 3 of the *Treatise on Faith, Hope, and Charity*, Aquinas discusses the act of faith. Question 2 takes up the interior, or mental, aspect of belief; and Question 3 deals with the exterior, or verbal, expression of faith. We might say that Aquinas sets forth in these two questions a theological evaluation of the psychology and ethics of belief—how a man comes to believe and how he should express his belief to other men.

These are the topics discussed in the ten articles of Question 2:

1   What is "to believe," which is the inward act of faith?
2   In how many ways is it expressed?
3   Whether it is necessary for salvation to believe in anything above natural reason?
4   Whether it is necessary to believe those things that are attainable by natural reason?
5   Whether it is necessary for salvation to believe certain things explicitly?
6   Whether all are equally bound to explicit faith?
7   Whether explicit faith in Christ is always necessary for salvation?
8   Whether it is necessary for salvation to believe in the Trinity explicitly?
9   Whether the act of faith is meritorious?
10 Whether human reason diminishes the merit of faith?

In Article 1, Aquinas defines the inward act of belief as an assent of the intellect, determined by an act of the will. To believe is "to think with assent," but the decision to assent comes from the will, not from the understanding, as in science. In scientific knowledge, the intellect assents to what is demonstrably true and cannot be otherwise. Science is purely a rational matter. But faith depends on a decision of the will which determines the mind to assent when denial or indecisive doubt would be equally possible. Thus faith differs from opinion as well as from science.

But some acts of the intellect have unformed thought lacking a firm assent, whether they incline to neither side, as in one who doubts; or incline to one side rather than the other, but on account of some slight motive, as in one who suspects; or incline to one side yet with fear of the other, as in one who holds an opinion. But this act "to believe," cleaves firmly to one side, in which respect belief has something in common with science and understanding; yet its knowledge does not attain the perfection of clear vision, in which respect it agrees with doubt, suspicion and opinion. . . . The intellect of the believer is determined to one object, not by the reason, but by the will, and so assent is taken here for an act of the intellect as determined to one object by the will. (Vol. 20, pp. 391d-392a)

But again the question is raised, whether faith is not superfluous since reason gives us solid knowledge of God's existence and nature. As before, Aquinas answers that knowledge through faith is quicker, more widespread, and more certain than similar knowledge attainable through reason. But here he adds a new argument. He says that since man is subordinate to God, his perfection requires both the knowledge that he can acquire by the use of his natural faculties and the knowledge that he can receive from God. Both the light of natural reason and the light of divine revelation are necessary for man's full perfection. Moreover, revelation alone can direct man to ultimate salvation.

. . . man's ultimate happiness consists in a supernatural vision of God, to which vision man cannot attain unless he be taught by God . . . And every one who learns thus must believe, in order that he may acquire science in a perfect degree. . . .

Hence, in order that a man arrive at the perfect vision of heavenly happiness, he must first of all believe God, as a disciple believes the master who is teaching him. (Vol. 20, p. 393b)

God is the teacher who enlightens man by the light of faith. In order to learn the special truths that God teaches we must first believe—we must "believe God." (In Art. 2, Aquinas distinguishes between believing God, believing in *a* God, and believing in God: "to believe God" means to believe His teaching or revelation; "to believe in *a* God" is to believe that God exists; and "to believe in God" means to direct the will to God as its end.)

Aquinas takes up in Articles 4-8 the question whether faith is a matter of believing precise, explicit propositions; or a general, implicit readiness and openness to the mind and will of God. The discussion here is a fuller development and refinement of the discussion in Question 1 about the articles of faith. Aquinas distinguishes between primary articles of faith, which all men are bound to believe explicitly; and secondary matters following from the primary articles, which may be believed implicitly by the common and unlearned people, though they must be believed explicitly by the learned. "Explicitly" here means consciously and expressly; "implicitly" means unconsciously, but implied in what is explicitly believed.

Therefore, as regards the primary points or articles of faith, man is bound to believe them, just as he is bound to have faith; but as to other points of faith, man is not bound to believe them explicitly, but only implicitly, or to be ready to believe them, in so far as he is prepared to believe whatever is contained in the Divine Scriptures. Then alone is he bound to believe such things explicitly, when it is clear to him that they are contained in the doctrine of faith. (Vol. 20, p. 395a)

For instance, all men are bound to believe explicitly in the Incarnation and the Trinity, but the various details of the Passion and Resurrection and the fine points of doctrine on the relations of the three persons of the Trinity are matters of implicit belief for most men, though explicit for the learned. By "all men" Aquinas means Jews and pagans as well as Christians. He insists that even before the coming of Christ, the Jews believed in the Incarnation, Passion, and Resurrection, since they prefigured these events in their ritual sacrifices, though this was apparent only to the learned. He also asserts that many pagans received explicit revelations of Christ before his coming, and that certain others were saved through faith in a mediator, implied in their explicit belief in divine providence and redemption. Thus the "unlearned" may be simply those who lived in a time and place where they could not have explicit knowledge of the mysteries of the Christian faith. But all men are bound to explicit faith after the event.

> After grace had been revealed, both learned and simple folk are bound to explicit faith in the mysteries of Christ, chiefly as regards those which are observed throughout the Church, and publicly proclaimed, such as the articles which refer to the Incarnation, of which we have spoken above (Q. 1, A. 8). As to other minute points in reference to the articles of the Incarnation, men have been bound to believe them more or less explicitly according to each one's state and office. (Vol. 20, p. 397a)

Aquinas' last point about faith is that it is meritorious (see Art. 9 and 10). Faith is one of the three theological virtues, the other two being hope and charity. But if faith depends on divine grace, how can it be regarded as meritorious? Why should we praise a man for being faithful, or why should God reward him for his faith? Aquinas answers that

> our actions are meritorious in so far as they proceed from free choice moved with grace by God. Therefore every human act proceeding from free choice, if it be referred to God, can be meritorious. Now the act of believing is an act of the intellect assenting to the Divine truth at the command of the will moved by the grace of God, so that it falls under free choice in relation to God. And consequently the act of faith can be meritorious. (Vol. 20, p. 398d)

God's grace moves the human will to command the human intellect to assent to the truths revealed by God. The believer's free assent is required, for faith, unlike science, is not compelled by the undeniable force of rational demonstration. The believer responds to both external and internal signs—to "the authority of Divine teaching confirmed by miracles, and . . . by the inward impulse of the Divine invitation." He responds; he says, "Yes," where another in his place might refuse, might say, "No."

In giving reasons for one's faith does one lessen its merit? The 19th-century Danish religious philosopher Sören Kierkegaard said giving reasons for believing in the existence of God is just as silly and out-of-place as giving reasons for believing in the existence of the person you love, or reasons to prove your love. Aquinas would agree, but only if the reasons and the "proofs" are the basis of the faith, instead of following after, as a kind of homage and service to one's faith.

Human reasons may be consequent to the will of the believer. For when a man's will is ready to believe, he loves the truth he believes, he thinks out and takes to heart whatever reasons he can find in its support; and in this way, human reason does not exclude the merit of faith, but is a sign of greater merit. (Vol. 20, p. 399d)

Moreover, the central mystery which is the object of faith still remains a mystery after all the reasons and "demonstrations" are set forth: the unseen still remains unseen.

The reasons which are brought forward in support of the authority of faith, are not demonstrations which can bring intellectual vision to the human intellect, and therefore they do not cease to be unseen. But they remove obstacles to faith, by showing that what faith proposes is not impossible. Hence such reasons do not diminish the merit or the measure of faith. (Vol. 20, p. 400a)

In Question 3, Aquinas deals with the overt act of "confession," that is, the profession of faith—the credo, or "I believe"—by which the individual believer bears witness to his faith publicly. He points out the essential importance of this outward act by quoting Paul's words: "With the heart we believe unto justice; but with the mouth, confession is made unto salvation." (See Romans 10:10.) This act of open confession honors God and serves fellow men.

Thus then it is not necessary for salvation to confess one's faith at all times and in all places, but in certain places and at certain times, when, namely, by omitting to do so, we would deprive God of due honour, or our neighbour of a service that we ought to render him; for instance, if a man, on being asked about his faith were to remain silent, so as to make people believe either that he is without faith, or that the faith is false, or so as to turn others away from the faith. (Vol. 20, p. 401c)

Aquinas advises us to affirm our faith openly when it serves good purposes, but not for mean motives of display, or to start a dispute. Stand up and be counted, he counsels; bear witness to your faith at the proper time and place.

V

Is the God of philosophical reason the same as the God of religious faith?

Aquinas explicitly recognizes that philosophy, based on natural reason, can provide sound knowledge about God. But is the God of the philosophers the same as the God of the patriarchs, prophets, and apostles? If they are different, where does the difference lie? It has been said that philosophy provides an abstract diagram of divine reality, while religious faith centers on a living, personal God. But even if this is so, are philosophy and religion concerned with the same reality—the one God—in different ways, or are they not? Which affords a truer picture of divine reality—philosophy or religion?

It is possible to affirm that philosophy provides an objective norm for the religious view, which often is fogged by emotional biases, historical tradition, and anthropomorphism (*i.e.*, seeing God in terms of human qualities). It is also possible to affirm that religious faith gives the only true picture of God's nature and attributes, beside which the God of philosophy is a flimsy idol made of cobwebs and abstraction. Finally, it is possible to affirm that both the philosophical and religious views do justice to the divine reality, though dealing with different aspects or levels, so that the God of philosophy and the God of religious faith are one and the same. Which position does Aquinas take? Is Aquinas' God the same as the God of the Bible?

Is a man free to refuse the gift of faith?

Aquinas says God's grace moves man's will to assent to revealed truths. Is man, then, compelled by God's action to believe, or is he free to disbelieve divine revelation when grace is operative? If compelled, then he lacks the free choice which Aquinas makes essential in the act of faith. If free to believe or disbelieve, then the omnipotence of God seems challenged. How would you answer this theological problem? For part of Aquinas' answer, see Article 1, Question 6, in Part II of the Second Part (Vol. 20, pp. 413d-414c).

How can sacred theology be a science if its origin is faith, and its aim salvation?

Aquinas deals with this question in Articles 2 and 4 of Question 1 in Part I (Vol. 19, pp. 4a-c, 5a-b). However, the question is still an open one for us, since Aquinas' answers are in terms of medieval notions of science and are inconclusive.

In Article 2, Aquinas compares sacred theology, which draws its first principles from divine revelation, to the sciences of perspective and optics, which draw their first principles from mathematics. But can principles not evident to reason be the basis of a true science? If we answer in the negative, we must then face the question whether science, based on reason alone, implies a trust in reason as a means of attaining truth. Is trust in reason, and in the unity and order of nature, required before we can engage in scientific inquiry? Does science, then, rest in an act of faith, so to speak?

In Article 4, Aquinas decides that sacred theology primarily provides theoretical knowledge about God, rather than practical knowledge about what man should do. But he also considers it partly a practical science, since it serves to guide man to his ultimate salvation. Is sacred theology formally the same kind of science as philosophical theology, or metaphysics, merely differing in the origin of its first principles, *i.e.*, divine revelation instead of natural reason? Or is it essentially the highest intellectual expression of the Church's function of preaching and teaching the Gospel of salvation through Christ? Is the sacred theologian's relation to his subject matter the same as the secular metaphysician's relation to his? Does the theologian's pursuit of truth have a practical effect on him as a man and a Christian that is quite distinct from the practical effect of philosophical inquiry upon the philosopher? Can a man be a sound theologian without being a genuinely religious man? Is a great, creative theological construction, like that of Aquinas, possible apart from living roots in religious faith?

How does the believer know that what he believes in is divine revelation?

The traditional answer is that he knows this through faith. But faith involves the gift of divine grace. How do we know that it is a genuine faith we have, and not mere conformity to what has been handed down to us? Aquinas notes that miracles —in the common sense of extraordinary events that contravene the laws of nature—comprise one of the factors which predispose a man toward faith. But most believers claim no personal experience of miracles. Belief in miracles is, again, a belief in what has been handed down, or in the assertions of others.

It is possible to believe that (1) the "miraculous" events did not take place as reported, or (2) they were not the work of divine power. One or the other of these attitudes is taken by Jews toward Christian miracles, by Christians toward Jewish miracles in the post-Biblical period, or by Protestants toward Catholic miracles in the post-Biblical era. Do believers simply believe what they are told—what they are taught by their elders and religious leaders? Or is this tradition the vehicle of divine revelation? But, in the latter case, there are so many traditions, and they are in disagreement at vital points.

For Aquinas and faithful Catholics, the Church is the mystical body of Christ, and its officiants and teachers have a sacred character. But on what is this faith, or trust, in the Church and its officials based? Aquinas makes it quite clear that only God is absolutely trustworthy and infallible, for the learned doctors of the Church can err. "Hence it is not human knowledge, but the Divine truth that is the rule of faith" (Vol. 20, p. 396a).

Is rationality the criterion of revelation, based on the assumption that revelation does not contradict reason, and in certain points is supported by reason? But many Jewish, Islamic, and secular philosophers deny the rationality of some essential Christian dogmas. Perhaps historical success—the world-wide spread and cultural creativity of Christianity—is a sign that this doctrine is from God. But it is difficult to prove transcendent truths from historical data; and, besides, there are equally noteworthy historical successes, such as the spread of Buddhism over Asia and the extraordinary expansion of

Islam. Another criterion might be the "inward impulse" that Aquinas talks of (the knowledge of the heart, the content of religious experience). But does such experience carry its own validation?

Perhaps these are the wrong questions to ask, because they are asked from outside the condition of faith, and with some critical doubt. Can plausible or impressive criteria for the divine origin of faith be offered to anyone who stands outside the community of the faithful? Does Aquinas claim to give a rational demonstration that the Christian faith is based on divine revelation, or does he start with that faith and go on from there?

Is it legitimate for theology, as a scientific discipline, to use figurative expressions?

Articles 9 and 10 of Question 1 in Part I deal with the interpretation of scriptural symbols. Aquinas defends the use of figurative expressions in Scripture to represent divine things. What does this have to do with the nature and scope of sacred theology? Is it the function of theology to use such symbolical expressions itself, or rather to make explicit in systematic fashion what the hidden meanings of scriptural symbols are?

Aquinas uses the terms "Holy Scripture" and "sacred doctrine" interchangeably in these articles. He says that "this sacred science may use metaphors . . . sacred doctrine makes use of metaphors . . . this science has the property that the things signified by the words have themselves also a meaning" (Vol. 19, p. 9a-d).

Is this use of figurative expressions a distinctive feature of sacred theology as compared with the philosophical sciences? Are the latter restricted to literal expressions?

Does "faith" mean anything besides intellectual assent to propositions?

Is the absolute trust in God that is expressed in the Psalms, Gospels, and passages like Isaiah 26:3-4 genuine religious faith? Is it similar to an assent that certain propositions are true, or is it more like trust in a person? To what, in Aquinas'

exposition of faith, does trust in God in the Biblical sense cor-
respond? If there are two types of faith (*i.e.*, creedal belief and
personal trust), how are they related? Does belief in articles of
faith lead to a personal trust in God, or does personal trust
in God lead to the affirmation of certain propositions about
God?

The following questions are designed to help you test the thoroughness of your reading. Each question is to be answered by giving a page or pages of the reading assignment. Answers will be found on page 269 of this Reading Plan.

1 Is sacred doctrine a practical or a speculative science?

2 Does Aquinas believe in a progressive advancement in man's knowledge of revelation?

3 Why does Aquinas think that material images, even very low ones, are a good way of indicating the highest spiritual truths?

4 What are the two basic forms of symbols in Scripture?

5 What three things are proposed for belief in the articles of faith?

6 What is the threefold confession commended by Scripture?

7 What end does faith have in common with charity?

D A N T E

The Divine Comedy

"Paradise"

Vol. 21, pp. 106-157

At rare moments in a cultural tradition, great works are created which sum up all the strands of thought and imagination that have gone into the making of that tradition. Such a unifying work is usually the creation of a poetic genius. In the case of Western Christendom, that moment comes in the early part of the 14th century; the work is *The Divine Comedy*, and the poet is Dante Alighieri.

Dante takes nothing less than man's ultimate destiny as his theme. To achieve his aim he deals with the whole of human life (man's history from Adam to his own era) and the whole physical universe as it was known in his day. He summons to his aid ideas and images and events from the great books of the Western world up to his time.

Through this work of original genius march Biblical patriarchs and prophets, Christian martyrs and saints, Homeric heroes and villains, Greek philosophers and

Church Fathers, medieval scholastics and mystics, and the prelates and politicians of Dante's own day. *The Divine Comedy* comprises an extraordinary combination of poetic imagination, religious faith, rational thought, mystical insight, and historical fact.

All of this goes to portray the state of man after death as the ultimate result of his life on earth. *The Divine Comedy* starts at the gateway to Hell and ends with the mystical vision of God at the summit of Paradise. Dante's poetic genius gives shape and body and color and voice to the highest and most abstract concepts of medieval Christian thought. Ideas take personal form here, and the virtues are given concrete life. The result is both a literary masterpiece and an unforgettable view of man's spiritual nature and destiny.

Seventh Reading

I

The original title of this work was *The Comedy of Dante Alighieri*. The adjective "divine" was first added to the title in the 16th century, expressing admiration for its wondrous artistry and intellectual power, as well as indicating its sacred theme. The term "comedy" refers to the happy ending of the work, for it starts in Hell and ends in Paradise.

The work breaks with literary tradition in many respects. For one thing, it is written in Italian (one of the "vulgar" tongues) instead of in Latin, the language of scholars and writers. For another, the author himself is the protagonist as well as the narrator of the story. His epic forerunners, Homer and Virgil, were never characters in their own works. Dante also peoples his *Comedy* with actual persons, including both famous characters of the past and contemporaries of the author. Like a historical novelist, he mixes fiction and history.

This so-called "comedy" does not have entertainment nor the purging of the emotions as its end. It is deadly serious— prophetic rather than aesthetic in intention. Dante's aim is to edify, to awaken his readers morally through appealing to their minds and hearts by means of his literary power—"to put into verse things difficult to think." In a letter to his patron, Can Grande della Scala, he states emphatically that his intention is not speculative, but moral—to affect human character and action. Here is what Dante has to say in this epistle about the theme of *The Divine Comedy*:

The subject of the whole work, taken merely in its *literal* sense, is the state of souls after death, considered simply as a fact. But if the work is understood in its *allegorical* intention, the subject of it is man, according as, by his deserts and demerits in the use of his free will, he is justly open to rewards and punishments.

Thus Dante forewarns us to seek the underlying meanings in this work, and not to be satisfied with the dramatic surface of the story. He also tells us that this is a *human* comedy, about man's condition and man's destiny, not merely an otherworldly panorama. In it we find human passions and aspirations, politics and religion, philosophy and theology, the history of Europe and Italy, Dante's personal experiences, his thought and his faith—all in the framework of the Christian scheme of man's creation, fall, and salvation. Dante tells us, in effect, that he has set his imaginative powers to work in order to reveal and embody, to recreate and represent moral and metaphysical reality.

II

Let us glance at the action in the preceding sections of this work before considering the concluding section called "Paradise." As the poem opens Dante is lost in a dark wood (worldly temptations) on the night before Good Friday in the year 1300. Early in the morning of Good Friday he tries to ascend a hill (felicity), but is prevented by a leopard, a lion, and a wolf (lust, pride, and avarice). The poet Virgil (natural wisdom) comes to Dante's aid. He has been sent by three heavenly ladies—the Virgin Mary, Saint Lucy, and Beatrice (divine grace, illuminating grace, and supernatural wisdom)—to lead Dante to Paradise by way of Hell and Purgatory.

(In the foregoing paragraph, the explanations we have put in parentheses are suggestive of the probable meanings of the places and figures. Additional meanings are possible, and may suggest themselves to you as you read.)

Virgil leads Dante through the Gate of Hell, where a sign warns newcomers to abandon all hope as they enter upon eternal woe. Hell is divided into three main divisions, corresponding roughly to Aristotle's classification of the vices: incontinence, brutishness or violence, and fraud or malice. The movement here is a descent to deeper and deeper levels of sin and punishment—nine levels in all—from the neutral zone of the "trimmers" rejected by Heaven and Hell alike, and the Limbo of the heathen unbaptized, to the nethermost depths where Lucifer is fixed permanently upside down in ice. On the way down, Dante meets notables of ancient history and of his own city of Florence—pagan philosophers, proud prelates, famous lovers, warriors, and poets.

After they reach the earth's center, Dante and Virgil ascend until they come to the foot of the Mount of Purgatory at dawn on Easter day. At the summit of Purgatory is the Garden of Eden, the Earthly Paradise from which man was expelled as a result of original sin. Man's first task is to return, through purgation, to his lost natural perfection before going on to the supernatural realm. As in Hell, there is a vestibule, an ante-purgatorial realm for tardy penitents and the excommunicated. Cato, the Roman Censor, the symbol of stern moral virtue, greets the two travelers as they begin the purgatorial ascent. They enter at St. Peter's Gate (the Church) and proceed through seven terraces, corresponding to the seven deadly sins. These are classified in a threefold division as types of distorted, defective, and excessive love. Dante and Virgil make the exceedingly difficult climb, undergoing some of the purgation and discipline imposed on souls in this realm. On the way they meet many of the most famous men of Dante's time. Finally, they reach the Earthly Paradise, man's lost Garden of Eden.

Here they meet first Matilda, the guardian spirit of Eden, who represents the active life in a state of innocence. Next they meet Beatrice, representing supernatural wisdom or revelation, who must now replace Virgil (natural wisdom or philosophy) as Dante's guide. It is Beatrice who is to lead Dante through the nine heavens to the Empyrean realm where he will experience the beatific vision. Before starting out, she instructs him on the corruption and usurpations of church and state, which have prevented man from regaining Eden and kept it a deserted place. Beatrice prophesies a coming purification and a just relation between church and state.

III

The physical analogue of Dante's spiritual ascent is taken from the Ptolemaic picture of the universe that was accepted in his time, with the earth at the center instead of the sun. (See the Sixth Reading in the Reading Plan for Physics and Mathematics.) Each of the seven planetary heavens is associated, in ascending order, with a defect in virtue, an earthly approximation to virtue, or one of the cardinal moral virtues, as follows:

1 Moon—inconstancy
2 Mercury—ambition
3 Venus—earthly love
4 Sun—prudence
5 Mars—fortitude
6 Jupiter—justice
7 Saturn—temperance

In the eighth heaven, the heaven of the fixed stars, Dante meets redeemed human souls; in the ninth heaven, or Primum Mobile, the angels. The tenth, or Empyrean, heaven is the place of God and His angels and the redeemed souls. It is the eternal present where, for a moment, Dante experiences the mystical vision of God.

At the beginning of their ascent, Beatrice tells Dante of the universal order in which all things have their place, with the Eternal Power which holds the world together as their source and their goal. Man's ascent to God is as natural as water's descent from a mountain, although—seduced by false pleasures—man may go down instead of up.

All things whatsoever have order among themselves; and this is the form which makes the universe like unto God. Herein the exalted creatures see the imprint of the Eternal Power, which is the end for which the aforesaid rule is made. In the order of which I speak, all natures are disposed, by diverse lots, more or less near to their source; wherefore they are moved to different ports over the great sea of being, and each with the instinct given to it which bears it on. This bears the fire upward toward the moon; this is the motive force in mortal hearts; this binds together and unites the earth. Nor does this bow shoot forth only the created things which are without intelligence, but also those which have understanding and love. (p. 107b-c)

Piccarda, who occupies the lowest level of heaven because of her inconstancy, proclaims her acceptance of the divine will and order, and her lack of resentment at not being more highly placed. Blessedness is to be at one with God's will. Every place in heaven is Paradise, for it is to be with God.

But tell me, ye who are happy here, do ye desire a more exalted place, in order to see more, or to make for yourselves more friends?

With those other shades she first smiled a little, then answered me so glad, that she seemed to burn in the first fire of love: "Brother, virtue of charity quiets our will, and makes us wish only for that which we have, and quickens not our thirst for aught else. If we desired to be more on high, our desires would be discordant with the will of Him who assigns us here, which thou wilt see is not possible in these circles, if to exist in charity is here of necessity, and if thou dost well consider its nature. Nay, it is the essence of this blessed existence to hold itself within the divine will, whereby our wills themselves are made one. So that as we are, from seat to seat throughout this realm, to all the realm is pleasing, as to the King who inwills us with His will; and His will is our peace; it is that sea whereunto everything is moving which It creates and which nature makes."

Then was it clear to me, how everywhere in Heaven is Paradise, even if the grace of the Supreme Good does not there rain down in one measure. (p. 110a-b)

Beatrice quickly points out to Dante that we are not to take literally these physical levels of the heavenly ascent. They merely indicate grades of spiritual grace. All the inhabitants of Paradise, from the seraphim on down, occupy the highest heaven together, though they are touched in greater or lesser degree by the eternal breath (see p. 111a). Paradise for Dante is the realm of divine love, which descends on all the inhabitants, though in different degrees according to their spiritual level. Hell, on the contrary, is characterized by the absence of love; and Purgatory, by imperfect love. Creation must inevitably strive upward from the states of absent and defective love to the state of perfect love—the ultimate end and resting place.

I V

Just as in the preceding sections of the poem, so here in "Paradise" the figures that Dante meets on his way up to the Empyrean circle are significant expressions of his main concerns and his basic view of things. For instance, Dante held that both the state (that is, the Holy Roman Empire) and the church were divinely instituted, each with distinct powers derived directly from God. He considered the Empire a universal power established by God to take care of man's secular life, just as the church was the universal institution set up by God to care for man's religious life. That is why we find the emperor Justinian, the great lawmaker of the Roman Empire, in the sphere of Mercury in heaven (Canto VI). And that is why we find Dante's work filled with vituperation against his contemporary, Pope Boniface VIII, for usurping the secular power. Church and state, for Dante, are two equal powers, subordinate only to God. This conflicts with the medieval Catholic view that the temporal power, though distinct, is subordinate to the spiritual power. (Note that justice ranks high in the heavenly order of virtues, and is associated with kingly power; see Cantos XVIII-XX.)

Reaching the sphere of the sun (Canto X), we find a reconciliation, or harmony, between the two great monastic orders —the Franciscan and Dominican—and their respective types of theology—the spiritual or mystical, and the intellectual. Thomas Aquinas, the author of our previous reading, points out the great medieval thinkers to Dante and eulogizes Francis and Dominic, the founders of the orders that bear their names. To balance the praise given by the Dominican Aquinas to Francis, the great Franciscan theologian Bonaventura in turn praises Dominic. Dante thus tells us that both speculative and mystical theology (represented, respectively, by Aquinas and Bonaventura) have a place in the divine scheme. The earthly clash between these two types of thought is resolved in heaven, in a spirit of gentle courtesy and love.

We expect theology to get a place in heaven, but what—we may ask—about philosophy? Does Dante consider philosophy a pursuit springing from merely natural powers, and undeserving of the heavenly state? From our reading of the first section, on Hell, we know that Dante put Aristotle, the typical representative of philosophy for most medieval thinkers, in Limbo—the highest circle in Hell, reserved for righteous heathens and the unbaptized. According to the traditional Christian view, Dante had no choice; he put Aristotle as high up in the scale of things as he could. Furthermore, we know from

Dante's other writings that he considered philosophy a divinely instituted pursuit in the realm of natural wisdom, just as the state was divinely established in the realm of secular power.

It is hard to find a representative philosopher in Dante's Paradise. However, one philosopher got through the needle's eye, and the insertion of this solitary figure, Siger of Brabant, into Dante's heaven has aroused much puzzled comment. Siger was the exponent of a type of Aristotelian philosophy that was condemned by the Church, and his contemporary Thomas Aquinas was one of his most vigorous opponents. But in Canto X, Dante has Aquinas eulogize "the eternal light of Siger, who, . . . syllogized invidious truths" (p. 121c-d); that is, truths which brought him hatred and condemnation. Dante has taken liberties here to express a viewpoint of his own.

Does Dante mean to say that secular philosophy, the fruit of natural wisdom, has a place in heaven beside sacred theology? Or does he put Siger beside Aquinas because both men recognized the power and virtue of natural reason?

Notice, again, Dante's independent viewpoint and poetic license in Canto XII, where Bonaventura eulogizes Joachim of Floris as one "endowed with prophetic spirit." (p. 125a) Joachim was a Cistercian abbot who preached that the age of the Holy Spirit would succeed the ages of the Father and the Son. In the new age of love and freedom, the worldly institutions and disciplines of the visible Church would be absorbed into the contemplative perfection of the spiritual church.

It makes no difference to Dante that Aquinas considered Joachim a false prophet, and that Bonaventura vigorously opposed Joachim and his influence among Franciscans. In the first place, Joachim expresses Dante's own view that the Church should be spiritualized and desecularized. In the second place, Joachim and Bonaventura are associated by Dante according to their essential type, as advocates of contemplation and spirituality. Their place in the poem does not depend on the attitude that one may have taken toward the other in actual history. In Dante's heaven they are friends and allies; in heaven, Dante might remind us, things are as they should be. Dante is not interested in reporting historical events, but in writing an imaginative work that will express his whole view of things. Bonaventura and Joachim, as Aquinas and Siger, function as characters in this work.

When Dante ascends with Beatrice to the sphere of Mars—the realm of the warriors who have fought for God—he meets his great-great-grandfather, the founder of his family (see Canto XV). This ancestor of Dante gives us a history of ancient Florence as well as predicts what suffering Florence will inflict upon Dante. (See the Biographical Note, pp. v-vi.) Dante, who referred to himself on the title page of *The Divine Comedy* as "a Florentine by birth but not by character," was unable to forget or forgive what his native city had done to him. Through his ancestor he rails against Florence, even in heaven.

In the next sphere, that of Jupiter, we meet the just rulers, including not only the Christian kings, Charlemagne and Godfrey of Bouillon, but also the pagan rulers, Rhipeus of Troy and Trajan of Rome. In response to his wondering questions, Dante is told that the pagans may have been open to divine revelation and that some of them may be saved. He is warned not to prejudge who is and who is not elect, nor to presume to know God's will (see Canto XX).

Dante ascends next to the seventh heaven of Saturn where he encounters Benedict, founder of the famous order at Monte Cassino and representative of the contemplative life. Benedict extols the contemplative way to God and castigates the degenerate state of present-day monastic orders. His appearance here in the highest of the planetary heavens reflects the high value Dante puts on contemplation. Benedict expresses Dante's low opinion of contemporary religious orders.

Before going up into the eighth sphere, Dante looks down on the universe below and smiles at the littleness of the earth so far below him, realizing that its concerns are of little account from the viewpoint of eternity.

In the eighth, or stellar, heaven, Dante sees Christ and Mary and the whole heavenly host for a moment before they ascend to the higher spheres. The description of this moment in Canto XXIII is a beautiful expression of medieval faith and imagination. It is there, in the stellar heaven, that Dante is examined by St. Peter on the Christian faith. Dante cites both Aristotle and Scriptures in defense of his beliefs. Next come the brothers James and John, Jesus' early disciples, to test Dante on hope; they are followed by the apostle John (author of the Fourth Gospel), who examines Dante on love (charity). Finally, we read a tirade against the usurpations of Pope Boniface VIII just before Beatrice and Dante rise to the ninth heaven, or Primum Mobile.

Here, in the Primum Mobile, is the starting point of the love and intelligence that move all things. Beatrice tells Dante:

On that Point Heaven and all nature are dependent. Look on that circle which is most conjoined to It, and know that its motion is so swift because of the burning love whereby it is spurred. (p. 149b)

She also instructs him about the heavenly hierarchy of the nine angelic orders. These consist of three triads: Seraphim, Cherubim, and Thrones; Dominations, Virtues, and Powers; Principalities, Archangels, and Angels.

When Dante ascends into the Empyrean heaven, Bernard of Clairvaux, the great contemplative and mystical monk, supplants Beatrice as Dante's guide to show him the highest reaches of heaven. Revealed knowledge now gives way to immediate vision: even sacred theology is not the ultimate spiritual attainment. Dante's son Pietro, who wrote a famous commentary on the *Comedy*, says of this moment in Canto XXXI:

He (Dante) pretends that he is abandoned by Beatrice. The metaphor is that we cannot see and know God through theology, but through grace and contemplation. Hence, through St. Bernard, that is, through contemplation, he obtains from the Virgin the privilege of seeing such things as cannot be apprehended through the written word.

Here is the panorama revealed to Dante: Just below Christ is Mary. Nearest to her are Adam and Peter, John and Moses, and then the other "patricians" of the heavenly empire. Heaven is divided between those who looked forward to Christ and those who looked back on him after he came: that is, the saints of the Old and New Testaments. But they are all there, centered on the primal love which moves the sun and the other stars.

The poem ends with a moment of mystical vision in which the poet sees the whole of things in their essential order. Although he cannot keep that vision in his earthly form, his desire and will are now permanently at one with that primal love which moves them as it moves all things.

O Light Eternal, that sole abidest in Thyself, sole understandest Thyself, and, by Thyself understood and understanding, lovest and smilest on Thyself! That circle, which appeared in Thee generated as a reflected light, being awhile surveyed by my eyes, seemed to me depicted with our effigy within itself, of its own very color; wherefore my sight was wholly set upon it. As is the geometer who wholly applies himself to measure the circle, and finds not by thinking that principle of which he is in need, such was I at that new sight. I wished to see how the image was conformed to the circle, and how it has its place therein; but my own wings were not for this, had it not been that my mind was smitten by a flash in which its wish came.

To the high fantasy here power failed; but now my desire and my will were revolved, like a wheel which is moved evenly, by the Love which moves the sun and the other stars. (p. 157c-d)

V

Are we to take Dante's story as an imaginative fiction or as an allegory of religious truth?

If we compare Dante's *Divine Comedy* with such works as Spenser's *Faerie Queene* or Bunyan's *Pilgrim's Progress*, we recognize that we are not dealing here with an allegory in the usual sense. Dante does not present personified virtues or vices, or abstractions expressed in human form and speech, although he does use allegories in the case of places (such as the dark wood) or in the case of animals (such as the lion, leopard, etc.). Dante's people are actual historical persons or legendary characters. Aquinas, Bonaventura, Bernard, Justinian, and Boniface are themselves as well as representative persons in the story. As we have seen above, they are not mere copies of their historical realities. They play their parts as living characters in the world which Dante created in this poem. We must remember that *The Divine Comedy* is above all a wonderful, entrancing, and moving story. If we do not appreciate it first as literature, we are unlikely to grasp any other meanings it may have to offer. But there are other meanings, are there not? Did not Dante announce that there were in the letter to his patron, quoted above (p. 111)?

Is not the "allegorical" intention he states there more properly a "moral" intention? Does not Dante want to affect human character and action by dramatizing man's damnation through sin and his salvation through penance and grace? Can we understand the whole work in a spiritual sense, and apply its meaning to life in this world? Would Hell then represent the darkness and degradation that ensue from our vices; Purgatory, our painful reformation and regeneration; and Paradise, the happy state of virtue or holiness? Or would we be false to Dante's vision if we interpreted the otherworldly setting in a this-worldly sense? Is the world of the poem a picture of how Dante sees the actual world—with all things and powers in their proper places, together forming a harmonious whole?

There are so many ways to take this poem: as story, history, philosophy, theology, politics, and, last but not least, biography. What does the Dante of the poem have to do with the Dante of actual history? Was Dante himself lost in a dark wood in the middle journey of his life?

Who was Beatrice? What does she represent in the poem?

Again we seem to be confronted with a mixture of the actual and the symbolical. Exactly what the symbolical meaning of Beatrice is, we can grasp only by reading and rereading the poem. Dante has furnished us with an announcement of his general intention, but not with a score card that identifies the players. There was a Florentine girl by the name of Bice Portinari, whom Dante loved at a distance with a romantic, chivalrous passion. Though she married another and died young, he retained his feeling for her. She was probably the Beatrice in Dante's earlier works, as well as in *The Divine Comedy*. In the *Vita Nuova* ("new life"), he cloaks his interest in Beatrice (at a church service) by flirting with a lady who stands between them. In the *Convivio,* or *Convito* ("banquet"), the lady, now identified as philosophy, eulogizes Beatrice. Who, then, is Beatrice?

We may get some indication of her role from the likeness between her name and the word "beatitude," or blessedness. But is it not Bernard who guides Dante to the beatific vision? Bernard, representing mystical contemplation, supplants Beatrice, as she had supplanted Virgil, and leads Dante to the summit of religious experience.

Thus on the one hand, we have philosophy (the lady); on the other, we have mystical contemplation, or the beatific vision (Bernard). What can be in between? Is Beatrice the symbol for theology or revealed truth, as contrasted with philosophy or rational truth on the one hand, and the immediate experience of the beatific vision on the other? Does this have anything to do with the two kinds of knowledge of divine things discussed by Aquinas in the Sixth Reading? (See above, p. 90.) What is it that Bernard represents that is higher than what Bonaventura, the mystical theologian, represents? (Note that Bonaventura is not put above Beatrice's level.)

What does all this have to do with Dante, in the poem and in actual life? Did he desert the pursuit of theology or give up a clerical vocation to follow secular interests, such as philosophy? Can you find any indication of this in the poem?

What are Dante's theological views?

In the first place, we must judge whether Dante accepts basic Christian theology, as expressed in medieval Catholicism, as really true, or whether he is merely using theological ideas and symbols—hell, purgatory, paradise, the gradation of beings from Lucifer to God—to people his fictional world. Is Dante a believing Christian or an aesthetic, poetic Christian? We might put this more objectively thus: Does the "Paradise" make sense apart from its Christian theological background?

In the next place, even if we grant that Dante is a believing Christian, we need not thereby interpret him as accepting the Catholic view expressed by a thinker such as Thomas Aquinas. The decisive points to look for here are the relative order assigned to philosophy and theology, and to church and state. Aquinas assigns natural reason a wide sphere of relative autonomy where it is competent to operate, but it remains subordinated ultimately to supernatural revelation, which directs man and his reason to the final end. Similarly, Aquinas assigns to the state a definite realm in which it is competent to contribute to man's earthly happiness, but it is subordinated to the church, which is entrusted with leading man and the political order to ultimate salvation.

Does Dante hold the same views as Aquinas on these points? It is difficult to find a direct statement on the relation of philosophy to theology, but the brief reference to Siger of Brabant undoubtedly has some significance (see p. 117 above). Does it mean that Dante finds natural philosophy equal to sacred theology? Or does it mean only that he thinks philosophy is divinely instituted to operate in the natural sphere?

On church and state, we have many more passages. What is the meaning of the passages we have cited above? Remember that Dante puts just kings, including pagan ones, high up in the heavens. And he is hard on the usurpations of the papal power. He even goes so far as to blame the church equally with the state for keeping man from regaining Eden. Church and state are equally to blame. Does Dante, therefore, regard church and state as equals, as subordinate arms of the divine power, both dealing with man's prebeatific state? Is the visible church concerned only with Purgatory, the inferior realm of repentance?

How, exactly, does Dante regard the corporate, institutional church? Is it significant that he stresses the mystical, contemplative, and spiritualistic aspects of the Christian faith, and places the heretical Joachim of Floris in Paradise? Would you say he took a negative or critical attitude toward the sacred or supernatural character of the visible, institutional church? Is Dante closer to certain "modern" or Protestant attitudes toward the church than to the medieval Catholic view of it? How does he regard the invisible, spiritual church in contrast to both the institutional church and the secular state?

The following questions are designed to help you test the thoroughness of your reading. Each question is to be answered by giving a page or pages of the reading assignment. Answers will be found on page 269 of this Reading Plan.

1 Who is both father and father-in-law to every bride?

2 In what type of wisdom was Solomon supreme?

3 Do miracles prove the Christian faith?

4 What was the greatest gift God gave to man at the Creation?

5 What pagan deity does Dante invoke to write the *Paradise*?

6 What Apocryphal, or deuterocanonical, wisdom for judges is spelled out in the sphere of Jupiter?

7 Where did the pagans go astray in deifying the heavenly bodies?

8 Why must there be a resurrection of the flesh?

9 In what respect is the universe like God?

HOBBES

Leviathan

Part I, Chap. 12; Part II, Chap. 31; Part III

Vol. 23, pp. 79-84, 159-246

T he relation between religion and the state has long been a subject of dispute in the Western world. In modern times it has been settled in most Western countries by the principle of liberty of conscience, with freedom of worship and civil rights guaranteed to the adherents of all faiths. In the United States, religious freedom and the separation of church and state are guaranteed by the Constitution.

But the tension and the problem are not completely ended. May the adherents of certain beliefs refuse to pledge allegiance to the flag, refuse to serve in the armed forces, refuse to be vaccinated or undergo other medical treatment? The Supreme Court as well as public opinion has split on these questions. In case of conflict between the civil law and religious belief, which shall prevail?

Thomas Hobbes, the great 17th-century political philosopher, was absolutely certain that he had the right answer—the power of the state should regulate all overt conduct and expression, both civil and religious. According to Hobbes, private persons are bound to obey the supreme civil power in all public matters, and that power is derived directly from God.

Hobbes sets forth this radical doctrine with magnificent vigor and style. His bluntness and his sledgehammer blows make it impossible to ignore or forget what he is saying. This doctrine of absolute state power has rarely, if ever, been set forth with such eloquence. It is an extreme doctrine, but Hobbes's virtue is that he makes us see what this doctrine means clearly and coherently.

What Hobbes says is bound to be offensive to many readers. It was offensive to laity and clergy in his own day. It is certain to offend Catholics, Protestants, and Jews nowadays, since it grants no autonomous powers to the religious community. It will also offend people who are antagonistic or indifferent to religion, since it grants no inalienable rights to the individual conscience. The state is total for Hobbes, and includes everything in its scope.

Perhaps this doctrine is not completely foreign to the modern temper. Is there not a tendency in our time to make the secular power supreme and to make the religious life of man subordinate to the needs of the state and society? In an ultimate conflict between the needs of the state—such as military defense or public health—and religious beliefs or practices, which side would most of us support?

Eighth Reading

I

Thomas Hobbes thought and wrote in the 17th century, which was the springtime of both modern science and nationalism. The cultural and religious unity of Europe had been exploded from within by the various Reformation movements, the rise of capitalism, and the growing power of centralized national states. The medieval world view, portrayed so magnificently by Dante, was no longer universally held. The leading thinkers of the era were developing a mechanical-materialistic view of the nature and behavior of things. Hobbes himself accepted this view, as is obvious to anyone who reads the *Leviathan* attentively. To Hobbes, whatever was real was material; the spiritual was merely an expression of material processes, and hence could be explained mechanically. Popular opinion and many churchmen in the England of his time held Hobbes to be an atheist.

Our major concern here is not with Hobbes's personal religious beliefs, but with his discussion of the relation of church and state. His masterpiece, the *Leviathan,* deals with the state, which, for Hobbes, is the solution to all of man's vital problems. The state alone can provide the peace and order which make it possible for men to live together and to develop the arts and sciences that characterize civilization.

Civil order, according to Hobbes, requires that absolute power over all individual behavior be concentrated in the hands of a sovereign (either one man or a group). Indeed, all private persons are members, or parts, of this corporate community, or Leviathan. (Hobbes derived the term from Chapter 41 of the Book of Job ([D] Chap. 40-41), where Leviathan, the sea-monster, is a symbol of almighty and awful divine power (see

p. 148b). The state is an artificial person which comes into being when men give up their natural liberty to constitute the sovereign power. The sovereign is the head, voice, and hands of the community, or corporate person. Law is what he says it is. (See Part II, Chap. XVII, pp. 99a-101a, and the Guide to the Eighth Reading in *The Development of Political Theory and Government*, pp. 101-115.)

What, then, is the place of religion in such an absolute, "totalitarian" political society? Hobbes's answer, as radical as his concept of state power, is that the sovereign alone is the final authority in religious matters, both in doctrine and worship. Anything else would lead to schism or civil war, and, besides, would be irrational, unnatural, and unjust.

Indeed, church and state are one. The original subtitle of the *Leviathan* was: *The Matter, Forme and Power of A Commonwealth Ecclesiasticall and Civil.* Before we go on to investigate Hobbes's extreme proposals, we should note that his solution, in one form or another, had many precedents in the history of Christianity. Church historians give it the aptly descriptive name of "caesaropapism." In Hobbes's time, it was called "Erastianism."

The Christian emperors of the Roman Empire took a leading role in the administration of the Church, convened ecumenical councils, handed down ecclesiastial decrees, decided matters of doctrine, approved the election of the Pope at Rome, and virtually appointed the Patriarch of Constantinople. Constantine, the first Christian emperor, assumed the ancient Roman title of *pontifex maximus,* or chief priest. The title and the function of directing religious life were retained by his successors. The great emperor Justinian was one of the most forceful directors of Church affairs.

After Constantine, the government of the Empire was divided between Rome in the West and Byzantium (Constantinople) in the East. Direction of Church affairs by the civil sovereign continued in the eastern part of the Roman Empire and later on in Russia under the tsars. (See Section I of the Guide to the Fourteenth Reading.) In the Western part of the Empire, as the imperial structure decayed the Church took over responsibility for the direction of Western society and culture. Great popes, such as Leo the Great, Gregory the Great, and Innocent III, virtually reversed the position of church and state. The Church reached the peak of its power in secular affairs early in the 13th century under Innocent III. During his reign the Church assumed political dominance in Italy, took a leading role in supporting and deposing kings and emperors, and held many kingdoms as papal fiefs.

After the Reformation the trend was reversed again, and the local princes and monarchs, both Protestant and Catholic, assumed at least administrative control of the churches in their domains. At the Peace of Augsburg (1555) the doctrine was adopted that each ruler should decide what was to be the religion in his realm. This doctrine, with modifications, prevailed in large parts of Europe at the time Hobbes was writing.

II

Our main text is Part III of the *Leviathan,* on the "Christian Commonwealth." However, to get some insight into the basic principles involved in the discussion, we shall start with Chapter 12 of Part I and Chapter 31 of Part II, which present Hobbes's views on religion in general, apart from Biblical revelation.

Chapter 12, in Part I, is entitled "Of Religion." It gives Hobbes's views on the nature, origin, and purpose of religion. Sometimes he seems to be talking of "natural religion" only; at other times he seems to be referring also to the Biblical faiths. Hobbes sees the natural origin of religion in fear and ignorance, but he hastens to add that this is true only of the Gentiles, who did not know the "one God, eternal, infinite, and omnipotent," who is the prime mover and first cause of all things.

The main point we should note here is that Hobbes takes the true end of religion to be civil concord. He sees two types of religion, natural and revealed, one arising from human invention, the other by divine command. Both, however, aim at making men fit for "obedience, laws, peace, charity, and civil society." Both fall under politics, which consists of two parts—"human politics" and "divine politics."

According to Hobbes, the religious beliefs inculcated by the great pagan founders of law codes and states had a single aim—"the peace of the Commonwealth." The ancient religio-political codes were craftily designed to produce law-abiding, orderly citizens or subjects by working on various fears and guilt feelings. As for Biblical religion, it affirms *a literal Kingdom of God,* created and ruled by God Himself, in which politics and religion are inseparable.

But where God himself by supernatural revelation planted religion, there he also made to himself a peculiar kingdom, and gave laws, not only of behaviour towards himself, but also towards one another; and thereby in the kingdom of God, the policy and laws civil are a part of religion; and therefore the distinction of temporal and spiritual domination hath there no place. (p. 82d)

Hobbes closes his discussion of religion by listing the causes for its decline: a deficiency in wisdom (logical consistency), sincerity (practicing what is preached), love (unselfish motivation), and signs (supernatural miracles). This may seem a curious list, in view of his account of the origin and purpose of religion, but the object of Hobbes's attack is the Roman Catholic Church. He sums up all the causes of decay in one: priestcraft, an evil which he says affects all religions.

So that I may attribute all the changes of religion in the world to one and the same cause, and that is unpleasing priests; and those not only amongst catholics, but even in that Church that hath presumed most of reformation. (p. 84b-c)

Note, however, that the main point in Hobbes's indictment of the Roman Church is its usurpation and disturbance of royal authority. Hobbes, like Dante, is certain that temporal power comes directly from God. But, as we shall soon see, he goes much further than Dante.

III

Chapter 31 of Part II treats "Of the Kingdom of God by Nature." This may seem an odd idea at first, but here is Hobbes's argument. It is a natural fact that God is King of the

Universe; but in order for the Kingdom of God to exist, His authority and law must be proclaimed and recognized. This is done universally through natural reason, or specially through prophetic revelation. In the Kingdom of God by nature, God's laws are proclaimed and received through natural reason. These laws deal both with what man owes to man and with what man owes to God, namely *worship.*

Pay close attention to Hobbes's idea of worship: it is man's relation to overwhelming power (aside from any consideration of justice and goodness). This is the "natural ground" of God's sovereignty. Worship consists in the weaker party, man, rendering *honor* to, or courting the favor of, the stronger party, God. It expresses love, hope, and fear in the form of praise, magnifying, and blessing. Our very statements about God's existence, nature, and attributes are ways of rendering Him honor; we talk in negatives and superlatives to show our recognition that God is wholly other than and beyond everything else.

But *someone* must decide what the forms of public worship should be. There must be uniformity of words and actions in common worship. There is no point, says Hobbes, in having more than one form of worship in the commonwealth. His recipe is: one state, one sovereign, one worship.

But seeing a Commonwealth is but one person, it ought also to exhibit to God but one worship; . . . And therefore, where many sorts of worship be allowed, proceeding from the different religions of private men, it cannot be said there is any public worship, nor that the Commonwealth is of any religion at all. . . . And because a Commonwealth hath no will, nor makes no laws but those that are made by the will of him or them that have the sovereign power, it followeth that those attributes which the sovereign ordaineth in the worship of God for signs of honour ought to be taken and used for such by private men in their public worship. (p. 163c-d)

IV

Our reading of the selections from Parts I and II has prepared us for the discussion of church and state in Part III of the *Leviathan,* "Of a Christian Commonwealth." For Hobbes, the two main grounds of natural religion, (that is, reason and sovereignty) also apply to revealed religion. Even in a revealed re-

ligion we must decide what is authentic revelation and interpret its meaning. For an interpretation of revelation we must
rely ultimately on reason, which is the "undoubted word of
God," and on civil sovereignty, which derives directly from
God. Revelation may be *above* reason, but it cannot be *against*
it. And hence it cannot be against legitimate authority.

Hobbes discounts private inspiration as unavailable to most
of us and, hence, useless for public purposes. Since the power
to work miracles is one of the signs of a true prophet—and the
days of miracles are over for Hobbes—he rules out present-day
prophecy as a guide. We may note in passing that another
sign of the true prophet for Hobbes is that he teaches established doctrine. Innovation is both religious heresy and rebellion against the established government; hence it is false.

In the end, says Hobbes, we must rely on Scripture, as interpreted by our natural reason "without enthusiasm or supernatural inspiration," and in conformity with the civil power
and established institutions. The Bible is *canon* (that is, law)
for all Christendom; but which books of the Bible are genuine
canon must be decided by the national sovereign, who decides
what both the civil and the canon law shall be. Hence Hobbes
accepts the ruling of the Church of England as to which books
of the Bible are canonical, because the king of England is the
head of the Church.

Hobbes also relies on his two main grounds, reason and sovereignty, as authority for making the Bible law. Insofar as
scriptural teaching is the same as natural law, it is confirmed
by human reason. Insofar as it is specially promulgated by
God, some public authority must confirm that it is God's
promulgation of law for the community. Why cannot the
church be that authority? Hobbes answers that this would be
all right if all Christians were bound together in a single commonwealth, under a single sovereign (in which case commonwealth and church would be one). But since this is not the case,
no church can call itself universal, and decide what God's law
is. The national sovereign alone has civil and religious authority. He alone has the power to make law.

For, whosoever hath a lawful power over any writing, to make it law, hath the power also to approve or disapprove the interpretation of the same. (p. 172a)

Notice that Hobbes has turned the question of whether God's law should be confirmed by the civil or religious authority into the question of whether the national sovereign or the Roman pope should have supreme religious power in a nation. But why could not a national church, independent of the state, decide the question in each nation? Such a solution is impossible for Hobbes because, for him, church and commonwealth are the same thing, and one person is both civil and religious ruler. There can be only one legitimate authority in a nation. Since there is no universal commonwealth (church), the sovereign is head of the church in each nation. May we conclude, then, that if there were a universal Christian commonwealth, the civil sovereign would also be *pontifex maximus*, head of the church in the full sense, and thus both pope and emperor?

Here is Hobbes's view of what a church is, and of the relation between civil and religious authority:

I define a *Church* to be: *a company of men professing Christian religion, united in the person of one sovereign at whose command they ought to assemble, and without whose authority they ought not to assemble.* . . . a Church . . . is the same thing with a civil Commonwealth consisting of Christian men; and is called a *civil state,* for that the subjects of it are men; and a *Church,* for that the subjects thereof are Christians. *Temporal* and *spiritual* government are but two words brought into the world to make men see double and mistake their lawful sovereign. (pp. 198d-199a)

Thus, for Hobbes, the Kingdom of God is the actual government of men on earth, a civil kingdom. Natural sovereigns are God's lieutenants by nature. Christian sovereigns are God's vicegerents in a special way. They are the direct descendants of the priests, prophets, and kings of Israel, who governed a kingdom instituted by special covenant between the people and God. This ancient covenant involved a special positive law, regulating civil government and social behavior as well as religious practices. In this "sacerdotal Kingdom," or "holy nation," sacred and secular were one. So it is now, says Hobbes, with those Christian sovereigns who are God's vicegerents on earth. (See the Guide to the Fourth Reading in *The De-*

velopment of Political Theory and Government, pp. 45-50.)

Hobbes contends that both Christian faith and natural law support his theory. All kings, whether Christian or not, are supreme pastors of their people by natural law. Hence, any ecclesiastical injunction to disobey legitimate sovereigns is null and void. Hobbes quotes the exhortations of Peter and Paul to Christians to obey the will of their pagan civil authorities. All legitimate power is from God.

Hobbes has a ready answer to the objection that the early Christian Church was governed by apostles, elders, deacons, and bishops before there were any Christian monarchs. The power of the apostles, he says, was simply to preach the Kingdom of *Christ,* which is *not of this world.* The mission of the clergy is to prepare and regenerate mankind for this otherworldly Kingdom through persuasion and reasoning, not by law and force. They cannot even excommunicate or condemn heresy in any effectual way, for they do not possess the power to expel or punish heretics physically. Only the civil power can deal with such matters. The power of the clergy is purely spiritual.

Hobbes seems finally to be setting up a distinction between spiritual and secular functions, but the ecclesiastical functions he assigns to the Christian sovereign make the special spiritual functions seem rather nebulous. For instance, all pastors (archbishops, bishops, priests) derive their authority from the sovereign alone. He makes all ecclesiastical appointments. The church's ministers are his ministers. Indeed, as supreme pastor, he has the right to preach, administer sacraments, consecrate, and exercise other priestly functions, although in practice he may not do so. If all preaching and teaching are subordinate to his command, where does the this-worldly Kingdom of God end, and the otherworldly Kingdom of Christ begin? What autonomous powers, spiritual or otherwise, does the clergy have?

Hobbes's view on the pope's power is consistent with his theory of the union of civil and religious power. The pope has supreme religious power only where he also has supreme civil power: that is, in the papal state and its dependencies.

He has no power to excommunicate people or rulers of other states, nor to pronounce on heresy beyond his own borders. Heresy is private judgment and action that is contrary to the common will, as expressed by the sovereign. It is not the intrinsic wrongness of the judgment that makes heresy wrong, but the private rebellion against authority. In this definition of heresy, Hobbes agrees with the Catholic Church, but he differs by placing authority in the civil sovereign rather than in the pope. Indeed, right and wrong *in words and actions* are, for Hobbes, what the sovereign says they are, through proclamations and edicts. Note the emphasis on "in words and actions," for the sovereign does not interfere with private thoughts; he reserves this apparently unimportant realm for the immediate relation between the individual and God.

One final question occurs, and it is a big one. What does a religious person do when his religious beliefs conflict with the commands of the sovereign? Nearly all religious persons would agree

that subjects owe to sovereigns simple obedience in all things wherein their obedience is not repugnant to the laws of God. . . . (p. 159d)

But what of the possibility, which Hobbes grants abstractly, that civil obedience may entail disobedience to God, that the word of man may conflict with the Word of God? Of course, says Hobbes, when this is the case the true believer must disobey his civil ruler and follow God's Word. But if we accept Hobbes's view that obedience to God is obedience to the civil laws, such a case can rarely occur.

Hobbes says that God's Word, which proclaims what is necessary for eternal salvation, requires us to believe in Christ and obey the laws. The laws to be obeyed are the civil laws, which are derived from the laws of nature, which are the laws of God. Thus the Word of God commands obedience to the civil laws. How, then, can there be a conflict between obeying the law of the state and obeying the law of God? The one distinction Hobbes makes is that God counts our will, our intent, as obedience, whereas the civil sovereign judges only actual conduct.

Suppose a sovereign forbids the expression of certain religious beliefs: Does a Christian who holds them have the right to profess them publicly, to disobey his sovereign? No, says Hobbes, for a private citizen cannot presume to disobey his sovereign in any matter involving *words and actions.* And who is in a position to decide that the king is wrong? He is the final authority. Besides, popes and apostles may err, too, in their conclusions from the original premises of faith. Even if the king is wrong, it is right to obey him.

It makes no difference to Hobbes whether or not the sovereign is a Christian. Disobedience to a non-Christian sovereign is also a sin against God. Christian belief is an internal, spiritual, otherworldly matter, whereas the sovereign is interested only in outward conduct in this world. There is no need to incur martyrdom, save where there is an undoubted command from God to bear witness to one's faith. This can only apply to a few, very rare souls. Since they go straight to heaven as a reward, they should not bear ill feeling against the sovereign who persecutes them. He is only doing what he has to do in order to preserve public peace and order; in addition, he is helping them to attain eternal salvation.

But what . . . if a king, or a senate, or other sovereign person forbid us to believe in Christ? . . . such forbidding is of no effect; because belief and unbelief never follow men's commands. Faith is a gift of God which man can neither give nor take away by promise of rewards or menaces of torture. And . . . what if we be commanded by our lawful prince to say with our tongue we believe not; must we obey such command? Profession with the tongue is but an external thing, and no more than any other gesture whereby we signify our obedience; . . . whatsoever a subject . . . is compelled to in obedience to his sovereign, and doth it not in order to his own mind, but in order to the laws of his country, that action is not his, but his sovereign's; nor is it he that in this case denieth Christ before men, but his governor, and the law of his country. (pp. 209d-210a; see also 245a-246c)

To make loyalty to the commands of conscience the ruling principle, says Hobbes, would sanction "all private men to disobey their princes in maintenance of their religion, true or false" (p. 210b). This would subvert the very basis of right and order in human society.

Even Christian faith, the essential belief that Jesus is the Christ, depends on the action of the civil sovereign. Christian faith, says Hobbes, is usually based on belief that the Bible is the Word of God. Why do we believe this? It is because our parents and our teachers told us so. The patriarchs and prophets had firsthand experience of God; the apostles and disciples, an immediate relation with Christ; but in these latter days we must rely on hearsay. We take the word of our parents and our pastors; we rely on authority. Ultimately, we rely on the sovereign and his ministers or teachers. Christian faith is limited for the most part to the subjects in a Christian commonwealth.

For what other cause can there be assigned why in Christian Commonwealths all men either believe or at least profess the Scripture to be the word of God, and in other Commonwealths scarce any, but that in Christian Commonwealths they are taught it from their infancy, and in other places they are taught otherwise? (p. 242a)

Hobbes grants that we may hear and not believe, for faith is the gift of God, who gives it to whom He wills; but it is received only through teaching, "for the immediate cause of faith is learning." And in a Christian commonwealth the teachers are under the sovereign's direction. Hence his authority is a necessary means for the Christian to attain faith.

V

This reading sets forth one of the most provocative and extreme theories of the relation of religion and government that has ever been proposed in the Western world. It raises many critical questions. Here are a few of them.

Is Hobbes's God the God of the Bible and of Christian faith?

Hobbes's notion of God is that He is the supreme power and lawmaker of the universe. At first sight, this seems to be the essence of the Biblical doctrine of God. But does the Bible mean this in the same sense that Hobbes does? Does the Bible have anything else to say about God in His relation to man? Is the Biblical view of God, as the power that created and sustains the world, exactly the same as Hobbes's definition of God as Prime Mover and First Cause?

What of such attributes as mercy and loving-kindness? To attribute such qualities to God, according to Hobbes, is just another way of paying honor to overwhelming power, power that may afflict the innocent along with the guilty. God's answer to Job, says Hobbes, is that He is overwhelming and unaccountable power. The elements of love, of mercy, of forgiveness, and an intimate personal relation between man and God are omitted. But are not these the elements that loom large in the Biblical accounts of the religious experience of the patriarchs, prophets, and apostles? Is the experience of the Divine Presence solely a confrontation with overwhelming power for Abraham? For Isaiah and Jeremiah? For Peter, Paul, and John?

Hobbes certainly pays much attention to Scripture. Indeed, he rests his case on his interpretation of the Bible, especially of the Old Testament. But is not Hobbes's main concern the public promulgation of law and the centralizing of communal authority, rather than the personal relation between man and God? Or is it more correct to say that he takes the relation of God to man—of sovereign lord to obedient subject—as the model for the relation between the civil sovereign and his subjects?

Do Scriptures support Hobbes's contention that the civil sovereign should rule in religious affairs?

Hobbes calls our attention to the unity of the sacred and secular realms in Old Testament times. However, is it always the sovereign who is the agent of God in the Bible? Are there not many instances where prophets, acting for God, struggle against kings whom they indict as godless men? The prophets are somewhat of a problem to Hobbes, and he solves it by considering them as the real rulers of the people. But was this really the case? There were prophets, priests, and kings in the Old Testament who played the principal roles in the indivisible religious and civil community of Israel, but all these functions were not always concentrated in the same person. There were high priests who were not civil rulers, rulers who were not priests, and prophets who were neither.

Consider the New Testament injunction to render unto God what is God's and unto Caesar what is Caesar's. Did that imply that the early Church recognized the pagan Empire is divinely instituted? When imperial edicts conflicted with Christian faith, did not stanch believers choose the way of civil disobedience and possible martyrdom? Do the injunctions of Peter and Paul to obey the civil authorities imply that Christians should obey their civil rulers in religious matters? Or do such injunctions apply only to the civil realm? Can you find any evidence in the New Testament that the apostles preached or practiced sub-mission to the civil sovereign in essentially religious matters?

Is it inevitable that more than one kind of public worship would lead to civil disorder?

If we look around us in present-day America or consider most of the countries of the Western world, Hobbes's view seems absurd.

History appears to have demonstrated that where toleration and full civil rights have been accorded to the adherents of various faiths, civil strife based on religious differences has dis-appeared. Have not some of the bloodiest revolutions and civil wars occurred in countries where one religion has had a virtual monopoly (for example, in France and Spain)? On the other hand, was the greatest civil war in history, our own, fought over religious issues?

During Hobbes's lifetime, religious wars between Protestants and Catholics had wreaked terrible havoc on Germany and France. Hobbes wrote the *Leviathan* in the midst of the Eng-lish Civil War, which arose partly from the struggle between Catholic and Puritan elements in the Anglican Church. Re-ligious doctrine and worship, as well as the relative power of King and Parliament, were at stake in the conflict. Men fought with steel and shot to make their religious faiths dominant.

What is the conclusion? Would our present Anglo-American system of tolerated diversity have achieved civil harmony in Hobbes's time? Or was the time not yet ripe for tolerance? Do you agree with Hobbes that uniformity, rather than plurality, of religious beliefs and practices is the way to civil concord?

Do you agree that varying religious beliefs divide people from one another and make them enemies? What about varying political and philosophical beliefs?

What argument does Hobbes offer for his belief that the sovereign has divine authority to rule in both civil and religious matters?

Hobbes's argument is that anything else would lead to anarchy and chaos; hence, we must have one ultimate authority, both civil and religious. This is "rational," "just," and "natural"; hence it is "divine," since natural law is the Word of God. Civil authority is decisive for Hobbes in all religious matters. Notice that he declines to voice his opinion on an important theological issue until one side or the other has won the Civil War and assumed the sovereign authority, which alone can decide what is right and wrong doctrine (see p. 193c).

Does Hobbes give any rational basis for religious faith? He advocates that we "captivate our understanding to the words" and swallow religious mysteries whole—without chewing them —as if they were pills (see p. 165b). This, he hastens to add, does not mean intellectual submission to another private person, but merely the will to obey lawful authority. Is Hobbes interested in attaining religious knowledge or in securing civil and ecclesiastical power? For Hobbes, is it *truth* or *authority* that decides which beliefs and practices are right and which are wrong?

The following questions are designed to help you test the thoroughness of your reading. Each question is to be answered by giving a page or pages of the reading assignment. Answers will be found on page 269 of this Reading Plan.

1 What great Catholic defender of papal power does Hobbes argue with at great length?

2 What does Hobbes regard as the essence of the Gospel According to St. Matthew?

3 What four things are the natural causes of religion?

4 What does the distinction between natural and conventional meanings have to do with the forms of worship?

5 Does Hobbes regard the Bible as historically accurate?

6 Why is Naaman the Syrian a model for Christian subjects under non-Christian sovereigns?

MONTAIGNE

The Essays

"That a Man Is Soberly to Judge of the Divine Ordinances," "Of Prayers," "Of Liberty of Conscience"

Vol. 25, pp. 98-99, 152-156, 324-326

Michel de Montaigne had an inborn distaste for dogmatic judgments and fanatical beliefs. The events of his time confirmed him in his lifelong revulsion against narrow-minded bigotry. In that era Catholics and Protestants waged implacable warfare on one another to make their own faith dominant and to control the state. In France, Catholic supremacy was menaced by Huguenot revolts; terrible massacres, such as that of St. Bartholomew's day, occurred; and horrible cruelties were committed by both sides.

Montaigne, himself a loyal Catholic, decided to withdraw from public life and live peacefully, as the only way to retain human decency and rationality. He sought tranquility of spirit and the cultivation of the mind. In his rural retirement he wrote the essays which made him one of the great writers of the Western world.

The essays may seem slight at times (an "essay" is only an attempt, a sketching out), but many of them bear echoes of the tumultuous times in which they were written. When you read these selected essays on religious themes, remember that the whole countryside around Montaigne was being devastated in an attempt to settle some of the issues he was writing about. These quiet, genial, direct writings on religious truth and inwardness represent a little oasis of peace and reason in a world of intolerance, cruelty, and passion. They are a permanent monument to a single individual's attempt to preserve human decency and moderation under the most unpropitious circumstances imaginable.

Ninth Reading

I

In the first essay assigned, on judging divine ordinances, Montaigne warns us against something with which we are very familiar—the association of religion with success, or the claim to have God on one's own side in wars and other enterprises. Have faith, some preachers tell us, and you will be successful in all your earthly endeavors. This country, some people assert, is "under God"; thus, we are bound to win out in any international conflict. This is the pragmatic view of religious faith.

Montaigne begins, and ends, by pointing out that we are being very presumptuous to claim that we know the secret workings of the divine mind. He charges that such a claim is impious. He closes the essay with these words from the Book of Wisdom: "Who amongst men can know the counsel of God? or who can think what the will of the Lord is?" (Wisdom 9:13)

He also charges that such a coupling of religious faith with material success is logically absurd. When we win, we conclude that God's approval of us is manifest; but when our enemies win, we do not conclude that God planned it that way, save maybe as a fatherly punishment. God is never on the side of our enemies. When people whose religious doctrines are opposed to ours die in a horrible manner, we see the hand of divine judgment at work; but not so when people of our own views suffer similar fates.

On the contrary, says Montaigne, God having shown us

. . . that the good have something else to hope for and the wicked something else to fear, than the fortunes or misfortunes of this world, manages and applies these according to His own occult will and pleasure, and deprives us of the means foolishly to make thereof our own profit. (p. 99a)

145

From the religious point of view, the best thing is to accept whatever happens as the will of God, without presuming to know the inscrutable divine purposes and meanings behind events. Montaigne would have approved of Abraham Lincoln's humble acceptance of the origin and result of the Civil War as the action of divine providence—not favoring either side, but a judgment on both. (See Lincoln's Second Inaugural Address.)

II

Our second selection, on prayers, is perfectly consistent with the first one. It inveighs against the pragmatic use of prayer to attain material ends, and urges that prayer arise out of purity of heart and a genuine turning toward God. In the middle of the essay there occurs a discussion of whether the Bible and theology should be made available to the ordinary worshiper. We shall consider this separately as a second topic.

Montaigne says that he is completely baffled by those people who are able to combine "devout" offerings and prayers to God with a life in which they do the very opposite of God's will. Indeed, they even implore God's help in their nefarious enterprises. What goes on in the minds of people who can jump so easily from fervent religious affirmations to unethical acts? They seem to be unconscious of their schizoid state. They are in what Montaigne calls "an indigestible agony of mind." (The original meaning of "agony" is "conflict.")

Their theology is oddly one-sided, says Montaigne. They realize that God is supreme power, but they do not seem to understand that He is also supreme righteousness and justice. To proceed as they do is like asking a judge to help you pick pockets or burglarize houses.

Montaigne sees the pragmatic attitude, the seeking of material results, at the bottom of such duplicity. The people who take such an attitude either do not realize that prayer is a spiritual matter, concerned with inner holiness and truth, or they simulate being in such a state in order to attain material rewards. Witness the man who told Montaigne that he had practiced a religion he detested solely to get ahead in the world.

The externalities of religious acts are easy to mimic, says Montaigne, because so much of it is mere routine, inane mumbling, and posturing.

We pray only by custom and for fashion's sake; or, rather, we read or pronounce our prayers aloud, which is no better than an hypocritical show of devotion . . . We seem, in truth, to make use of our prayers as of a kind of gibberish, and as those do who employ holy words about sorceries and magical operations; and as if we reckoned the benefit we are to reap from them as depending upon the contexture, sound, and gingle of words, or upon the grave composing of the countenance. (pp. 153b, 156c)

The "hypocritical show" and "gibberish" result from the fact that we fail to perceive that prayer is inwardness. We do not recognize that we can only pray to *be* better, not to *have* more. It is blasphemous to give "one hour to God, the rest to the devil," says Montaigne. It is our whole life that attests to our devotion, repentance, at-one-ness with God. God finds the sacrifice of a contrite heart more pleasing than a stockyard full of burnt offerings or other outward show.

III

Now let us take up Montaigne's views on the reading and translation of the Bible. Montaigne speaks as a good and loyal Catholic. He makes this clear from the beginning, although he claims only the status of personal opinion for his views. He supports the policy of the Church of his day in not making the Scriptures available to the mass of the laity. He is aghast at the widespread circulation they have received as a result of the Reformation and of the translation of the Bible from Latin into the common tongues.

In the first place, he asserts, the Bible is something very special and sacred, and can only be approached with deep spiritual preparation. Secondly, what it has to say can only be understood by profound study, and is not a matter of merely literal meanings expressible in ordinary everyday language. Only a select, authorized few can understand the Bible.

Neither is it a book for every one to fist, but the study of select men set apart for that purpose, and whom Almighty God has been pleased to call to that office and sacred function: the wicked and ignorant grow worse by it. (p. 154b)

Montaigne extends his advocacy of exclusiveness to the study of dogma and theology. "The pure mysteries of piety" should not be "profaned by the ignorant rabble," a group in which Montaigne would include princes, as well as the gabbling women and children who, he claims, discuss canon laws. He sides with the view that

. . . all contentions and dialectic disputations [on theological subjects] were to be avoided, and men absolutely to acquiesce in the prescriptions and formulas of faith established by the ancients. (p. 154d)

Indeed, Montaigne would keep theology entirely separate from philosophy and the humanistic disciplines; sacred doctrine is not to be stained by contact with profane learning. He would approve an edict preventing anyone who is not a "public professor of divinity"—including himself—from writing unreservedly about religious subjects. He sets up as a model for our admiration a legendary Christian community whose inhabitants are paragons of religious practice and ethical conduct, but "so simple that they understand not one syllable of the religion they profess and wherein they are so devout" (p. 155a).

Should we take this last remark of Montaigne's literally, or does he intend it ironically?

IV

Our third and last selection is the essay on liberty of conscience. This is a short and seemingly slight essay, apparently not doing justice to the deadly seriousness of the topic at the time in which Montaigne lived. But the author prefers an indirect approach. He tries to evoke the sense of his theme in his readers' minds by describing concrete cases of intolerance.

Montaigne refers at the very start to the situation in which he and his readers found themselves at the time he wrote: a religious civil war. He proclaims himself unequivocally on the Catholic side, but he expresses uneasiness over the passion, violence, and injustice which sway even the most sincere persons on his own side. Thus, he starts from the immediate situation and notes something disturbing with which his readers were familiar.

Then he jumps suddenly to the ancient past, and summons up examples of Christian intolerance against things pagan. First, he refers to the destruction of pagan learning and letters— an obvious loss, which few in Montaigne's time would condone. Next, he brings up the case of Julian the Apostate, the Roman emperor who recanted the Christian faith and tried to restore the old-time pagan religion. (For a full account of Julian, see Chap. XXII-XXIV of Gibbon's *Decline and Fall of the Roman Empire*, Vol. 40, pp. 330-381.)

Montaigne devotes the greater part of the essay to a discussion of the noble character of Julian. Only at the end of this apparent digression does he come to the topic of the essay. Montaigne sees Julian as the prime example of the Christian tendency to approve all emperors who were pro-Christian and to condemn completely all emperors who were anti-Christian. Montaigne demonstrates that it is possible to give a perceptive and honest account of a man whom he considers "wrong throughout" in religious matters. He ridicules gently what he considers Julian's superstitiousness, but shows an open understanding of the man's religious attitude. He also demonstrates that a striving for historical truth can accompany a firm Christian faith. He questions the authenticity of the legend that Julian recanted his "apostasy" at the time of his death (referring to the supposed utterance, "Thou hast conquered, O Nazarene").

Finally, at the end, we see the connection between the discussion of Julian the Apostate and the problem of liberty of conscience. Montaigne says that Julian introduced freedom of worship in order to produce factions in the Christian Church. Just the opposite purpose motivates princes in Montaigne's time.

Wherein this is very worthy of consideration, that the Emperor Julian made use of the same receipt of liberty of conscience to inflame the civil dissensions, that our kings do to extinguish them. So that a man may say on one side, that to give the people the reins to entertain every man his own opinion, is to scatter and sow division, and, as it were, to lend a hand to augment it, there being no legal impediment or restraint to stop or hinder their career; but, on the other side, a man may also say, that to give the people the reins to entertain every man his own opinion, is to mollify and appease them by facility and toleration, and to dull the point which is whetted and made sharper by singularity, novelty, and difficulty: and I think it is better for the honour of the devotion of our kings, that not having been able to do what they would, they have made a show of being willing to do what they could. (p. 326a-b)

Montaigne is saying here that the princes of his day were not able to establish the doctrine that the religion of a country must follow that of its ruler. They could not impose one faith as the sole faith. But they were able to institute freedom of religion, which affords liberty of conscience to individuals and bestows concord on the state.

V

Now that we have listened to this genial conversationalist— this marvelous raconteur, this persuasive example of tolerance and openness—let us ask a few questions about what we have heard from him.

Is religion, for Montaigne, a purely spiritual matter, without relation to the everyday, empirical world?

Montaigne, in these essays, vigorously opposes the view that religion is intended to affect our "fortunes or misfortunes of this world" and to result in "our own profit." Does he mean that what happens in this world has no religious significance? Would he not, then, be opposing the stand of the Judaeo-Christian faiths that God works in history, directing events and men's lives toward an appointed goal? Is not Job rewarded for his righteousness by the restoration of his goods and children?

But if we reread Montaigne's essays on divine ordinances and on prayers, we may find that these questions do not do him justice, do not really get at the meaning of his thought. Does he not demand that inner adherence to God's will be demonstrated in ethical conduct in the world, rather than in "one hour to God, the rest to the devil"? Does he deny that events are directed by God's providence? Consider this passage from his essay on divine ordinances:

'Tis enough for a Christian to believe that all things come from God, to receive them with acknowledgment of His divine and inscrutable wisdom, and also thankfully to accept and receive them, with what face soever they may present themselves. (p. 98c)

Compare the above sentence with the following words from Lincoln's Second Inaugural Address:

The prayer of both [North and South] could not be answered. That of neither has been answered fully. The Almighty has His own purposes. . . . American slavery is one of those offences which, in the providence of God, must needs come, but which having continued through His appointed time, He now wills to remove, and. . . . He gives to both North and South this terrible war as the woe due to those by whom the offence came. . . . the judgments of the Lord are true and righteous altogether.

Compare both of these passages with the final chapters of the Book of Job. Do they agree or disagree on what man's attitude should be toward God's action in the world?

Does prayer have any effect?

Montaigne devotes so much time to the perversions of prayer that we may miss what he thinks the purpose or essence of prayer is. Most people would agree that prayer should not be an attempt to profit pragmatically in the world (as, for example, winning a bet on a horse race, or coming out on top in an athletic contest or business deal). But we pray for peace and that wisdom and prudence be granted to our statesmen; we pray that the sick and the troubled be made whole and unanxious, and we pray for personal virtue and strength. Are such prayers "efficacious," or mere talk to soothe the mind of the person who prays?

Does Montaigne think about prayer in this way? Does he not consider it rather as a means of becoming at one with God—a means of "reconciliation," of attaining inner purity and complete submission to the divine will? He points to the Lord's Prayer of the Christian faith as the model prayer, good on any and all occasions. Why did he make it his personal prayer? Is it not because it is a prayer centered utterly in God, putting the will of the petitioner in accord with the divine will and imploring spiritual and ethical purification? But the first petition is for "our daily bread." Is this not a request to fulfill a practical need? Or is it rather an assertion that all things come from God, an expression of gratitude rather than a pragmatic device for filling one's stomach?

To Montaigne, the end of prayer, its "effect," is being with God. To be with God requires us to be like God; hence, free of rancor, anxiety, or avarice. Praying is not a matter of asking for specific, finite things. Indeed, it is possible to pray without using words. Praying is an inner attitude, an intention of the heart.

Would Montaigne countenance the prayer of a bad or imperfect person to become good or better? Does not the Lord's Prayer implore deliverance from evil? Would Montaigne consider the evil person good at the moment he prays for repentance? (See the end of the essay "Of Prayers.")

How does Montaigne regard the social expression of religion?

Putting the outward success of a party, nation, or church at the center of things is regarded by Montaigne as blasphemy and idolatry. He calls for individual righteousness and inwardness. But is religion only a personal matter for Montaigne? Is the communal, or corporate, aspect of religion unimportant when it is not baleful—as in religious intolerance and fanaticism? What does Montaigne have to say about religious institutions and communities? Is religion, for him, solely a matter between the individual soul and God?

Can ordinary believers understand the Bible?

When we recall what the Bible, in popular translations, has meant for the spiritual edification of individuals and the great role it has played in shaping the Western mind, we are amazed that Montaigne should advocate that Bible reading be prohibited to the laity. But actually Montaigne is only making an extreme and provocative statement of the traditional

Roman Catholic position on the Scriptures; namely, that the Church is the authority which transmits and expounds the Scriptures. Tradition, shaped by the fathers and doctors of the Church, is as important as the Bible for the Catholic faith. In the Roman Catholic view, the words of the Bible, whether in the original or in translation, require an authoritative interpretation in conformity with dogmatic norms.

The Protestant position originally was quite different. The Reformers' battle cry was "Back to the Bible!" For them, the Bible was the Word of God speaking to every believer. Luther's call for the "priesthood of all believers" implied that the individual believer did not require the formal interpretation of a church official to understand the Bible. Tradition was regarded as an arbitrary addition to the Biblical Word of God. Reading and study of the Bible by the laity have played a central role in Protestant churches. Of course, the confessions, creeds, and traditions that have arisen since the Reformation have influenced Protestant interpretations of the Bible.

The Jewish position is a mixed one. On the one hand, it makes the reading and study of Scripture central. In the worship service, lay members of the congregation read the scrolls of the Law, including the whole of the Pentateuch, along with copious selections from the Prophets, in the course of the religious year. On the other hand, Judaism has a body of tradition in the Talmud and custom, which the orthodox consider divinely instituted and equally authoritative with the Bible. Literalism, or fundamentalism, has played a part in Judaism only as an ephemeral medieval heresy. In the modern forms of Judaism, there is reliance on literary and historical interpretation, as well as an informal and nondogmatic acknowledgment of tradition.

Let us consider the following questions: Can the religious meaning of the Bible be understood without some method of interpretation? If interpretation is needed, where should the ultimate norms of interpretation reside? Should they rest in the mind and conscience of the individual believer and reader, or in the authoritative spokesmen of a religious community, or in the warranted consensus of secular scholarship? If we leave it to the individual believer, how can there ever be an agreement as to what the Bible says? If we leave it to the church authorities, will we not again get a wide variety of views, depending on the theological and creedal positions of the various denominations and churches? On the other hand, even if there is an agreement among scholars as to textual meanings, sources, context, etc., how can that determine the religious meaning of the Bible for believers?

The following questions are designed to help you test the thoroughness of your reading. Each question is to be answered by giving a page or pages of the reading assignment. Answers will be found on page 269 of this Reading Plan.

1 What does Montaigne say about the charge that distinguished persons profess Catholicism for outward reasons alone?

2 What does Montaigne point to as another proof that women are not fit to treat of theological matters?

3 Why are men apt to believe almost anything they are told about divine things?

4 Does Montaigne look on "divine law" as a yoke or a joy?

5 Why does Montaigne consider Julian "superstitious"?

6 What previous reading in this Reading Plan does Montaigne refer to as listing false beliefs about the gods? What are they?

7 What is Montaigne's interpretation of "forgive us our trespasses"?

MILTON

Paradise Lost

Books I-III

Vol. 32, pp. 93-151

T he presence of evil in the world is a great challenge for religious faith. When confronted with the problem of evil, religion may deny the reality of evil, and say that it is a mere appearance to our undeveloped minds. Or it may set up evil as a rival power, equal or almost equal to divine good. Or it may ascribe evil to some weakness or perversion in creatures, and affirm a divine redemption that brings good out of evil.

The third response to the problem of evil is that of Christianity. The Christian faith affirms a primal fall of man through an original act of sin, and a redemption from man's fallen state by God's own atonement in human form, through the Passion and Resurrection of Christ.

This is the theme of Milton's grand epic poem. Like Dante, he makes use of magnificent language and imaginative genius to enliven, dramatize, and embody abstract religious ideas. Fully characterized persons give body to bare concepts. Colorful and exciting actions make theological thought concrete.

This vividness is most evident in Milton's portrayal of the power of evil. On the basis of a few passages in Biblical and Apocryphal literature and of scattered images from popular lore and legend, Milton has given us an unexampled portrayal of the Devil and his cohorts. Few readers are likely to forget Milton's Satan, that magnificent epitome of pride, perversity, and defiance. Milton does not content himself with moralistic condemnation, but gives us a convincing and understanding portrait of the Devil, of a villain who is magnificent and almost heroic in his villainy.

Here again, as with Dante, we have a writer of tremendous learning, wide experience, and great artistic power who fuses all these elements into one masterwork. *Paradise Lost,* like the *Divine Comedy,* has a thousand facets, but one central vision. It is a unified whole containing a multitude of insights. It gives us a profound and impressive view of man's nature and destiny in relation to the eternal order of things.

Tenth Reading

I

Of Mans First Disobedience, and the Fruit
Of that Forbidden Tree, whose mortal tast
Brought Death into the World, and all our woe,
With loss of *Eden* ... (p. 93b)

Such is the theme of Milton's epic poem *Paradise Lost.* The
Bible takes a single chapter (Genesis 3) of no more than
twenty-four verses to tell the tale. Milton takes twelve books
and thousands of verses to do it. Out of the terse essentials of
the original story he has constructed a literary masterpiece, a
poetic fiction, into which he has fused all his erudition and his
creative genius.

Milton imagines details and scenes that were not in Genesis.
Like Paul, Milton presents the story of the fall of man in the
light of the Crucifixion, which he sees as atonement for and
redemption from man's original sin. He also introduces many
pagan literary and mythological allusions that are anachronis-
tic with regard to the original story. Moreover—and this is
most interesting to us here—he introduces a Devil and demons
that are not in the Biblical account. These devils, with definite
names and characters, add interest and color to his story:
Satan, Beelzebub, Moloch, Belial, Mammon, the pagan gods
and goddesses, the whole resplendent company of the powers
of evil, the infernal host of Pandemonium.

Milton employs the ancient prerogative of poetic license to
make these abstractions come alive. (Remember what Dante
did with historical personages.) In his identification of the
devils with the pagan gods, Milton has tradition behind him,
for that was a prevalent belief in the early Christian Church.
The devils, or demons, remain angelic beings, even though
they are fallen angels.

159

Milton takes certain liberties in his treatment of Beelzebub and Belial. In the New Testament, Beelzebub is a synonym for Satan; here, however, he is Satan's lieutenant and prime minister, a separate personality. Perhaps Milton was thinking also of the Philistine god mentioned in the Old Testament. (Beelzebub means "lord of flies.") Similarly, the name Belial, or Beliar, is a synonym for Satan in the New Testament, whereas in the Old Testament it is a general term for wickedness, sometimes applied as a term of opprobrium to persons. Milton makes Belial the vilest of the fallen angels. Moloch is a pagan god of Old Testament times, notorious for the horrible forms of worship he required. Mammon is covetousness personified in the New Testament, and in medieval times was the devil of covetousness. Here again Milton has tradition, as well as imagination, with him. Milton dramatizes and personifies the power of evil in various forms. Though he uses a Biblical theme, he creates a poetic fiction, not a scholarly work on demonology.

In ancient Judaism, the rigorous monotheistic theology prevented any attribution of real substance, or personality, to the evil forces in man or the universe. But in late Judaism—perhaps because of the encounter with Babylonian and Persian religious beliefs—Satan played a leading role in the popular religious mind, especially in folklore and Apocryphal literature. In the New Testament, he became the archenemy, the prince of this world—man's tempter and God's adversary. Indeed, the original meaning of the name Satan is the "hinderer," or "accuser," the one who goes against. He opposes God and tempts man. He is associated with sin and death.

The only clear Biblical text that relates to Milton's story is in Chapter 12 of the Book of Revelation ([D] The Apocalypse). It contains a reference to a war in heaven, and the fall of the rebellious angels with their leader, "that old serpent, called the Devil, and Satan, which deceiveth the whole world" (Revelation ([D] The Apocalypse) 12:9; see also 20:2). The apocryphal Wisdom of Solomon ([D] Book of Wisdom) implicitly identifies the serpent and Satan when it says that "by the envy of the devil, death came into the world" (Wisdom of

Solomon ([D] Book of Wisdom) 2:24). The taunt against the King of Babylon in Isaiah 14 likens him to the vainglorious Lucifer, who fell from heaven (see Isaiah 14:12-15). And, of course, the first chapter of Job shows us Satan as the divinely ordained tempter and accuser of man before God (see Job 1:6-12; see also Zechariah ([D] Zachariah) 3:1-2, and I Chronicles ([D] I Paralipomenon) 21:1). The Jewish Talmud identifies the "evil impulse" in man with Satan, and finds that impulse as essential to the ultimate working out of the divine purpose as the "good impulse." A passage in the Gospel of Luke associates devils and serpents, and speaks of the fall of Satan "as lightning" from heaven (see Luke 10:17-19).

All these elements are present in the portrait of Satan in *Paradise Lost*. He opposes God and tempts man. Sin and Death follow in his wake. These elements are dramatized, characterized, and narrated with masterful poetic power. To get the full sweep of Milton's magnificent literary rendition of this ancient religious theme, you must read the whole poem. The present discussion of the first three books will help you get started in your reading of the epic.

Of course, a work such as this has many unfamiliar literary allusions and, moreover, often uses the English language in a different sense than we do nowadays. You will, of course, notice that the "argument" at the beginning of each book is a summary of the theme or subject matter, and not a debating term. But you may have to go to a good dictionary to find that "assert" means "vindicate," or that "Grand Parents" means "original parents," or that "prevent" means "precede."

The best procedure is to wait until the end of each book to look up all the unfamiliar words and references. In addition to a good dictionary, you may find one of the guides to classical allusions very useful. A handy one listed in Everyman's Library is called *A Smaller Classical Dictionary*. Or you may use the very fine *Oxford Companion to Classical Literature*. And if you are hazy about Biblical events and characters, there are many Bible dictionaries which will both explain the unfamiliar references and indicate the Bible passages in which they appear.

II

The main theme of the first three books of *Paradise Lost* is Satan's journey from the depths of Hell to Earth, in order to tempt God's newest creature, man, and stain the goodness of God's new-made world. (Compare this journey with Dante's in the *Divine Comedy*.) In the background and watching over all—prepared to undo Satan's temptation and man's misstep— are God and the Son and the heavenly host.

You may be interested in tracing Milton's use of the physical symbols of light and darkness to indicate spiritual qualities. Hell is utter darkness, Chaos is middle darkness, Earth is in the sphere of reflected light, and Heaven is pure light. Note also that Satan is called Lucifer, meaning "light-bringer," "day-star," or "shining one," referring to his high station before his fall (see Isaiah 14:12).

To see what Milton has to say in these introductory books, let us first look at his portrait of the evil power of perversion and rebellion, the leader of the fallen angels, Satan. Then we will see how Milton sets off the powers of light and good against this personification of darkness and evil.

There is no doubt that Satan is the dominant figure of this part of the poem. He has more speeches and is portrayed with more force than any other character, including God and Christ. Indeed, many perceptive readers have considered Satan to be the "hero" of Milton's poem. Let us see what there is in Milton's portrait to give rise to such an interpretation.

At the very beginning of the poem this utterly beaten archrebel, cast down from the topmost heights to the lowest depths, hurls his defiance out of complete darkness and despair. His pride, his rancor, his rebellion are absolute, unaffected by the most cataclysmic events.

> What though the field be lost?
> All is not lost; the unconquerable Will,
> And study of revenge, immortal hate,
> And courage never to submit or yield:
> And what is else not to be overcome?
> That Glory never shall his wrath or might
> Extort from me. (p. 95b-96a)

Satan's mood is that he has only lost a battle. The war is to be continued, and he must regroup and rally his forces, gaining "resolution from despare." If the result is not victory and the reconquest of Heaven, at least he may accomplish his aim to do evil in the universe and to frustrate God's designs.

> To do ought good never will be our task,
> But ever to do ill our sole delight,
> As being the contrary to his high will
> Whom we resist. If then his Providence
> Out of our evil seek to bring forth good,
> Our labour must be to pervert that end,
> And out of good still to find means of evil;
> Which oft times may succeed, so as perhaps
> Shall grieve him, if I fail not, and disturb
> His inmost counsels from their destind aim. (p. 97a)

Thus Satan sets himself up as the perfect opponent, the true adversary of God, whose aim is to achieve the good.

This Prince of Angels, who still bears much of his superb form and "Original brightness" (see comment on Lucifer, above), cannot bear to be second to anyone, not even to God, so that he welcomes his new lordship over Hell.

> Here we may reign secure, and in my choyce
> To reign is worth ambition though in Hell:
> Better to reign in Hell, then serve in Heav'n. (p. 99a)

Satan is not content to remain secure as the Lord of Hell. He must act and carry on the fight against God and the good. But he is no mere bullheaded warrior; he is also a crafty statesman. In the present state of the forces of evil, he urges cunning as the better part of valor.

> our better part remains
> To work in close design, by fraud or guile
> What force effected not: that he no less
> At length from us may find, who overcomes
> By force, hath overcome but half his foe. (p. 107b)

He sits on his throne while his council debates the question: "Whether of open Warr or covert guile." When the chief speakers have had their say and his proposal has won assent, Satan, in "transcendent glory" and "with Monarchal pride," decides that he alone must carry out the mission to discover the new world and subvert man. He takes the ancient valorous attitude that to the leader belong the greatest risks; he can ask no one else to undertake them. He will go it alone: "this enterprize None shall partake with me." He tells his chiefs to keep the home fires burning while he is out on his dangerous quest to bring freedom for them all. Notice that he allows no discussion, shrewdly aware that some may offer to go, now that they know they will not have to, in order to gain standing over the others. They bow to his will

> With awful reverence prone; and as a God
> Extoll him equal to the highest in Heav'n:
> Nor fail'd they to express how much they prais'd,
> That for the general safety he despis'd
> His own: for neither do the Spirits damn'd
> Loose all thir vertue. (p. 121b)

They extol "thir matchless Chief," and enviable concord reigns among these fallen angels.

While the other devils entertain themselves in various ways, including engagement in philosophical and theological discussions, "the Adversary of God and Man" journeys to the gates of Hell. He finds it guarded by a woman-serpent and a shapeless monster. When the monster challenges him and tries to frighten him away, Satan, undismayed, prepares to give battle, but "the Snakie Sorceress" steps in between them. She tells Satan that he is raising his hand against his own son and hers, for she is Sin, both Satan's daughter and his "darling." She gave birth to the monster Death, here in Hell after the fall from Heaven. Their son has continued the family tradition of incest and has begotten a host of "yelling Monsters" out of his mother.

Satan, full of guile and cunning, delivers a courtly speech in the foul circumstances and pleads with his daughter-darling and son-son-in-law to let him through the gates of Hell. He promises them freedom and prosperity on earth, where Sin and Death will find abundant opportunities. Seduced by Satan's argument, Sin opens the gates of Hell with "the fatal Key, Sad instrument of all our woe," and Satan enters the limitless ocean between Hell and Heaven, the realm of Chaos

and Night. Chaos is so angry because much of his domain
has been taken away from him (first Heaven and Hell, and
now Earth, too) that he accedes to Satan's request for directions to the new world. Satan promises to return it to its
original chaos and darkness (see Genesis 1:1).

Satan finds the way to earth a hard and risky one, but the
author tells us that after this pioneer journey and the subsequent trips of Sin and Death, it became a broad, well-
traveled highway. Satan reaches the border where Nature
begins and Chaos ends. As "the sacred influence of light"
appears, Satan sees both the Empyreal Heaven from which
he has been exiled and the new globe.

> This pendant world, in bigness as a Starr
> Of smallest Magnitude close by the Moon.
> Thither full fraught with mischievous revenge,
> Accurst, and in a cursed hour he hies. (p. 134a)

Satan takes the form of a stripling cherub in order to get
directions from the archangel Uriel ("the light of God"), one
of the chief messengers of God and the Regent of the Sun.
Uriel tells how the world was created from chaos, light from
darkness, order from disorder, with the elements in their places
and the stars in their courses. He points to "earth, the seat
of Man," and to "Paradise, Adam's abode." As we come to the
end of Book III, Satan renders Uriel mock reverence and takes
off on his terrible errand of subverting God's creation and
burdening "this new happie Race of Men" with sin and
remorse.

III

What figure or figures does Milton set off against this power
of evil? At the beginning of Book III, we see the forces of
light (see the hymn to light on pp. 135-136), led by God and
Christ. High on his empyrean throne, the Almighty Father
sits and views all, with his Son, "the radiant image of his
Glory," at his right hand. He sees the bliss of Adam and Eve
in Paradise, and Satan speeding to put an end to it. That
Satan will tempt man and that man will fall are foreknown
to God: the future is present to him. Why, then, does not

God intervene? The reason is that God has given man free will. Man stands or falls by his own choice. This is central to the theme of Milton's poem.

> So will fall
> Hee and his faithless Progenie: whose fault?
> Whose but his own? ingrate, he had of mee
> All he could have; I made him just and right,
> Sufficient to have stood, though free to fall.
> Such I created all th' Ethereal Powers
> And Spirits, both them who stood & them who faild;
> Freely they stood who stood, and fell who fell.
> Not free, what proof could they have givn sincere
> Of true allegiance, constant Faith or Love,
> Where onely what they needs must do, appeard,
> Not what they would? what praise could they receive?
> What pleasure I from such obedience paid,
> When Will and Reason (Reason also is choice)
> Useless and vain, of freedom both despoild,
> Made passive both, had servd necessitie,
> Not mee. They therefore as to right belongd,
> So were created, nor can justly accuse
> Thir maker, or thir making, or thir Fate;
> As if Predestination over-rul'd
> Thir will, dispos'd by absolute Decree
> Or high foreknowledge; they themselves decreed
> Thir own revolt, not I: if I foreknew,
> Foreknowledge had no influence on their fault,
> Which had no less prov'd certain unforeknown.
> So without least impulse or shadow of Fate,
> Or aught by me immutablie foreseen,
> They trespass, Authors to themselves in all
> Both what they judge and what they choose; for so
> I formed them free, and free they must remain,
> Till they enthrall themselves: I else must change
> Thir nature, and revoke the high Decree
> Unchangeable, Eternal, which ordain'd
> Thir freedom, they themselves ordain'd thir fall. (pp. 137b-138a)

Note, however, that God distinguishes between two types of sin: (1) purposeful sin for sin's sake, or self-temptation; and (2) sin through being tempted by others. The first, Satan's, is unforgivable; the second, Adam's, can be forgiven.

> The first sort by thir own suggestion fell,
> Self-tempted, self-deprav'd: Man falls deceiv'd

> By the other first: Man therefore shall find grace,
> The other none. (p. 138a)

The Son, the voice of divine compassion and infinite love, speaks on man's behalf, urging mercy for God's "youngest son" and the frustration of the malicious aims of the Adversary. God answers that man cannot, by his own power, redeem himself from sin, which is essentially disobedience and treason. Man is utterly condemned unless someone else suffers vicariously for him and pays "the rigid satisfaction, death for death." The Son offers to take the burden of man's atonement on himself—to condescend from his eternal being, to take on human, mortal form, to suffer man's fate but also to conquer it, and to raise man with him. Christ shall be the victor over the powers of death and sin. Hell and the powers of darkness shall be conquered.

God the Father hails the Son as the new Adam and the redeemer of the world. He proclaims the doctrine of the Christ.

> And be thy self Man among men on Earth,
> Made flesh, when time shall be, of Virgin seed,
> By wondrous birth: Be thou in *Adams* room
> The Head of all mankind, though *Adams* Son.
> As in him perish all men, so in thee
> As from a second root shall be restor'd,
> As many as are restor'd, without thee none.
>   . . . So Man, as is most just,
> Shall satisfie for Man, be judg'd and die,
> And dying rise, and rising with him raise
> His Brethren, ransomd with his own dear life.
> So Heav'nly love shal outdoo Hellish hate, . . .
> Therefore thy Humiliation shall exalt
> With thee thy Manhood also to this Throne;
> Here shalt thou sit incarnate, here shalt Reigne
> Both God and Man, Son both of God and Man,
> Anointed universal King. (pp. 141b-142a)

The risen Son shall rule over the universe until the final judgment, after which no rule will be necessary, for "God shall be All in All." (See also Romans 5:12-21; I Corinthians 15:20-28, 45-49; Philippians 2:5-11.)

There follows a hosanna by the heavenly host of angels.

Their song proclaims God the Father and Christ the Son, but omits the Holy Ghost. (William Blake notes in "The Marriage of Heaven and Hell" that, in Milton, "the Holy-ghost [is] Vacuum!") First is the Father-Creator, followed by the first-born of Creation—the Son, who is God's image ("Divine Similitude"), and his agent of creation. This is Milton's version of the doctrine of Christ as the Word, which you can find sketched at the beginning of the Gospel According to St. John. But notice that, in John, the Word *is* God in addition to being from God (see John 1:1). Milton has God call the Son "My word, my wisdom, and effectual might" (p. 139a). The Son is not only the thirty or more years of human life in Jesus of Nazareth, but also the eternal Word, or expression, of God, existing before the rest of Creation and working in it. The Word is the divine intermediary between the utterly transcendent and eternal God and the universe of space and time.

> Thee next they sang of all Creation first,
> Begotten Son, Divine Similitude,
> In whose conspicuous count'nance, without cloud
> Made visible, th' Almightly Father shines,
> Whom else no Creature can behold; on thee
> Impresst the effulgence of his Glorie abides,
> Transfus'd on thee his ample Spirit rests.
> Hee Heav'n of Heavens and all the Powers therein
> By thee created, and by thee threw down
> Th' Aspiring Dominations. (pp. 143b-144a)

The last reference in the above passage is to the rebellion of Satan and his cohorts, put down by the Son single-handed, as portrayed in Book VI. God first aroused Satan's enmity and rebellion by appointing His newly begotten Son to be His right hand and head of the Angels, Dominations, and Powers. Satan could not endure having the Son rule over him. God's appointment and Satan's rancor are narrated in Book V, pages 188b-195a.

There you have the principal characters of Milton's epic: God the Father, the Son, and Satan. Adam and Eve are the victims in the struggle between God (Father and Son) and Satan. Satan's disobedience and rebellion lead to man's disobedience and rebellion, and to man's loss of Paradise.

IV

Is Satan like Prometheus?

Remember from our First Reading how obdurate Prometheus, the rebellious Titan, was against Zeus's attempts to subdue him to obedience. Is Satan a Promethean figure? Does the fact that Zeus, in the poem by Aeschylus, is not the ultimate power in the universe and is acting tyrannically make Prometheus' case different from Satan's? Does not Satan also think that he has been unjustly treated? Does it make any difference that Prometheus tried to help man, and that Satan plots to hurt him? But is that an essential difference? Did Satan fall because he wanted to hurt man? Did Prometheus, like Satan, aim at holding second place, or even first, in Olympus? Is Prometheus a Satanic figure?

Is Satan's fall analogous to Adam's?

If you compare Milton's account of Satan's fall with the story of Adam's fall in Genesis 3, what similarities and differences do you find? Of course, we know that both Satan and Adam fell from a glorious and happy state because of sin (that is, disobedience or rebellion against God). But let us look for more specific similarities or differences.

Satan wanted to be like God, to sit at his right hand, or even to take his place—at the top. Did Adam also aim so high? The fear is expressed in Genesis 3:22 that man has become like God through attaining knowledge of good and evil, and will become immortal if he eats of the tree of life. Hence Adam is cast out of Eden.

Shall we conclude, then, that Adam's aim was the same as Satan's—to be like God or to take God's place? But does not Milton distinguish between Satan's purposeful sin and Adam's succumbing to external temptation? Do you disagree with Milton's interpretation? In the Genesis story, Adam puts the blame on Eve, and she puts the blame on the serpent. Were Adam and Eve wholly innocent in motivation, or did they welcome the opportunity? Will either Satan or Adam accept his place in the divinely created order of things?

We might also inquire whether the fallen state of Satan is

identical with that of Adam. Satan is condemned to absolute and eternal separation from God, to perpetual alienation from the center of being and meaning, to utter and permanent darkness. Is this true of Adam also? (See Book XI, pp. 299b-300a, li. 22-44.)

Why are sin and death linked in Milton and in the Bible?

The Genesis story has Adam condemned to return to the dust he came from, Paul has death entering the world with Adam's original sin, and Milton repeats this theme. What is the meaning of this connection? Are we to take it literally as pointing back to an actual state and time when there was no death in the world, as an indication of the way Creation was intended to be before it was alienated from God by man's sin? Or are we to take it figuratively as a symbol for the spiritual degradation and void that result from the act of sin, that is, for the *state* of sin? But are finitude, mortality, and temporality considered evil? Are not these characteristics involved in the essential distinction between God and his creatures? If death is a punishment for sin, wherein have the animals been at fault? Or is the rest of Creation affected by man's sins of commission and omission? (See Book XI, p. 300a-b, li. 45-71.)

Why is the portrait of Satan so much more vivid than that of God and the Son?

Do you think it is because Milton is on Satan's side—that poets are always in the Devil's party, as William Blake says? Or do you think that Milton, writing in Puritan England, had to be very circumspect in his portrayal of the divine? Could he have made a living image of God the Father—"Omnipotent, Immutable, Immortal, Infinite, Eternal King"—even if he had wanted to? Or would such a portrait have been aesthetically, as well as religiously, in bad taste? How do you present God in art without being offensive or unconvincing?

Of course, there has been great literature, painting, and sculpture dealing with the Son in human form, but here Milton is dealing with the Son in heavenly residence. Perhaps, Milton is simply a good storyteller, and realizes that the terribly bad is always much more interesting than the wonderfully good. If you have read Dostoevsky's *The Brothers Karamazov*, who stands out most vividly in your mind—that roistering sensualist Dmitri, or the sweet and gentle Alyosha? Yet does not the Bible make God the Father a living and impressive figure? How did the Biblical writers accomplish this without being offensive? Wherein is the difference between a Biblical poet and a poet like Milton?

What is Milton's doctrine of Christ in this poem?

Read the passages dealing with the Son in Book III, pages 139a-144b. Then ask yourself such questions as these: Is the Son in this text equal or second to God the Father? Does he become the Son through virtue and sacrifice, or is he the Son eternally? Is the Son created by God? Is he of the *same* substance as God the Father, or only *similar*? If Milton seems to answer these questions both ways, where do you think his real opinion lies? How does Milton's view of Christ accord with such orthodox summations of Christian belief as the Creed of Nicaea (A.D. 325)? How does his view compare with other expressions of Christian belief before and since Nicaea? (See the discussion of the 4th-century creedal controversies in Chap. XXI of Gibbon's *The Decline and Fall of the Roman Empire*, Vol. 40, pp. 305-330.)

The following questions are designed to help you test the thoroughness of your reading. Each question is to be answered by giving a page or pages of the reading assignment. Answers will be found on page 270 of this Reading Plan.

1 Are Heaven and Hell mental states?

2 What sort of religious persons occupy the limbo called Fools' Paradise?

3 Who or what does Milton invoke for success in making this poem?

4 Where does Milton refer to his blindness?

5 Are the fallen angels mortal?

6 Which is the only invisible vice?

7 Why cannot envy and faction arise in Hell?

8 Did Satan arise from the burning lake through his own will or God's?

9 What three religious acts does man owe God?

10 Which fallen angel, even in Heaven, had his thoughts on material things?

PASCAL

Pensées

Sections III-IV

Vol. 33, pp. 205-225

Blaise Pascal's *Pensées* (or "Thoughts") belong to that group of writings which describe man's plight as he seeks God and at the same time doubts God. These writings point to the perils and insecurities of man's situation in this world, and proclaim God the eternal rock on which man's faith abides. The Psalms belong to this same type of literature, and so does Augustine's *Confessions* with its revelations of the terrible abysses of the human soul. In modern times, Kierkegaard's *Sickness Unto Death,* depicting the despair which afflicts the man without faith in God, joins this company.

Pascal's *Pensées* is one of the greatest of such works. Seldom has religious experience been expressed so perfectly. The author speaks from firsthand knowledge and is a master of language. Because he himself has known it, he can speak with piercing intensity about the anguish of that odd creature, man, who realizes that he is finite—almost nothing—and yet possesses the hunger for eternity. Pascal knows personally that man can sink into the utter depths of misery, but also that he can mount to the height of bliss.

Reading the *Pensées* is, in itself, a great experience. It makes us aware of the depths within us and reminds us of our ultimate concerns as human beings. This keen perception of man's religious situation is couched in a style which makes every word count. These fragments, jotted down in the living thought of the moment, still retain for us centuries later the freshness and bite of their original conception and composition.

Eleventh Reading

I

Blaise Pascal was one of that great company of scientists and mathematicians who laid the foundations of modern science in the 17th century—"the century of genius." Pascal wrote a treatise on sound at the age of twelve, another on conic sections at sixteen, and most of his mathematical works by the time he was twenty-six. We have collected his main treatises on physics and mathematics on pages 355-487 of Volume 33. See the Reading Plan on Science and Mathematics for a discussion of Pascal's scientific contributions.

Here we shall consider the background of Pascal's religious thought. The main influence under which he fell was Jansenism, a French Catholic movement which emphasized personal religious experience, especially the sudden conversion which it believed brings the soul into direct relation with God. Pascal's family was Jansenist, and he came under the tutelage of certain confessors at the convent of Port Royal, a famous Jansenist center.

In 1654 Pascal had a decisive religious experience, usually referred to as his "conversion." Some stories associate this with a near escape from death. From that time on, Pascal devoted himself to religious meditation and concerns. He became closely associated with Port Royal and took the side of the Jansenists in their controversy with the Jesuits. He wrote (anonymously) the scathing *Provincial Letters* as part of this struggle. This work appears on pages 1-167 of Volume 33. (Jansenist doctrines were declared heretical by papal decrees in 1653 and 1713.)

It is characteristic of Pascal that personal experience, rather than philosophical speculation, was the basis for his religious meditations. At the moment of his "conversion" experience he wrote down his thoughts on a scrap of parchment. This confession, called "The Memorial," was found after his death, sewn into the lining of his doublet. He carried it on his person all the time. Here it is in full:

The Year of Grace, 1654.

Monday, November 23rd, day of St Clement,
Pope and Martyr, and others in the Martyrology.
Eve of St. Chrysogonous, martyr, and others.

From about half past ten at night to about
half past twelve.

Fire.

God of Abraham, God of Isaac, God of Jacob.
Not of the Philosophers and the men of Science.
Certainty, Certainty, Feeling, Joy, Peace.
God of Jesus Christ.

Deum meum et Deum vestrum.
Thy God shall be my God.

Forgetfulness of the world and of all apart from God.

He can be found only by the ways taught in the Gospel.

O righteous Father, the world has not known thee, but I have known thee.

Joy, Joy, Joy, tears of Joy.
I have separated myself from him.
Dereliquerunt me fontem aquae vivae.
Wilt thou leave me, O my God?
May I not be separated from him for ever.

This is life eternal that they may know thee the only true God and Jesus Christ whom thou hast sent.

Jesus Christ.
Jesus Christ.

I have separated myself from him; I have fled, renounced, crucified him.

May I never be separated from him.

He maintains himself in me only in the ways
taught in the Gospel.
Renunciation total and sweet, &c.[1]

The phrase, "God of Abraham, God of Isaac, God of Jacob, not of the Philosophers," has thundered down the ages and is still the subject of discussion. Can the God of religious faith and the God of philosophical speculation be reconciled? Must we choose between them? (See our discussion of this question in the Guide to the Sixth Reading.) Pascal, together with a line of illustrious religious thinkers both before and after him, chose the God of the Biblical patriarchs, as against the First Cause, Prime Mover, and Pure Act of the philosophers. You will note in this reading that Pascal rejects the reasons of the intellect in favor of the reasons of the "heart" as the basis of religious faith.

II

Pascal's *Pensées* belong to that class of religious writings called "apologetics." Indeed, the *Pensées* comprise notes for a work which Pascal intended to call an *Apology for the Christian Religion*. The term "apology" here has its original meaning of "defense," rather than the common, loose meaning of "excuse." Pascal intended to present a systematic defense of the Christian faith against unbelievers.

Christian apologetic writing in the early centuries was mainly directed against pagan attacks on Christian beliefs. Justin Martyr, Tertullian, and Origen are outstanding examples of early Christian apologists. Later, Aquinas' *Summa Contra Gentiles* ("Against the Gentiles") offers a defense of the Christian faith against a certain type of Arabic Aristotelian philosophy. This philosophy was making inroads on Christendom in Aquinas' time. In modern times, the defense of Christian faith within Christendom has become the most important task of apologetics. Many contemporary historians consider Chris-

---

[1] Blaise Pascal, *Thoughts*, selected and translated by Moritz Kaufmann (Cambridge, 1908), pp. 217-219.

tianity a minority movement in Western culture, fighting for its life against dominant secular forces.

This crisis had already begun in Pascal's day. The new science, the voyages of discovery, the developing knowledge of other cultures and religions, the radically new social and political order that was emerging—all these contributed to the shaking of traditional religious beliefs. Some of the keenest minds and most expressive pens of the era were directed to casting doubt on the foundations of Christian faith. Indeed, Pascal tells us that "shaking off the yoke" had become quite fashionable, and many ordinary people were putting on a show of being doubters, even when they were not, in order to be in style (see pp. 208-209). Pascal decided to meet this situation by devoting his gifts for keen thought and apt expression to the defense of the Christian faith. His "apology" consists of a description of the misery of man without God and the cure of that misery through the Christian faith.

In reading the *Pensées* you must understand that this is a posthumous work, edited and arranged by other hands after Pascal's death. Thus it is not really a book, but notes for a book, put together by various editors in whatever order each of them considered best. This explains the fragmentary and sometimes disjointed and repetitive nature of the text. This may prove annoying at times, but it also gives a genial, firsthand quality to our reading. It is as if we were looking over Pascal's shoulder as he writes, or recalling scraps of conversation with him.

Because of the unusual structure of this work, we are departing from strict adherence to page references for texts cited. Most of the time we will cite the fragment by number, thus: (#1). Sometimes, in the longer fragments, we will pinpoint the reference by the usual page-and-letter combination, thus: (p. 208b).

III

Pascal says that man is miserable without God, that he must seek Him in order to attain eternal life. First he must admit his misery and his need, and then seek with all his heart.

The worst form of misery is the unconscious and indifferent state of those who do not care about being cut off from God and do nothing to attain salvation. Like his fellow spirit Sören Kierkegaard, Pascal saw the worst form of despair in the unconscious type which hides itself by attaching infinite importance and anxiety to trifles—the passing show. Our author considers unconcern for one's eternal salvation as the most irrational and vicious attitude imaginable.

There are only three kinds of persons; those who serve God, having found Him; others who are occupied in seeking Him, not having found Him; while the remainder live without seeking Him and without having found Him. The first are reasonable and happy, the last are foolish and unhappy; those between are unhappy and reasonable. (#257)

The attitude of the last group, for Pascal, betrays a lack of virtue as well as of reason. This apathetic indecisiveness about man's ultimate concern shows lack of character. No one would trust a person like that in the ordinary affairs of life, says Pascal. He gives doubters the classical advice to abate their passions, renounce pleasure, and hunger after righteousness. He harps on the transitoriness of life before the vast infinity of eternity which will see us "either annihilated or unhappy forever." How frivolous of man to think only of the moment's satisfaction and forget the ultimate end of life!

Between us and heaven or hell there is only life, which is the frailest thing in the world. (#213)

Here is his terrible version of the confession of the indifferent doubter:

"I know not who put me into the world, nor what the world is, nor what I myself am. I am in terrible ignorance of everything. I know not what my body is, nor my senses, nor my soul, not even that part of me which thinks what I say, which reflects on all and on itself, and knows itself no more than the rest. I see those frightful spaces of the universe which surround me, and I find myself tied to one corner of this vast expanse, without knowing why I am put in this place rather than in another, nor why the short time which is given me to live is assigned to me at this point rather than at another of the whole eternity which was before me or which shall come after me. I see nothing but infinites on all sides, which surround me as an atom and as a shadow which endures only for an instant and returns no more. All I know is that I must soon die, but what I know least is this very death which I cannot escape.

"As I know not whence I come, so I know not whither I go. I know only that, in leaving this world, I fall for ever either into annihilation or into the hands of an angry God, without knowing to which of these two states I shall be for ever assigned. Such is my state, full of weakness and uncertainty. And from all this I conclude that I ought to spend all the days of my life without caring to inquire into what must happen to me. Perhaps I might find some solution to my doubts, but I will not take the trouble, nor take a step to seek it; and after treating with scorn those who are concerned with this care, I will go without foresight and without fear to try the great event, and let myself be led carelessly to death, uncertain of the eternity of my future state." (p. 207b)

What of the honest doubter who seeks? How is he to find God? Hobbes, we recall, made authority and established tradition the ultimate guide in religious matters. But Pascal is talking here of inner belief, not merely of words and actions. He counsels us not to rely on authority, tradition, or the common view, but to listen to our inner voice.

Authority.—So far from making it a rule to believe a thing because you have heard it, you ought to believe nothing without putting yourself into the position as if you had never heard it.

It is your own assent to yourself, and the constant voice of your own reason, and not of others, that should make you believe. (#260; see also #285)

How about looking to nature for the presence and glory of God? Philosophers and theologians have long attempted to base proofs of God's existence on the evidence afforded by the natural world. But Pascal will have nothing to do with this kind of demonstration of God. It is futile; it proves nothing, save to those who already believe.

I admire the boldness with which these persons undertake to speak of God. In addressing their argument to infidels, their first chapter is to prove Divinity from the works of nature. I should not be astonished at their enterprise, if they were addressing their argument to the faithful; for it is certain that those who have the living faith in their hearts see at once that all existence is none other than the work of the God whom they adore. But for those in whom this light is extinguished, and in whom we purpose to rekindle it, persons destitute of faith and grace, who, seeking with all their light whatever they see in nature that can bring them to this knowledge, find only obscurity and darkness; to tell them that they have only to look at the smallest things which surround them, and they will see God openly, to give them, as a complete proof of this great and important matter, the course of the moon and planets, and to claim to have concluded the proof with such an argument, is to give them ground for believing that the proofs of our religion are very weak. And I see by reason and experience that nothing is more calculated to arouse their contempt. (#242)

Pascal complains, for himself and for doubters in general, that nature is ambiguous about the divine presence, teasing us with apparent revelation, but not letting us see enough to put our hearts at ease, our hearts that hunger for eternity and will find no rest without attaining it.

This is what I see and what troubles me. I look on all sides, and I see only darkness everywhere. Nature presents to me nothing which is not matter of doubt and concern. If I saw nothing there which revealed a Divinity, I would come to a negative conclusion; if I saw everywhere the signs of a Creator, I would remain peacefully in faith. But, seeing too much to deny and too little to be sure, I am in a state to be pitied; wherefore I have a hundred times wished that if a God maintains Nature, she should testify to Him unequivocally, and that, if the signs she gives are deceptive, she should suppress them altogether; that she should say everything or nothing, that I might see which cause I ought to follow. Whereas in my present state, ignorant of what I am or of what I ought to do, I know neither my condition nor my duty. My heart inclines wholly to know where is the true good, in order to follow it; nothing would be too dear to me for eternity.

I envy those whom I see living in the faith with such carelessness and who make such a bad use of a gift of which it seems to me I would make such a different use. (#229)

Like Luther, Pascal revives the notion of the "hidden" God, not evident in nature, reason, or history, and knowable only to the pure of heart. Even the visible signs of His presence in the Church are so disguised "that He will only be perceived by those who seek Him with all their heart" (p. 206a). Indeed, it is good that He has not

revealed Himself to haughty sages, unworthy to know so holy a God.

Two kinds of persons know Him: those who have a humble heart, and who love lowliness, whatever kind of intellect they may have, high or low; and those who have sufficient understanding to see the truth, whatever opposition they may have to it. (#288)

The "haughty sages" are the philosophers, and the hidden

God is not their God (First Cause, Prime Mover, Pure Act, One Substance). Man, in his state of corruption since the Fall, can know the hidden God "only through Jesus Christ, without whom all communion with God is cut off" (#242).

IV

What about reason, a traditional Western path to God? At the beginning of Section III we find the affirmation that reason is the way God puts religion into the human mind (see #185). Pascal insists that religion is not contrary to reason (see #187). The indifferent doubters are condemned as irrational; indeed, "it is the glory of religion to have for enemies men so unreasonable" (p. 208a). Pascal says that reason is one of the sources of belief and finds this to be a unique characteristic of the Christian religion; but we soon find that reason is not enough.

Pascal distinguishes between the finite realm of ordinary experience, which can be measured, described, and explained, and the infinite realm beyond sensual experience and conceptual reasoning. Everything about God—his existence and his nature and attributes—is infinite, and, hence, beyond our finite cognitive powers. We can never know *what* God is, but through faith we can believe *that* He is. But how are those who are in doubt to attain faith?

Pascal rules out rational demonstration of God's existence. He sees a vast gap between knowing by reason and believing through faith, a gap which reason itself cannot bridge. "Reason can decide nothing here" (p. 214b). Christians offer no proofs of their beliefs, for a proven faith is no faith at all. Faith is a venture which involves personal commitment, rather than a rational conclusion which accords with logical necessity. Indeed, from the latter viewpoint faith appears quite risky. "If we must not act save on a certainty, we ought not to act on religion, for it is not certain" (#234).

But, says Pascal, we do act in life on a number of things that are even more uncertain than religion—such as trade and war—and it is reasonable to take such chances. Indeed, we must take chances if we are to act at all. Why not, then, take a chance on God's existence, asks this master mathematician and student of probabilities. Take a chance, says Pascal to the doubters; wager, bet on the positive—that God is. What have you got to lose? Nothing; you are going to die anyway, that is certain. What have you got to gain? Eternal salvation, infinite good, and happiness. Can you imagine a game of chance, asks Pascal, which could give you more favorable odds?

The odds are infinitely in favor of a bet that faith is right. Play it on the nose, advises Pascal; play on faith to win. Here is Pascal's argument in his own words:

Yes; but you must wager. It is not optional. You are embarked. Which will you choose then? Let us see. Since you must choose, let us see which interests you least. You have two things to lose, the true and the good; and two things to stake, your reason and your will, your knowledge and your happiness; and your nature has two things to shun, error and misery. Your reason is no more shocked in choosing one rather than the other, since you must of necessity choose. This is one point settled. But your happiness? Let us weigh the gain and the loss in wagering that God is. Let us estimate these two chances. If you gain, you gain all; if you lose, you lose nothing. Wager, then, without hesitation that He is. "That is very fine. Yes, I must wager; but I may perhaps wager too much." Let us see. Since there is an equal risk of gain and of loss, if you had only to gain two lives, instead of one, you might still wager. But if there were three lives to gain, you would have to play (since you are under the necessity of playing), and you would be imprudent, when you are forced to play, not to chance your life to gain three at a game where there is an equal risk of loss and gain. But there is an eternity of life and happiness. And this being so, if there were an infinity of chances, of which one only would be for you, you would still be right in wagering one to win two, and you would act stupidly, being obliged to play, by refusing to stake one life against three at a game in which out of an infinity of chances there is one for you, if there were an infinity of an infinitely happy life to gain. But there is here an infinity of an infinitely happy life to gain, a chance of gain against a finite number of chances of loss, and what you stake is finite. It is all divided; wherever the infinite is and there is not an infinity of chances of loss against that of gain, there is no time to hesitate, you must give all. And thus, when one is forced to play, he must renounce reason to preserve his life, rather than risk it for infinite gain, as likely to happen as the loss of nothingness. (pp. 214b-215a)

To the unbeliever who admits the logic of this argument, but who says that he still cannot bring himself to believe,

Pascal offers two pieces of advice. The first is to follow the way of virtuous self-denial and moderation. The second is to go through the motions of the faithful—kneeling, taking holy water, participating in the Mass and public prayers. Act as if you believe, advises Pascal, and "this will naturally make you believe, and deaden your acuteness" (p. 216a).

Overt action occurs before inner assent. In effect, Pascal says to unbelievers, first you kneel, then you believe. He associates "custom" with reason and inspiration as an irreplaceable component of faith.

There are three sources of belief: reason, custom, inspiration. The Christian religion, which alone has reason, does not acknowledge as her true children those who believe without inspiration. It is not that she excludes reason and custom. On the contrary, the mind must be opened to proofs, must be confirmed by custom and offer itself in humbleness to inspirations, which alone can produce a true and saving effect. (#245)

The external must be joined to the internal to obtain anything from God, that is to say, we must kneel, pray with the lips, etc., in order that proud man, who would not submit himself to God, may be now subject to the creature. To expect help from these externals is superstition; to refuse to join them to the internal is pride. (#250)

For we must not misunderstand ourselves; we are as much automatic as intellectual; and hence it comes that the instrument by which conviction is attained is not demonstrated alone. How few things are demonstrated! Proofs only convince the mind. Custom is the source of our strongest and most believed proofs. It bends the automaton, which persuades the mind without its thinking about the matter. Who has demonstrated that there will be a to-morrow and that we shall die? And what is more believed? It is, then, custom which persuades us of it; it is custom that makes so many men Christians; custom that makes them Turks, heathens, artisans, soldiers, etc. (Faith in baptism is more received among Christians than among Turks.) Finally, we must have recourse to it when once the mind has seen where the truth is, in order to quench our thirst, and steep ourselves in that belief, which escapes us at every hour; for always to have proofs ready is too much trouble. We must get an easier belief, which is that of custom, which, without violence, without art, without argument, makes us believe things and inclines all our powers to this belief, so that our soul falls naturally into it. It is not enough to believe only by force of conviction, when the automaton is inclined to believe the contrary. Both our parts must be made to believe, the mind by reasons which it is sufficient to have seen once in a lifetime, and the automaton by custom, and by not allowing it to incline to the contrary. (#252)

Notice that Pascal meets the usual objections of philosophers to overt acts by linking them with rational proof and spiritual faith. He is trying to see all the aspects of the concrete reality of religious experience together. He does not make quite the same use of the operative power of custom on belief that Hobbes does, for Pascal stresses "inspiration," feeling, the inner message of the heart. Custom, working on the "automaton"—the unconscious and involuntary aspect of our nature—acts as an intermediary for the spirit.

On the other hand, Pascal regards "too much docility"—mere submission to authority, creed, and tradition—as superstition and the destruction of true piety, which proceeds from "a feeling in the heart." (See #254, 255, 256, 259, 260.) Pascal continually stresses "the heart," not "reason," as the organ of faith. The "heart" may be thought of as intuition, feeling (in the sense of immediate experience), or as loving will.

The heart has its reasons, which reason does not know. . . . I say that the heart naturally loves the Universal Being, and also itself naturally, according as it gives itself to them; and it hardens itself against one or the other at its will. . . . It is the heart which experiences God, and not the reason. This, then, is faith: God felt by the heart, not by the reason. . . . The knowledge of God is very far from the love of him . . . We know truth, not only by the reason, but also by the heart, and it is in this last way that we know first principles; and reason, which has no part in it, tries in vain to impugn them. . . . those to whom God has imparted religion by intuition are very fortunate and justly convinced. But to those who do not have it, we can give it only by reasoning, waiting for God to give them spiritual insight, without which faith is only human and useless for salvation. . . . The heart has its own order; the intellect has its own, which is by principle and demonstration. The heart has another. We do not prove that we ought to be loved by enumerating in order the cause of love; that would be ridiculous. (#277, 278, 280, 282, 283)

We do not love mechanically or routinely, and we do not want to be loved in that way. It is ridiculous, says Pascal, to give reasons for loving someone! Wanting to be with God is not a matter of reasoning. The happiness of being with God can be known only by the heart—the core of man—not by his intellect.

Pascal seems to deny the part that reason has played in the

traditional exposition of the Christian faith—in such works, for example, as Aquinas' *Summa Theologica.* But if we look closely, we will see that Pascal does not deny the validity of human reason within the sphere which he considers its own. He wants to make sure that reason recognizes its limits.

The last proceeding of reason is to recognise that there is an infinity of things which are beyond it. It is but feeble if it does not see so far as to know this. But if natural things are beyond it, what will be said of supernatural? (#267)

We must know where to doubt, where to feel certain, where to submit. He who does not do so understands not the force of reason. There are some who offend against these three rules, either by affirming everything as demonstrative, from want of knowing what demonstration is; or by doubting everything, from want of knowing where to submit; or by submitting in everything, from want of knowing where they must judge. (#268)

There is nothing so conformable to reason as this disavowal of reason. (#272)

He holds these things to be true generally, outside of religious matters. The first principles from which reason starts—our basic intuitions of space, time, motion, and number—are not discovered by reason. "Reason must trust these intuitions of the heart, and must base every argument on them." (#282). This is especially important in religious matters, where reliance on reason alone would take the essential mystery out of faith. Faith, Pascal insists, is something *in addition to* and *beyond* reason, *not against* reason.

Two extremes: to exclude reason, to admit reason only. (#253)

If we submit everything to reason, our religion will have no mysterious and supernatural element. If we offend the principles of reason, our religion will be absurd and ridiculous. (#273)

V

Is Pascal's "wager" an offensive and invalid argument for faith?

Pascal seems to make faith a game of chance, like roulette or dice, and to promise a "system" that is a sure thing. Like a tipster at the race track, he appears to advise us to bet on God's existence—to cash in, getting infinity for an infinitesimal risk. Both Christians and skeptics have been shocked by this argument. Are they justified? Wherein is Pascal's "wager" open to criticism?

Let us first examine carefully the content and purpose of the argument. The argument is not a demonstration of the existence of God, but a calculation of the risks involved in affirming or denying God's existence. It is addressed to the unbeliever as a dialectical device to lead him out of his doubt. Pascal fights doubt dialectically with doubt. He tries to reduce doubt to absurdity, to make doubters think their doubt through. It is a stroke of finesse in a game of argument that Pascal takes quite seriously.

Did Pascal hope to convert anyone to a genuine Christian faith through this argument alone? He specifically cites the case of the unbeliever who is convinced by the "wager" argument, but still does not believe. The "wager" has dialectical force, but faith remains voluntary (see p. 215b). Did Pascal hope to destroy the unbeliever's negative attitude and open his mind to the possibility of accepting Christian faith? Then the "wager" argument would be an act of preliminary prophylaxis before the real therapy begins with the performance of overt acts *as if* one believed (see p. 216a).

There are other critical questions that we may ask about this unusual argument. Do not Pascal's calculations smack of the religious pragmatism which we discussed in the Guide to the Ninth Reading? Is personal gain, even when it concerns eternal salvation, a proper motivation for belief? Just believe here, and you will succeed hereafter: this seems to be Pascal's advice. Would God be more likely to reward a religious opportunist than an honest doubter?

Exactly what kind of belief is it which enters into the wager? It is the belief *that God exists*. But is this the same as the religious belief or trust *in God*? (See the discussion of this problem in the Guide to the Sixth Reading.) Remember Jesus' warning that men shall not enter Heaven merely through acknowledging him as Lord. (See the Guide to the Fourth Reading, p. 57.) And James points out that the devils also believe that there is one God, and tremble, for they remain devils and in hell (James 2:19). In apparent contrast to these passages are such texts as Matthew 10:32-33, and John 3:18, 6:29, 6:47, with their emphasis on belief as the prerequisite for salvation. But is the belief enjoined there belief *in the existence of God* or *in Jesus* as the Christ, *i.e.*, belief *in Christ?*

Turn back to the Guide to the Third Reading, where there is a discussion of Abraham's venture of faith (see especially p. 34). Is the essence of Abraham's faith the belief that God exists? Is Abraham's venture motivated by the same considerations as Pascal's wager? If different, how do they differ?

Would the performance of religious acts without inner belief encourage hypocrisy rather than faith?

We have already seen Montaigne's condemnation of "an hypocritical show of devotion." (See Guide to the Ninth Reading, pp. 146-147.) We may recall the plight of the king in *Hamlet*, who finds that "Words without thoughts never to heaven go." (Vol. 27, p. 54) Remember also our discussion of the relation of religious acts to moral character. (See Guide to the Second Reading, p. 29.)

Does "going through the motions" always result in the desired beliefs? Is it mere automatic conformity that is attained, or true inwardness and faith? Or is inner sincerity in the individual less important religiously than adherence to the communal forms of belief and action? Could this mechanical type of inculcation work just as well for religions or beliefs that Pascal would have deemed false?

The first question is psychological. What Pascal advocates has also been proposed by modern psychologists. The second and third questions are religious, dealing with what faith is or is not. The last question is metaphysical or theological, raising a question of objective truth.

Be sure to reread Pascal's remarks on custom, cited above on p. 184. If this is a true account of the psychology of belief, can true beliefs be inculcated in this way? Would the result be faith, described by Pascal as "God felt by the heart"?

Would the "deadening of acuteness," which Pascal promises as a result of the postures of belief, encourage the passive docility and submission which he scorns as superstition? Or would it lead instead to the active faith of the loving will?

Does Pascal have two levels of religion in mind—one a religion of the heart, the other a religion of formal beliefs and practices? If so, does he see one as leading to the other? Does the adherence to corporative beliefs and acts lead to a personal relation to God? Or does Pascal have in mind two separate levels of faith—one for a religious elite and one for the masses of adherents?

Why cannot the reason know "the reasons of the heart"?

By "reason" Pascal obviously means demonstrative reasoning from premises to conclusions. The "heart" proceeds by immediate intuition. You may want to question Pascal's limitation of the term "reason" and regard intuition as a proper act of human reason. But then we must quarrel about the meaning of terms with Pascal.

The point is this: Are there two different forms of human awareness, such as Pascal has described them, or not? Is there a "reasoning" reason on the one hand, and "spiritual insight" on the other? If so, is there any relation between these two forms of awareness?

Can "reasoning" systematically expound "the reasons of the heart"? Is that what systematic theology tries to do? Or is "reasoning" incompetent to say anything about immediate religious intuition, except that it cannot say anything about it?

Pascal says that there is a place for reason in religion. Where exactly is that place? If the intuitions of space, time, etc., furnish the basis for reason's understanding of nature, can "the reasons of the heart" provide a similar basis for rational thought in religion? Is there an essential distinction between the two types of intuition?

Is Pascal's aphoristic style suited to his subject?

Would you prefer an expository presentation in formal topics, chapters, and sections instead of this combination of assorted aphorisms? Or do you get something out of this kind of presentation which you would not obtain from the systematic order of a formal treatise or textbook? Do you think religious and philosophic subjects are better expressed in aphoristic or systematic form? Can you think of any other religious or philosophical writings which are expressed in aphorisms?

The following questions are designed to help you test the thoroughness of your reading. Each question is to be answered by giving a page or pages of the reading assignment. Answers will be found on page 270 of this Reading Plan.

1 Can people accept the Christian faith without knowing the Bible?

2 Is it incomprehensible that God should exist, or that he should not exist?

3 What Old Testament prophet is cited on the hiddenness of God?

4 Is imagination the same as the feelings of the heart?

5 Is believing propositions the same as having faith?

6 What is the main assumption we should make about our chances in this world?

7 Why is Pascal frightened by the idea of infinite spaces?

LOCKE

A Letter Concerning Toleration

Vol. 35, pp. 1-22

An Essay Concerning Human Understanding

Book IV, Chap. XVIII-XIX

Vol. 35, pp. 380-388

Can a civil community tolerate a diversity of religious beliefs and practices? This has been a problem in the Western world ever since the Protestant Reformation. We have already had Thomas Hobbes's answer to this disturbing question. Hobbes utters a resounding "No." His reason is that toleration endangers social solidarity. The security of the civil community comes first, and it demands that there be one established national religion. All citizens must openly adhere to the national religion, whatever their private beliefs.

John Locke takes direct issue with this kind of thinking. He says that there can and should be religious diversity. In reading both Hobbes and Locke, we are able to witness a dramatic encounter between two great thinkers who take opposite positions on the same issue. Locke not only says that the use of state power to enforce religious uniformity is morally and religiously wrong. He also says that it is a danger to the security of civil society. Contrary to Hobbes, he holds that enforced religious uniformity produces disloyalty and sedition, that it endangers the national welfare.

Locke goes beyond such practical considerations to insist that religious faith involves a personal, inner act that cannot be forced by any external power. The state is not only acting unjustly and imprudently when it tries to dictate religious beliefs. It is also acting foolishly and vainly by trying to accomplish what is beyond the scope of the civil power.

Locke's view is the prevalent one in the Western world today. It may help us better to understand present-day attitudes if we look closely into this early proclamation of religious tolerance.

Twelfth Reading

I

John Locke is one of the great spokesmen for traditional political liberalism in the English-speaking world. His emphasis on government by consent of the governed and on man's inalienable rights to life, liberty, and property influenced the men who drafted our own Declaration of Independence and Constitution. Locke's political philosophy is dealt with in *A General Introduction to the Great Books*. (See, there, the Guide to the Eleventh Reading, which you might find an instructive companion guide to this one.)

Here we will take up Locke's religious views. We shall see how he applies the principles of consent and natural reason to religious matters. Our first selection is the complete text of *A Letter Concerning Toleration*, which will receive most of our attention. The second selection consists of two chapters from *An Essay Concerning Human Understanding*, which discuss reason, revelation, and inspiration.

Locke wrote the letter on toleration while he was a political refugee living in Holland (see Biographical Note, p. x). The letter was published anonymously. (Note the signature "FAREWELL," p. 21c.) Locke was reluctant to admit authorship, even after his return to England under the new regime of William and Mary. The piece was first written in Latin, and later translated into the English version that we have here.

To whom is it addressed? Who is the "Honoured Sir"? He is Philipp van Limborch, a Dutch theologian with liberal views similar to Locke's. The original title was EPISTOLA DE TOLERANTIA *ad Clarissimum Virum T.A.R.P.T.O.L.A. scripta a P.A.P.O.J.L.A.* This has been deciphered to mean *A Letter Concerning Toleration, to the Illustrious Man, Professor of*

Theology among the Remonstrants, Hater of Tyranny, Limborch, of Amsterdam, Written by A Friend of Peace, Hater of Persecution, John Locke, Englishman. The initials stand for Latin words which indicate the addressee and the author of the letter, and apparently were another device used by Locke to keep his authorship secret.

The point in Locke's letter that caused the greatest stir in the England of his time was his advocacy of toleration for those groups who wished to separate from the Anglican Church and form their own churches. Locke, though not himself a separatist, defended their right to do this. The controversy continued throughout his lifetime, during which he wrote three more letters on toleration.

II

Locke's plea for religious tolerance is based on his view of the nature of religious faith and the nature of civil society. Religious faith, for Locke, is essentially an inner matter, an affair of the private conscience, and its ultimate concern is eternal salvation. Men join together to express and practice a faith they hold in common, but they do so freely and voluntarily, according to the dictates of their individual consciences.

No one else can believe for you, nor can they tell you what to believe, says Locke. Religious truth cannot be certified by some external authority. It must be freely believed by the individual to be truth for him. The things of faith cannot be professed in a merely external manner, without wholehearted inner assent. God will not be mocked. The profession of objectively true beliefs or the practice of divinely instituted rites becomes blasphemous idolatry if it represents no more than conformity with external pressure.

. . . no man can so far abandon the care of his own salvation as blindly to leave to the choice of any other, whether prince or subject, to prescribe to him what faith or worship he shall embrace. For no man can, if he would, conform his faith to the dictates of another. All the life and power of true religion consist in the inward and full persuasion of the mind; and faith is not faith without believing. Whatever profession we make, to whatever outward worship we conform, if we are not fully satisfied in our own mind that the one is true and the other well pleasing unto God, such profession and such practice, far from being any further-ance, are indeed great obstacles to our salvation. For in this manner, instead of expiating other sins by the exercise of religion, I say, in offer-ing thus unto God Almighty such a worship as we esteem to be dis-pleasing unto Him, we add unto the number of our other sins those also of hypocrisy and contempt of His Divine Majesty. (p. 3b-c)

Reasoning, persuasion, and admonition are proper ways of influencing religious belief and inner moral states. But law and force—taking away a man's life, liberty, and property or depriving him of natural and civil rights—are utterly out-of-place and of no effect in the realm of religious faith. It is particularly absurd for Christians (who profess the religion of love *par excellence* and supposedly follow the precepts of charity, meekness, and good will toward all men) to engage in persecution. Again and again in this essay, Locke castigates the tyrannical impulse to dominate other men's lives and minds, which he thinks underlies the show and cant of re-ligious zealots.

But what of the power of the religious community over individual believers? Locke recognizes that men come together to worship God publicly. They do this, he says, for mutual edification—to bear witness openly to their faith, and to in-fluence others to adhere to it. Besides, certain religious acts have to be done in common, rather than in private (see pp. 10d-11a).

Locke holds a church to be

a voluntary society of men, joining themselves together of their own accord in order to the public worshipping of God in such manner as they judge acceptable to Him, and effectual to the salvation of their souls. . . . No member of a religious society can be tied with any other bonds but what proceed from the certain expectation of eternal life. A church, then, is a society of members voluntarily uniting to that end. (p. 4b-c)

Each church, being a private association, has the sole right to make rules concerning its affairs, such as time and place of meeting, membership requirements, type of government, etc. Neither the civil power nor any other church has the right to regulate a particular church's affairs. On the other hand, a given church has no power over anyone but its own com-municants. It does have the right to admonish, exhort, and persuade recalcitrant members; and also the right, when persuasion fails, to cast the obstinate offender out of the religious community, that is, to excommunicate him. That is the only punishment it can inflict. It cannot use force, it cannot deprive the offender of life, liberty, or property, nor prejudice his civil life in any way.

The whole force of excommunication consists only in this: that, the resolution of the society in that respect being declared, the union that was between the body and some member comes thereby to be dissolved; and, that relation ceasing, the participation of some certain things which the society communicated to its members, and unto which no man has any civil right, comes also to cease. (p. 6a)

Note that by the term "church," Locke means a religious denomination or faith—such as the Anglican, Roman Catholic, or Baptist—not merely a local congregation.

III

Locke distinguishes sharply between the sphere of the church (the religious community) and that of the state (the political community). The church takes care of man's eternal salvation, and works through persuasion and love. It exercises "charitable" care. The state takes care of man's life, liberty, and property in this world, and works through law and force. It exercises "magisterial" care.

The commonwealth seems to me to be a society of men constituted only for the procuring, preserving, and advancing their own civil interests.

Civil interests I call life, liberty, health, and indolency of body; and the possession of outward things, such as money, lands, houses, furniture, and the like.

It is the duty of the civil magistrate, by the impartial execution of equal laws, to secure unto all the people in general and to every one of his subjects in particular the just possession of these things belonging to this life. . . . all civil power, right and dominion, is bounded and confined to the only care of promoting these things; and . . . it neither can nor ought in any manner to be extended to the salvation of souls. . . . (p. 3a-b)

Locke is convinced that religious matters are no concern or business of the civil power. The state has neither the right nor the power to compel persons to believe or act against their conscience. The civil authority cannot decide questions of religious truth, which concern man's ultimate destiny and salvation.

This does not mean that the civil authority has no power over anything which goes on in a church. It can forbid and punish any act in a religious community that is prohibited by civil law, such as infanticide, polygamy, or sexual immorality. There may be borderline cases in which the state may step in to protect the common welfare, as, for instance, prohibiting animal sacrifices in a time of famine. But the civil power cannot forbid anything that is civilly lawful to the church, such as kneeling, standing, going bareheaded, covering one's head, eating bread, or drinking wine.

Locke directly opposes Hobbes's view of church and state when he says that "there is absolutely no such thing under the Gospel as a Christian commonwealth" (p. 14c). Christ prescribed no form of government for his followers, says Locke. His Law of Love has nothing to do with the things of this world. He never advocated giving the civil arm the power to force men to adhere to the Christian faith. A Christian commonwealth is a contradiction in terms.

What should a citizen do when obedience to God, as he sees it, conflicts with the civil law—with the will of the civil authority? Again Locke is utterly in opposition to Hobbes. A man must always obey his conscience, and undergo whatever punishment the civil power may inflict. Locke trusts that in a justly administered state this will never occur, but he envisages certain cases where private religious judgment and public law may both sincerely intend the right. In such cases, the private person must resist, and the civil authority must punish him, each acting according to the right as he sees it. Where the sincere judgments of the private citizen and the civil magistrate differ, God alone is the ultimate judge. In the meantime

The principal and chief care of every one ought to be of his own soul first, and, in the next place, of the public peace; though yet there are very few will think it is peace there, where they see all laid waste. (p. 17b)

IV

Locke sets up a division of jurisdiction between state and church in regard to man's moral life. Insofar as it is an inner matter—concerning man's service to God, and under the jurisdiction of conscience—it belongs to religion. The civil power deals with moral conduct only insofar as it affects the public peace and interferes with other men's security and property. But Locke grants no authority to the civil magistrate in the sphere of religious opinions. The civil power can neither direct nor coerce belief. Although Locke holds that certain Catholic, Jewish, and "heathen" views are "false and absurd," it is not the state's business, he says, to suppress them in order to make the truth prevail.

For the truth certainly would do well enough if she were once left to shift for herself. She seldom has received and, I fear, never will receive much assistance from the power of great men, to whom she is but rarely known and more rarely welcome. She is not taught by laws, nor has she any need of force to procure her entrance into the minds of men. Errors, indeed, prevail by the assistance of foreign and borrowed succours. But if Truth makes not her way into the understanding by her own light, she will be but the weaker for any borrowed force violence can add to her. (p. 15c)

In addition to all the theoretical reasons of religion, reason, and justice, there is one very strong practical reason why Locke urges religious toleration. He believes that it is intolerance, not the diversity of religious opinions, which causes civil discord. Locke held that the supposed seditious attitude of the dissenters in his day would disappear once they were granted civil toleration. Persecuting men for their religious beliefs and subjecting them to deprivation of natural rights, he says, is bound to goad them into taking up arms to secure the justice which is their due. All residents of the community are entitled to religious liberty, whether they be Christians, pagans, or Jews. A man can be punished only for his own actions, according to regular and just civil laws. He is not guilty by reason of belonging to a religious association that is regarded unfavorably by the established state religion.

There could be no clear affirmation of religious toleration in principle. But Locke is not willing to tolerate all religious views and affiliations in practice. He makes at least two important exceptions—atheists and Roman Catholics. His view on atheists is set forth quite openly:

Lastly, those are not at all to be tolerated who deny the being of a God. Promises, covenants, and oaths, which are the bonds of human society, can have no hold upon an atheist. The taking away of God, though but even in thought, dissolves all; besides also, those that by their atheism undermine and destroy all religion, can have no pretence of religion whereupon to challenge the privilege of a toleration. (p. 18b)

Locke does not openly express his view on the toleration of Catholics. He refers often in this essay to churches which favor charity and toleration when they are in the minority, but practice persecution and intolerance once they are in power. This appears to be Locke's indirect way of attacking the Catholic Church. The key passage revealing Locke's attitude toward Catholics is on pages 17c-18a, where he inveighs against a sect which, he says, teaches disloyalty toward sovereigns not of their faith. Its members believe, Locke declares, that all Christians who are not of their faith are heretics; hence that one need not be bound by promises to them, and that heretical kings may be excommunicated and deposed. They claim special rights and authority over those of other faiths, says Locke.

I say these have no right to be tolerated by the magistrate; as neither those that will not own and teach the duty of tolerating all men in matters of mere religion. For what do all these and the like doctrines signify, but that they may and are ready upon any occasion to seize the Government and possess themselves of the estates and fortunes of their fellow subjects; and that they only ask leave to be tolerated by the magistrate so long until they find themselves strong enough to effect it? (p. 18a)

Locke's denial of tolerance to Catholics is probably motivated by local political concerns and rooted in special circumstances in English history, such as the struggle for dynastic power between Catholics and Protestants. Locke also opposed the toleration of Jews in practice, for reasons which are not quite clear. Possibly he felt that the Jews were an alien group in English society. Does Locke's attitude toward these religious

minorities—in striking disagreement with his expressed principles—reflect the prejudices of his time and place, or are they
the conclusions of reason and prudence?

V

Granted that belief is a matter of the individual conscience,
what decides whether the belief is true? In the selection from
An Essay Concerning Human Understanding, Locke vigorously opposes exclusive reliance on an "inner light" as warrant
for religious belief. He acknowledges the existence and validity
of revelation—direct communication from God to man—but he
insists that revelation cannot be contrary to reason. Indeed,
reason and revelation are closely bound together.

> *Reason* is *natural revelation,* whereby the eternal Father of light and
> fountain of all knowledge, communicates to mankind that portion of truth
> which he has laid within the reach of their natural faculties: *revelation*
> is *natural reason enlarged* by a new set of discoveries communicated by
> God immediately; which reason vouches the truth of, by the testimony
> and proofs it gives that they come from God. So that he that takes away
> reason to make way for revelation, puts out the light of both, and does
> much what the same as if he would persuade a man to put out his eyes,
> the better to receive the remote light of an invisible star by a telescope.
> (p. 385b)

Locke concedes that revelation may communicate truths not
knowable by natural reason, but he also insists that reason
alone can judge whether we are confronting a genuine revelation from God. How do we know that what is claimed to be
revelation is such? Locke repeats this question again and again.
Absolute inner assurance, "enthusiasm," or strong conviction
are not decisive. They prove nothing, since they accompany
contradictory beliefs. We may—with utter assurance and enthusiasm—believe that mere fancies of the human mind or
diabolical possession are divine revelation. As for the "inner
light," asks Locke, was not Lucifer a false angel of light as
well as the Prince of Darkness? (See p. 387c.)

There are, for Locke, only two sure criteria of divine revelation: reason and Scripture. The written Word of God and right
reason are our infallible guides. You will notice in *A Letter
Concerning Toleration* that Locke makes the literal text of

Scripture the test of whether specific tenets of doctrine or sacramental acts are essential to Christian faith. Thus he regarded only baptism and the Eucharist as essential sacraments, and found a good deal of traditional Christian theology to be without a Biblical basis and hence nonessential. (On the certainty and criteria of revelation, see also the passage on page 387b-c.)

Locke sees a basic connection between intolerance and the separation of reason from religious faith. In what may seem an astonishingly modern psychological insight, he interprets our zeal to impose our beliefs on other persons as a consequence of our first imposing them on ourselves. First we tyrannize over our own minds, says Locke, and force ourselves to accept what our reason does not assent to. Then we compound the wrong of self-abuse by dictating to others what they should think.

For how almost can it be otherwise, but that he should be ready to impose on another's belief, who has already imposed on his own? Who can reasonably expect arguments and conviction from him in dealing with others, whose understanding is not accustomed to them in his dealing with himself? (p. 385a)

VI

How would Locke's views apply to present-day problems of church and state?

Locke says there are borderline cases in which the state may interfere with religious practices and beliefs to assure the common welfare. Would he approve forcing persons to undergo vaccination or other preventive medical measures if doing so conflicted with their religious beliefs? Would he oppose using force in such cases as a regular procedure, but approve it in time of epidemic or public disaster?

Locke says the state cannot forbid anything to be done within the church that is lawful outside it. But if a state prohibits the production and consumption of alcoholic beverages, does it have the right to forbid the use of wine in the Christian communion or Jewish sanctification services? And what of conscientious objection to saluting the flag, entering military service, or taking oaths in courts? Are these borderline cases, where both the individual and the civil authority must act as each thinks right and risk the conflict of private conscience and public requirement?

Locke protests against finding a man guilty merely for belonging to an unpopular religious association. Should a man be liable only for his own acts, regardless of his religious or political association? Can you think of a similar protest against "guilt by association" in modern American political life?

Are church and state completely distinct in their spheres of operation?

Like Hobbes, Locke gives this world to the state, and the next to the church. But has not the church usually striven to embody Christian principles in actual social life? What about church councils for social welfare? Are they contrary to the principle of separation of church and state? Do you think the church's function is restricted to caring for eternal salvation, or does it also have a mission to influence political and social developments?

Is Locke's attitude toward atheists and Catholics consistent with his views on toleration?

Locke's essential thought on toleration is that no person should be forced to assent to religious beliefs and practices which he does not believe in. He regards religious compulsion or persecution as wrong in principle and harmful to the public concord and welfare. Yet he refuses toleration to atheists and Catholics. Is he contradicting himself?

Locke's reasoning seems to be as follows. The political community grants tolerance to all religious beliefs. But it cannot grant tolerance to expressions and practices which endanger its own existence and the principle of tolerance itself. Atheists and Catholics, according to Locke, are subversive of the state; furthermore, they are not entitled to religious toleration because atheists do not have any religious beliefs to tolerate, and Catholics will not tolerate non-Catholic religious beliefs.

Locke's argument amounts to saying that the state cannot

be expected to tolerate its own subversion. But is this not the type of argument on behalf of established state religion that he has been attacking? Is this not the argument usually advanced against unorthodox views by spokesmen for both state and church? And would not repression result in disobedience and civil discord?

Does our constitutional guarantee of freedom of religion extend to the expression of atheistic beliefs? Should it? Is the testimony of atheists admissible in our courts? Should it be? Is it just to refuse toleration to a religious group on the grounds that it does not advocate or would not practice religious toleration itself? Is it prudent for the political community to refuse such toleration? Suppose there were a religious group that, in a particular situation, was politically subversive. Would it be right to forbid its religious practices and prosecute individual adherents? Would such prohibition and prosecution be an instance of "guilt by association," or a justifiable measure against conspiracy? Should religious groups be immune from civil prosecution? Would the Canadian government be justified in prosecuting the Dukhobors for the acts of barn burning and nudism which are charged against this sect?

Do Pascal and Locke agree or disagree on the nature of religious faith?

Both Pascal and Locke insist on the inner nature of faith. Would Locke agree that the criterion of true faith is a feeling in the heart? Pascal and Locke both disapprove of authoritarian dictation in religious matters? Would Locke agree that a person can come to believe in certain doctrines and practices by acting *as if* he did? Does Locke understand the psychology of faith in the same way as Pascal? Wherein do Pascal and Locke agree in regard to the role of reason in religion? Wherein do they disagree? Would Pascal say that reason is natural revelation and that revelation is a more developed natural reason? Is Locke closer to Pascal or to Hobbes in his view of religious faith (ignoring Hobbes's views on church-state relations) and the relation of reason and revelation?

If reason and revelation are about the same, what need is there for revelation?

If we reread Chapter XVIII in Book IV of Locke's *Essay Concerning Human Understanding,* we see that he distinguishes between what man can know by rational deduction from sense experience and what he assents to because it is communicated by God. Locke also distinguishes between *original* revelation, a firsthand communication by God, and *traditional* revelation, coming down from other men who claim to transmit original revelation. Like Aquinas, Locke acknowledges divine revelation as containing absolutely certain truth, to be accepted on "bare testimony" alone. But reason and evidence are to decide whether that which claims to be revelation from God is such. This means not only questioning traditional revelation, such as the Scriptural accounts, but also original revelation. "Even original revelation cannot be admitted against the clear evidence of reason" (p. 382a). Indeed, we cannot accept anything on faith that contradicts rational knowledge. What need, then, is there for revelation?

Locke's reply is that revelation is unnecessary to disclose truths attainable by natural reason. He uses Euclid's mathematical propositions as examples of such truths. Is revelation also unnecessary for the knowledge of the existence of God? (See pp. 349c-354c.)

To the sphere of revelation Locke assigns things which are above reason, not contrary to reason, or not absolutely ascertainable by reason. What sort of things does he have in mind? He mentions only two: the revolt of the angels and the resurrection of the dead. Where would he put the Creation, the Incarnation, and the Trinity—in the sphere of reason or revelation? (See Locke's remarks on creation, p. 354a-c.)

What traditional religious doctrines would Locke treat as being contrary to reason, and hence unbelievable? Locke's assertion (p. 382b) that it is impossible to believe that a body can be in two places at the same time is generally interpreted as an attack on the Catholic doctrine of transubstantiation (*i.e.*, that the bread and wine of the Mass change into the body and blood of Christ). Would Locke view the doctrine of the

Trinity as above reason or contrary to reason? Locke accepts the literal word of Scriptures as divine revelation, as truth coming from God. Does he do so on rational grounds, through faith, or because it has been traditionally believed to be so?

Does natural reason disclose to man the moral law, and also God's purpose and providence? If so, why is special (Biblical) revelation needed? Is it to instruct the unlearned masses who lack perceptive and enlightened minds? But what of the peoples outside the Biblical dispensation? Does reason act for them as a general revelation from God? If so, does Biblical revelation add anything to this general revelation, or does it merely reiterate what is disclosed by natural reason to all peoples?

You remember that, in *A Letter Concerning Toleration*, Locke refers to "heathen" doctrines as false and absurd. Does Locke take Christian revelation as the norm for religious truth, or is he merely inveighing against the absurdities which he finds characteristic of all religion? (See p. 384b.)

What is the difference between Locke's view of religious faith and that of Aquinas?

Both Locke and Aquinas view faith as an assent of the mind to propositions disclosed by divine revelation. Aquinas further describes this assent as determined by an act of divine grace. Does Locke, too, bring in an act of the will and divine grace? If not, in what faculty or act does he place the decision to assent?

Does Aquinas regard religious experience, inspiration, or "enthusiasm" in the same way as Locke? Does he put it higher or lower than a rational inquiry into revelation? Does Aquinas advise consulting reason—which Locke calls "our last judge and guide in everything" (p. 387d)—in order to decide whether that which claims to be divine revelation really is such?

How do Locke and Aquinas differ about the relation between reason and revelation? Does the term "reason" mean the same thing to both thinkers? (For Locke's view of reason, see pp. 371c-380d.)

The following questions are designed to help you test the thoroughness of your reading. Each question is to be answered by giving a page or pages of the reading assignment. Answers will be found on page 270 of this Reading Plan.

1 What is Locke's definition of heresy?

2 Is "apostolic succession" a sign of the true church?

3 What is the difference between "traditional" and "original" revelation?

4 What decides whether men belong to the same religion?

5 Is the church more likely to be influenced by the court, or the court by the church?

6 Which part of worship is essential and which is indifferent?

7 Is tradition to be considered a guide to right doctrine and practice?

HUME

An Enquiry Concerning Human Understanding

Sections X-XI

Vol. 35, pp. 488-503

W e have heard from many thinkers concerning
the place of reason in religion. Thus far, the most critical view has been that of Blaise Pascal, who considered reason incapable of attaining knowledge about
God and his relation to man. Pascal, however, accepted the basic Christian beliefs, devoted himself
to their defense, and tried to show doubters how they
could reach assent.

David Hume, too, questions the power of reason
to attain religious knowledge. But he goes far beyond
Pascal in limiting the power of the human mind to
attain knowledge beyond the physical sphere, and—
whatever his intentions may have been—he raises
rather than quiets doubts. In the end he, too, points to
faith as the final answer, but it is unlikely that he
raised these doubts in order to defend the faith.

Hume does not merely question the power of deduc-
tive reasoning to provide knowledge about divine

things. He questions whether there is anything in human experience which can afford even a probable basis for religious beliefs. Where Pascal appealed to personal inwardness—"the reasons of the heart," the data of religious experience—Hume, who scorned this aspect of religion, merely points to the material facts of life as they are apprehended in sense experience. This, says Hume, is the only reality that man can know with his own powers; any belief in a realm beyond this rests on blind, unquestioning faith.

Hume presents the Christian faith with one of the greatest philosophical challenges it has ever faced. He does not openly deny the reality of God's existence, perfection, miracles, and providence. He simply questions whether belief in such things can be grounded in human experience and reason. His questions of "how we know" and "what we can know" are typically modern ones. They sound a new note in the great debate we have been following in this Reading Plan. The doubts that Hume raised have been the subject of lively controversy up to the present day.

Thirteenth Reading

I

David Hume, in common with other 18th-century philosophers, wrote on many subjects. His writings include not only works on philosophy and religion, but a famous five-volume *History of England* and numerous essays in politics, economics, and literature. He is most famous in the history of thought for his theory of knowledge, and was most notorious in his own time for his essay on miracles, which is included in this reading. The main passion of his life was study and inquiry into philosophical questions, but because of his failure to secure a university post, he had to take a number of jobs. These gave him a wide variety of experience, as well as a living. For an account of these jobs, including that of tutor to a lunatic marquis and various diplomatic posts, see the Biographical Note, pages 447-448.

Of Hume's personal religious background little is known, save that he was born and brought up as a Presbyterian, and that he dropped the Calvinist faith at an early age. According to James Boswell, who interviewed Hume on his deathbed, "He said he never had entertained any belief in Religion since he began to read Locke and Clarke [exponents of Deism and natural religion] . . . I asked him if he was not religious when he was young. . . . He said he was."

Like Locke, Hume found the emotional and affective aspect of religion repellent, both in the devotion of the ordinary worshiper and in the experience of remarkable religious personalities. This negative or uninterested attitude in religious experience was characteristic of the British empirical philosophers, of whom Hume was one. Hume's attitude toward religion is usually that of the cool and aloof observer. His main interest in religion is in abstract speculative problems rather than in what goes on in the religious life.

The arguments of Hume that we are about to examine scandalized upholders of traditional Christian beliefs. We will understand Hume's radical and unique position better, however, if we realize that his attack was directed against any rational justification of religious doctrines, whether of Deism and natural religion or of revealed religion. A prominent school of thinkers in England in Hume's time rejected Biblical revelation and propounded beliefs in God as creator and orderer of the world—beliefs they considered to be based on reason alone and available naturally to all men in all times and places. Hume's criticism of what he considered bad reasoning in support of religious beliefs applied to these Deists and natural religionists. It also applied to thinkers like Joseph Butler, the Anglican bishop and theologian, who wrote a famous apology for Christian doctrine on the grounds that ordinary experience and reason could justify even the most supernaturalistic tenets of Christian faith. It is probable that Hume's essay on providence and the afterlife, included in this reading, is directed against Butler's famous work, *The Analogy of Religion,* which is a defense of both natural and revealed religion.

Hume's main works on religion were the *Dialogues concerning Natural Religion* and the *Natural History of Religion.* The *Dialogues* (published posthumously for reasons of prudence) contains Hume's major criticism of the traditional and current arguments for God's existence, nature, and purpose. Many of the lines of argument in Section XI of the present reading— such as the criticism of the arguments from design, analogy, and cause—are developed more fully in the *Dialogues.* The *Natural History* is actually a speculative rather than a historical work. On the basis of an admittedly constructed and imagined state of primitive religion, Hume contends that man in a "natural" state, before civilization and philosophy, adored anthropomorphic deities made in his own image. It is these personalizations and projections of human emotions and feelings—and not the universal, infinite deity of the Deists—that are, for Hume, the center of natural religion. (You may recall that Hobbes, too, constructed a speculative history of early religion, and saw it arising from need and fear. Sigmund Freud, the subject of our final reading, continues in this tradition.)

Hume also wrote a short essay entitled "Of Superstition and Enthusiasm." "Superstition" is his term for the religion of ecclesiastical institutions with formal dogmas and a priesthood, such as Roman Catholicism and High-Church Anglicanism. "Enthusiasm" is his term for the religion of nonconformist sects which stress personal piety or religious experience, such as the Quakers and Methodists. Hume considers both "superstition" and "enthusiasm" to be "corruptions of true religion," derived from human passions and weakness. However, he considers "enthusiasm" to be more favorable in the long run to reason, toleration, and liberty.

II

David Hume's criticism of the arguments on behalf of traditional religious doctrines is based on his theory of knowledge. It will help us to follow his criticism of the attempt to found religious belief on rational grounds if we know something about what he thought man can know and how he thought man attains knowledge. And we may understand his criticism of the traditional argument for God as cause of the world if we know a little about what he thought of the nature of causality and how we come to know causes. Let us, therefore, glance briefly at Hume's theory of knowledge before we take up his criticisms of the arguments on behalf of miracles, providence, and a future state.

Hume held that our knowledge of the world rests on immediate sense experience, or "impressions," and on images, or "ideas," derived from sense experience. The only knowledge that is valid, for him, is knowledge that arises from sense experience and is verifiable by it. The test of the truth of an idea is its verification by sense experience. Hume excepted mathematical knowledge from this criterion, for he regarded mathematical relations as formal truths knowable apart from sense experience.

The novelty of Hume's position does not lie in his view that knowledge originates from sense experience and from an inductive survey of particular facts. This procedure was an accepted starting point among traditional philosophers, such as Aristotle and Aquinas. What is new with Hume is that sense experience is also made the sole test of rational principles and universal abstractions.

Hume's test casts doubt on traditional philosophical ideas. How could such a metaphysical notion as that of universal and primal being be verified by sense experience or traced to it? How can we talk of an underlying substance in things that is not apparent to the senses? How can we even accept such a common philosophical or scientific notion as causal necessity on the basis of sense experience?

Hume's criticism of this last idea—that one event or state follows from another with necessity—lays the ground for much of his attack on the philosophical attempt to justify religious beliefs. Hume asks some searching questions: How do we arrive at our notion of cause and effect? Is the idea derived from experience? How can we know by experience that a certain effect, or type of effect, will follow necessarily from a certain cause or type of cause?

Hume's answer is that we cannot know. All that experience tells us is that certain events regularly follow certain other events. Our notion of causality is derived from the repeated experience of a certain conjunction of events. This repetition, which Hume calls "custom" or "habit," becomes a felt connection in our minds, beyond mere chance or temporal succession. If the connection occurs with regularity, our minds ascribe necessity to the association of the prior and subsequent events. We expect the same connection to be repeated in the future as in the past.

We have no *rational* basis, Hume argues, for attributing necessity to the connection between two events—one of which we call "cause" and the other "effect." We have no assurance that what has occurred regularly in the past, so far as we know, will occur regularly in the future. The necessary character we ascribe to the connection lies in our mind, not in the things, so far as we know. It expresses our mental assurance or anticipation about the present and future, based on instances of experience or sense impressions in the past.

It may be that the regularity we experience in events is actually there, but we do not know this with the same kind of certainty that we know necessary connections in mathematics. Only experience can give us knowledge about matters of fact, and we have not had all the possible experiences. Hence, our so-called laws of nature are merely tentative generalizations having great probable truth, but the world picture may change at any minute. One exception would take away the necessity that we ascribe to a law.

The foregoing states Hume's view of what we can honestly say we know about causality. Anything beyond this is, for him, metaphysical abstraction, cobwebs, or moonshine, not traceable to our experience and not verifiable by it. You may wonder what all this has to do with religion and theology, but Hume's interpretation of causality is directly relevant to his criticism of theology.

There is a tradition in Western philosophy, going all the way back to Aristotle, that God is the First Cause, the ultimate origin of all things, the source behind the whole of nature, the beginning of the whole series of causes and effects. This idea was a commonplace in Hume's day, even with opponents of revealed religion. You may remember that even Hobbes, however radical he was, upheld this traditional view.

Obviously, Hume's reduction of causality to a merely psychological reflex, or a practical device for accounting for the appearances of things, puts this traditional philosophical interpretation of God in jeopardy. Also, as we shall see, it casts doubt on other traditional arguments for the existence and nature of God. Moreover, adherence to Hume's criterion of sense experience as the test of truth makes difficult, if not impossible, the rational justification of beliefs in miracles, providence, and an afterlife.

III

This reading consists of Sections X-XI of Hume's *Enquiry Concerning Human Understanding*. Section X deals with miracles, and Section XI discusses providence and a future state (an afterlife). It was Section X that caused the greatest stir in Hume's time, and it is often published separately. However, Sections X and XI form a unit dealing with the same subject—the attempt by philosophers and theologians to justify religious beliefs on grounds of reason and experience. In both sections Hume is attacking Bishop Butler and similar thinkers, as well as the whole tradition of natural theology. If we keep this in mind, we will not get lost in the details of the argument on miracles in Section X.

In the Bible, the essence of a miracle is that it is a "sign" of God's presence, power, and purpose. The wonder and awe which miracles evoke (the term *miracle* means "wonder") lies in man's witnessing the divine presence in these events and deeds, not merely in their departure from the regular course of nature. In the Biblical world-view, extraordinary deeds of magic and witchcraft were regarded as real, but they were not considered miracles. There were false wonder-workers just as there were false prophets. The essential element in a miracle is that it be an act of God.

Hume is aware of this, but he does not stress it. Instead, he emphasizes the merely extraordinary character of a miracle as "a violation of the laws of nature." He finds this rationally incredible, no matter to whom the act be ascribed—God, man, or devil. Of course, the notion of inviolable laws of nature is foreign to the Biblical mind; it is a product of Greek thought and, later, European science. However, Hume's notion of a miracle as a departure from the ordinary course of nature was a common, traditional Christian notion, which you will find expressed systematically in Aquinas' *Summa Theologica* (see Vol. 19, pp. 543b-545b).

Miracles, for Hume, are such events as a man's walking on water, living in the belly of a whale, walking through a wall, or rising from the dead. Such events as the opening and closing of the waters of the Red Sea or Joshua's making the sun stand still are what Hume means by miracles. He also considers as a miracle any event which could happen in the ordinary course of nature, but occurs in the particular case through divine power. Such events are the sudden cure of the

sick, the sudden death of the healthy, the falling of rain, or the
blowing of wind—through agencies outside the usual course of
nature. Even raising a feather in the air, says Hume, may be
a miracle if it is done by a particular act of the divine will or
through an invisible agent of the divine power. In this essay,
however, Hume concentrates on the types of miracles that are
obvious violations of the laws of nature.

A miracle is a violation of the laws of nature; and as a firm and unalterable experience has established these laws, the proof against a miracle,
from the very nature of the fact, is as entire as any argument from
experience can possibly be imagined. Why is it more than probable, that
all men must die; that lead cannot, of itself, remain suspended in the
air; that fire consumes wood, and is extinguished by water; unless it be,
that these events are found agreeable to the laws of nature, and there is
required a violation of these laws, or in other words, a miracle to prevent them? Nothing is esteemed a miracle, if it ever happen in the common course of nature. It is no miracle that a man, seemingly in good
health, should die on a sudden: because such a kind of death, though more
unusual than any other, has yet been frequently observed to happen. But
it is a miracle, that a dead man should come to life; because that has never
been observed in any age or country. There must, therefore, be a uniform experience against every miraculous event, otherwise the event
would not merit that appellation. And as a uniform experience amounts
to a proof, there is here a direct and full *proof*, from the nature of the
fact, against the existence of any miracle; nor can such a proof be destroyed, or the miracle rendered credible, but by an opposite proof,
which is superior. (p. 491a-b)

But what possible evidence could oppose such "firm and
unalterable experience," such "direct and full *proof*" against
miracles? If, as Hume says, the most certain evidence in matters of fact is the testimony of our senses, which flatly denies
miracles, what stronger evidence can counter it? Well, Hume
points out, we cannot go just by our own experience. Individual experience is limited and, hence, is not an infallible
guide to truth in matters of fact. Persons who live in a tropical
climate might be unable to conceive the freezing of water because it is completely outside their experience. Hence, even in
everyday affairs, we have recourse to the testimony of other
men, who claim to have witnessed things outside of our personal experience.

One thing is necessary, though, in dealing with the testimony of others. We must weigh the value of this secondhand testimony by the final standard of experience and observation, especially in matters of the extraordinary and marvelous. We must assay its likelihood by its harmony or discrepancy with the structure of common experience. Even the testimony of an apostle is not, by itself, stronger than the evidence of our own senses—"The incredibility of a fact . . . might invalidate so great an authority" (see p. 490c). Testimony to the miraculous, which directly contradicts the evidence of our own experience —"our only guide in reasoning concerning matters of fact"— must have tremendous weight to enlist our belief (see p. 489b). An early biographer of Hume suggested that the famous Section X should be entitled "The Principles of Belief in Human Testimony."

Here is the striking criterion which Hume propounds for accepting human testimony to miracles:

"That no testimony is sufficient to establish a miracle, unless the testimony be of such a kind, that its falsehood would be more miraculous, than the fact, which it endeavours to establish; and even in that case there is a mutual destruction of arguments, and the superior only gives us an assurance suitable to that degree of force, which remains, after deducting the inferior." When anyone tells me, that he saw a dead man restored to life, I immediately consider with myself, whether it be more probable, that this person should either deceive or be deceived, or that the fact, which he relates, should really have happened. I weigh the one miracle against the other; and according to the superiority, which I discover, I pronounce my decision, and always reject the greater miracle. If the falsehood of his testimony would be more miraculous, than the event which he relates; then, and not till then, can he pretend to command my belief or opinion. (p. 491b-c)

Hume goes on to say that "there never was a miraculous event established on so full an evidence." We have never, he says, had enough witnesses of proper intelligence and character attesting to a miraculous event of a public and verifiable nature. He points to the human propensity to believe in the big lie, the "utterly absurd and miraculous" tall tale, as against normal caution about ordinary absurdities. He points also to various possible motivations for telling miracle stories: self-deceit, the desire to promote a holy cause, vanity, and self-interest. And why is it, he asks us, that miracle stories are always about events far away and long ago, that usually occur in ignorant and barbarous times and places? *"It is strange . . . that such prodigious events never happen in our days"* (p. 493a).

Hume pulls no punches here. He daringly pushes his point home against the authenticity of the Biblical miracle stories, singling out the Pentateuch in particular. It recounts all kinds of "prodigies and miracles," he says, which are incredible in the light of our ordinary experiences and, moreover, rest on the testimony of the most dubious witnesses (an ignorant people, says Hume, trying to puff itself up about its early origins and future destiny).

Hume adds one more reason against believing in miracle stories, and he considers it decisive. It is the fact that all religions have such stories. Hume assumes that only one religion can be the true one; hence, all the others must be false. If certain miracles prove the truth of one religion, then they must prove the falsity of all other religions and their miracle stories. Hence, if we consider the testimony of all the religions, they are mutually contradictory, and the testimony of any one religion is overborne by the weight of all the others.

In the end, though, Hume says that we are naturally bound to deny any miracle story, *no matter how reliable the testimony nor how public the circumstances.* Hume takes his cue here from the Cardinal de Retz who disbelieved the story of the one-legged man in Saragossa who recovered his missing limb by rubbing holy oil on the stump, even though he saw the man (with two legs) and heard from respectable churchmen and all the townspeople that the miracle had occurred. Cardinal de Retz, says Hume,

concluded, like a just reasoner, that such an evidence carried falsehood upon the very face of it, and that a miracle, *supported by any human testimony,* was more properly a subject of derision than of argument. (p. 494d, italics added)

Hume feels the same about the healing miracles said to have occurred at the Abbé Paris' tomb. Despite the host of reliable and distinguished eyewitnesses—in a time contemporary with his own, on a scene open to public view—Hume refuses to believe what he considers to be absolutely impossible.

> And what have we to oppose to such a cloud of witnesses, but the *absolute impossibility* or miraculous nature of the events, which they relate? And this surely, in the eyes of all reasonable people, will alone be regarded as a sufficient refutation. (p. 495a, italics added)

Hume is unwilling to believe that the laws of nature have been violated. He simply will not believe that a man who has *really* died and been buried can be brought to life again. No constellation of reliable witnesses and public circumstances will avail against this firm conviction in the inviolability of the laws of nature. Common sense and past experience tell us, says Hume, that violation of truth by witnesses is much more likely and probable than the violation of the laws of nature.

> As the violations of truth are more common in the testimony concerning religious miracles, than in that concerning any other matter of fact; this must diminish very much the authority of the former testimony, and make us form a general resolution, never to lend any attention to it, with whatever specious pretence it may be covered. (p. 496c)

Thus, Hume advocates an absolute will to disbelieve miracle stories to safeguard our rational belief in natural laws—"a general resolution never to lend any attention to it." It makes no difference that the wonders are ascribed to the Almighty, for we can know of His deeds only from our ordinary experience of the regular course of things.

It would seem that Hume leaves a rational person with no alternative save to disbelieve in all miracle stories. But that is not the way he ends his essay on miracles. He says that the miracle stories can be believed by faith alone, against reason and common sense. Faith is the real and basic miracle, says Hume. It takes the miracle of faith to make a rational man believe in Christianity. A sure way to destroy Christianity, says Hume, is to try to make Christian beliefs rest on rational grounds. Here is Hume's remarkable conclusion:

> . . . we may conclude, that the *Christian Religion* not only was at first attended with miracles, but even at this day cannot be believed by any reasonable person without one. Mere reason is insufficient to convince us

of its veracity: And whoever is moved by *Faith* to assent to it, is conscious of a continued miracle in his own person, which subverts all the principles of his understanding, and gives him a determination to believe what is most contrary to custom and experience. (p. 497b)

IV

This startling passage puts the reader in a quandary. It is not clear now which side Hume is on, or what he himself believes. Perhaps he is being ironic here and is poking fun at traditional Christian beliefs. Or perhaps he is a sincere fideist—one who wants to rest religious belief on faith alone. Or could he be thinking of his own personal experience, as told to Boswell? But one thing is clear: Hume wanted to refute rational arguments for religious beliefs—Christian, Deist, or any other. Hume was convinced that the traditional arguments were full of holes, and that any belief which rested on such a basis could not long endure. (Whether or not he wanted any of the beliefs to endure is quite another matter.)

Section XI, which discusses providence and a future state, clearly demonstrates Hume's opposition to basing religious beliefs on rational grounds. Hume expresses his thoughts in the form of a fictitious dialogue with a friend. First, an introductory conversation between Hume and his friend sets the theme. Next, there is a long monologue in which the friend, assuming the role of the ancient materialist philosopher Epicurus, harangues Hume, who plays the part of a captive audience (the Athenian people). Finally, the conversation between Hume and his friend—in their own persons—is resumed, and they discuss the points raised in the harangue. This indirect form of presentation has a certain quaint literary charm, although it may make it hard to follow the line of argument. Besides, Hume's friend may speak more for the real Hume than the Hume of the dialogue.

1. In the opening discussion, the friend holds philosophy responsible for religious bigotry, because it constructed the "speculative dogmas" which are the occasion for present-day persecution of dissenters, including philosophers. He says that in ancient Greece, religion relied on traditional myths, while philosophy minded its own business—speculation. Religion, ap-

pealing to the ignorant masses, and philosophy, addressed to the brainy few, did not interfere with one another.

Hume interrupts to ask whether philosophic denials of divine existence, providence, and an afterlife may not be subversive of public morality and civil order. This is the ostensible subject of Hume's dialogue. Are ideas about the origin and government of the world mere speculation, or do they have practical effects on human conduct and society? Within this framework of discussion, Hume raises critical doubts about the traditional arguments for providence and a future life. The raising of these doubts is the main purpose of his dialogue. (Note how close the ostensible subject of the dialogue is to that of Book X of Plato's *Laws*, discussed in the Second Reading.)

2. At the beginning of his harangue to the Athenian people, "Epicurus" states the basic proposition of the dialogue.

The religious philosophers, not satisfied with the tradition of your forefathers, and doctrine of your priests (in which I willingly aquiesce), indulge a rash curiosity, in trying how far they can establish religion upon the principles of reason; and they thereby excite, instead of satisfying, the doubts, which naturally arise from a diligent and scrutinous enquiry. (p. 498c)

He proceeds at once to attack the traditional argument that the order of nature points to a supreme intelligence, or design, as cause of the world. Epicurus makes two counterarguments: (a) that experience and reason do not provide certain knowledge of such a cause, and (b) that even if we grant such an hypothesis, we can say nothing about the perfection and goodness of such a cause.

You then, who are my accusers, have acknowledged, that the chief or sole argument for a divine existence (which I never questioned) is derived from the order of nature; where there appear such marks of intelligence and design, that you think it extravagant to assign for its cause, either chance, or the blind and unguided force of matter. You allow, that this is an argument drawn from effects to causes. From the order of the work, you infer, that there must have been project and forethought in the workman. If you cannot make out this point, you allow, that your conclusion fails; and you pretend not to establish the conclusion in a greater latitude than the phenomena of nature will justify. (p. 498d)

Epicurus' second argument is based on the proposition that we cannot ascribe any more perfection to the cause than we find in the effect. Even if we assume that the world is the work of a divine designer, he argues, we can attribute to the designer only that degree of order, good, and wisdom that we find in our common experience of the actual world. We have no rational warrant to jump from the hypothetical cause we have inferred from this effect to other effects of a higher order.

Allowing, therefore, the gods to be the authors of the existence or order of the universe; it follows, that they possess that precise degree of power, intelligence, and benevolence, which appears in their workmanship; but nothing farther can ever be proved, except we call in the assistance of exaggeration and flattery to supply the defects of argument and reasoning. So far as the traces of any attributes, at present, appear, so far may we conclude these attributes to exist. The supposition of farther attributes is mere hypothesis; much more the supposition, that, in distant regions of space or periods of time, there has been, or will be, a more magnificent display of these attributes, and a scheme of administration more suitable to such imaginary virtues. We can never be allowed to mount up from the universe, the effect, to Jupiter, the cause; and then descend downwards, to infer any new effect from that cause; as if the present effects alone were not entirely worthy of the glorious attributes, which we ascribe to that deity. The knowledge of the cause being derived solely from the effect, they must be exactly adjusted to each other; and the one can never refer to anything further, or be the foundation of any new inference and conclusion. (p. 499b)

Following his principle that we can ascribe no more perfection in the cause than we find in the effect, Epicurus points to the evil and disorder of the actual world as obviously discordant with the superlative order, good, and wisdom attributed to its maker. This is the reason, he maintains, why philosophers and theologians invent a perfect state, before or after the present one—a golden age or paradise. But he insists that this jump from actual perfection to ideal perfection has no grounds in reason and experience. All such talk is mere conjecture, a figment of the imagination. We cannot rationally go beyond what is obvious in present experience.

Whence, do you think, can such philosophers derive their idea of the gods? From their own conceit and imagination surely. For if they derived it from the present phenomena, it would never point to anything farther, but must be exactly adjusted to them. That the divinity may *possibly* be endowed with attributes, which we have never seen exerted; may be governed by principles of action, which we cannot discover to be satisfied: all this will freely be allowed. But still this is mere *possibility* and hypothesis. We never can have reason to *infer* any attributes, or any principles of action in him, but so far as we know them to have been exerted and satisfied. (pp. 500d-501a)

Epicurus treats religious belief as if it were a scientific hypothesis. Indeed, he speaks of "the religious hypothesis [of providence] as a particular method of accounting for the visible phenomena of the universe." And the ultimate test of all hypotheses, he insists, as well as the only sure guide in regulating human conduct, is actual experience of the course of events.

His final objection to religious assertions which go beyond experience is that they are uncertain and useless. There is a notable modern, pragmatic tone in his complaint that such beliefs make no difference to our knowledge of matters of fact or the guidance of human conduct. Epicurus maintains that a well-disposed mind will inevitably choose a virtuous over a vicious life on the basis of experience alone, apart from any speculative hypothesis about divine providence. This, you remember, was the ostensible point that he set out to demonstrate. The religious hypothesis

is uncertain; because the subject lies entirely beyond the reach of human experience. It is useless; because our knowledge of this cause being derived entirely from the course of nature, we can never, according to the rules of just reasoning, return back from the cause with any new inference, or making additions to the common and experienced course of nature, establish any new principles of conduct and behaviour. (p. 501b)

All the philosophy, therefore, in the world, and all the religion, which is nothing but a species of philosophy, will never be able to carry us beyond the usual course of experience, or give us measures of conduct and behaviour different from those which are furnished by reflections on common life. No new fact can ever be inferred from the religious hypothesis; no event foreseen or foretold; no reward or punishment expected or dreaded, beyond what is already known by practice and observation. (p. 502d)

3. At the beginning of the final discussion, Hume points out that in actual life we not only infer causes from effects, but

also proceed to infer further effects from the causes. We jump from the sight of a half-finished house to the idea of a designer, a plan, and the finished building. We are not limited in our judgments to what is actually present in the moment of experience. Hume points to an analogy between human and divine plans and planners.

Hume's friend counters that the argument from analogy is false, because we know much about man's mind, nature, and works by repeated experiences. Our inferences about the finished state of a human work will be based on much observation and experience. But in the case of God and the universe, we have only a single case of cause and effect. If God is single in his kind, how are we to infer anything about his nature and intent? There are many men, and their works are even more numerous. But we have no other worlds on which to base inferences going beyond our actual experience to a more perfect state of goodness, wisdom, and order.

The argument from analogy, says Hume's friend, arises from man's inveterate tendency to make God in his own image, to account for Him in terms of human qualities and purpose. But God is wholly other, and incomprehensible in terms of anything else. It is extremely improbable that the ways of God are like the ways of man.

At this point the discussion takes a strange turn. Hume takes over his friend's argument and goes beyond it. Remember that, according to Hume's theory of causality, it is only when we constantly associate one type of event with another type of event that we consider one the cause and the other the effect. If, as Hume's friends says, God is utterly unique, and if the universe is also unique, how are we to infer that God is the cause of the universe, let alone anything about his nature and purpose? We infer causes from types of effects, and we connect effects with types of causes, but we do not have anything to go on here. How can we make comparative judgments when we have only a single case?

Hume's friend had argued earlier that it was dubious to infer anything about the God that we infer to be the cause of the world. Hume argues now that it is even dubious to infer a God as cause of the world. This is Hume's attempt at a knockout blow against the doctrine of God as cause, which has played so large a part in the Western tradition.

I much doubt whether it be possible for a cause to be known only by its effect (as you have all along supposed) or to be of so singular and particular a nature as to have no parallel and no similarity with any other cause or object, that has ever fallen under our observation. It is only when two *species* of objects are found to be constantly conjoined, that we can infer the one from the other; and were an effect presented, which was entirely singular, and could not be comprehended under any known *species*, I do not see that we could form any conjecture or inference at all concerning its cause. If experience and observation and analogy be, indeed, the only guides which we can reasonably follow in inferences of this nature; both the effect and cause must bear a similarity and resemblance to other effects and causes, which we know, and which we have found, in many instances, to be conjoined with each other. (p. 503b-c)

These final words conclude Hume's theoretical argument on the ideas of providence and a future state; but remember that we ostensibly had a practical problem as our subject—whether the denial of these ideas was injurious to the common good. The dialogue ends with Hume in agreement with his friend that the ideas in question are merely speculative and offer no guidance or inducement to moral conduct beyond what ordinary experience and reflection offer. He disagrees, however, that it follows that these ideas are of no effect in actual practice among the common run of men. Hume takes the pragmatic view that belief in such ideas induces hope of reward or fear of punishment in a supernatural realm, and thus does influence human conduct.

You conclude, that religious doctrines and reasonings *can* have no influence on life, because they *ought* to have no influence; never considering, that men reason not in the same manner you do, but draw many consequences from the belief of a divine Existence, and suppose that the Deity will inflict punishments on vice, and bestow rewards on virtue, beyond what appear in the ordinary course of nature. Whether this reasoning of theirs be just or not, is no matter. Its influence on their life and conduct must still be the same. And, those, who attempt to disabuse them of such prejudices, may, for aught I know, be good reasoners, but I cannot allow them to be good citizens and politicians; since they free men from one restraint upon their passions, and make the infringement of the laws of society, in one respect, more easy and secure. (p. 503a)

V

If Hume's view of causality is accepted, are violations of the laws of nature possible?

According to Hume, laws of nature are nothing but expressions of constant and common experience—such as that men die, heavy bodies fall, fire consumes wood, and water extinguishes fire. But there is no inherent reason why future experience may not turn up exceptions to the so-far uniform rules. The state of the world may change, or facts may become apparent that were hidden from us before. How, then, can Hume talk about the absolute impossibility of a violation of the laws of nature?

Would Augustine's view that miracles occur "not contrary to nature, but contrary to what we know as nature," be more consonant with Hume's theory of causality? (See Vol. 18, p. 567c.)

There are two kinds of questions which we must pursue here: (1) questions of what *is* or what *is possible;* and (2) questions of *how we know* the answers to (1). In the first category belong the questions of whether there are inviolable laws of nature and whether intervention by a supernatural power can cause an event to occur contrary to those laws. This is apart from questions of how we come to know the laws or the exceptional events which violate them.

Does Hume say that there are no absolute laws of nature, or that we cannot know them with absolute certainty through experience? Does he say that miracles, as violations of the laws of nature, are absolutely impossible in general, or that it is impossible to accept human testimony that a particular miraculous event took place? Is there or is there not a contradiction between Hume's apparent view that casual laws are nearly probable generalizations and his seemingly dogmatic rejection of the miraculous violation of such laws before and apart from experience?

Would Hume distrust his own sense experience of a particular event if it appeared to contradict a law of nature? Or would he decide that the law was not absolutely universal, and that a new law should be formulated? How does this affect the question of whether a special act of God is involved?

Would Hume's criticism apply if miracles are not literally violations of the laws of nature?

For Augustine, the greatest miracle of all is the world itself and all the creatures in it, seen as the work of God (see vol. 18, pp. 306d-307b). The modern Protestant theologian Friedrich Schleiermacher said that for the religious man "every event, even the most natural and usual, becomes a miracle." Some great present-day religious thinkers hold this view of miracles, although they would add that some events are more specifically miracles (that is, signs of the divine presence and power) than others—for the persons or groups involved.

How does Hume's criticism apply to this view of the nature of miracles? It would seem that Hume's analysis, based on the definition of a miracle as a literal, visible, material violation of natural laws and on the theory that knowledge is derived from sense experience, does not apply here. Or could Hume say that he has reached that result anyway, in resting belief in miracles on faith alone—against reason, experience, and common sense?

Would Hume's criticism of human testimony apply here, too, in regard to belief in the experience claimed by others? Or would it be less applicable here, where we are not asked to believe in violations of natural laws? Would we still be pushed back to Hume's criticism of the argument that God is the cause of the world? How do you know that the world is the work of God? Can the man of faith offer any objective criterion for his belief that God is present in an event, or in every event? If everything is miraculous when viewed "before God," is nothing miraculous in Hume's sense?

Do the miracle stories in the various religions disprove one another?

Hume attacks the argument that miracles furnish "external" proof of the truth of the Christian revelation. The basic assumption is that there is only one true religion, in which God's will and presence is uniquely revealed. Miracles, prophecies, and inspiration attest to that revelation. It is such traditional assumptions that Hume subjects to critical attack. He argues that if miracles prove the unique truth of one religion, then they prove the falsity of every other religion, including its miracle stories. Hence, in the end, all the "proofs" disprove one another, if we weigh the various testimonies and calculate the probabilities involved—one against all the rest (see p. 493c-d).

What do you think of Hume's logic? Might one religion's miracle stories be true, and all others false? Could some religions have true stories and others, false ones? Could each religion have both true and false stories? Or do all religions have false miracle stories? Hume chooses the last alternative, on the assumption that all religions contradict one another, since only one can be true. What are the grounds for such an emphatic assumption? And how does Hume jump from that to denying the validity of the stories (and, hence, the truth) of all religions?

If the traditional believer accepts the Biblical miracle stories, does he thereby commit himself to the possibility that God may demonstrate his presence and power in other times and places? If the believer commits himself to that possibility, can he limit the area of these demonstrations to the Jewish and Christian faiths? Is there any inherent reason, once this possibility is accepted, why true miracles cannot occur in religions that are not rooted in Biblical revelation? What would this do to the idea of miracle as a proof of religious truth?

Is there any rational justification for the traditional argument for God as cause?

The traditional argument rests on the assumption that the whole process of cause and effect in the world depends on an

ultimate cause which is not itself caused, and which is outside
the series of natural causes. The problem Hume raises is
whether we can proceed from the temporal sequence of causal
connections, derived from the moments of our sense experience, to this primal and perfect cause. Does this argument or
any other argument for the existence of God, he asks, rest on a
belief which precedes rather than follows from the argument?
Do men first believe in God, and then argue that He is the
first cause, or do they first reach the rational conclusion that
there is a first cause, and then assent to the belief in God?

Hume also raises the problem of whether, granted the existence and necessity of this first cause, we are able to attribute
perfect qualities to it, especially the attributes of the Christian
God. Is the first cause He whom men mean by the word
"God"? You may remember that, in our Second Reading, Plato
concluded from a similar argument about motion that the
world was full of gods, not just one first cause or self-moved
mover. Similarly, Aristotle argues for a number of prime
movers. Did Plato and Aristotle believe in the God that
Christian theologians try to prove by the argument from cause?

Where would you find the link between the philosophical
notion of a first cause and the religious understanding of God?
In the Biblical idea of divine creation? In the universal notion
of divine power? In the will and purpose attributed to God in
Western religion? Is God, as first cause, the constant sustainer
as well as the originator of the universe? Can we reach any of
these religious notions of God as cause by reason alone?

Does Hume deny any possibility of attaining re-*
ligious truth from reason and experience?

We have already seen that Hume rests belief in the Christian
religion on faith, even against all principles of reason. But does
Hume rule out reason entirely, or does he only hold that "mere
reason" is insufficient to attain religious conviction? At the end
of the present essay he says that theology, in its proof of God's
existence and the immortality of the soul, is founded on reason
so far as experience extends, but that "its best and most solid
foundation is *faith* and divine revelation" (p. 509c). What kind

of reasoning and experience does Hume have in mind here? How far would it extend in the proof of God's existence and the soul's immortality? Does Hume rule out entirely the possibility of our becoming aware of a divine or transcendent realm through our experience of this world?

Is Hume's criticism of the traditional arguments for God, Providence, and an afterlife irreverent and irreligious?

Let us leave aside the question of Hume's intentions, about which philosophers still dispute, and concentrate on his acts. Is it the cogency of certain human arguments or the service of God that is at stake here? Would it have been more holy and pious for Hume to assent to these arguments, if he really saw deficiencies in them, or to keep silent? Is Hume's criticism of the concept of cause so destructive that it subverts the whole idea of a divine creator and sustainer of the universe? Or is Hume more pious than the theologians in not confining God within a certain causal order? (See Hume's final footnote, p. 509d.)

The following questions are designed to help you test the thoroughness of your reading. Each question is to be answered by giving a page or pages of the reading assignment. Answers will be found on page 270 of this Reading Plan.

1 What are the possible answers to the question of the existence of distributive justice? What is Hume's interpretation of the answers?

2 Are prophecies miracles?

3 Has testimony amounting to mere probability ever attested to a miracle?

4 What specific physical example does Hume use to show that a cause must not exceed its effect?

5 What writer included in the *Great Books* set suggested collecting and scrutinizing cases of extraordinary events?

6 Can experience give us grounds to predict events with certainty?

Fourteenth Reading

DOSTOEVSKY

The Brothers Karamazov

Book VI, "The Russian Monk"

Vol. 52, pp. 146-170

Fyodor Dostoevsky has played a remarkable role
in the thought of our time. Although he speaks to us
from a culture strangely different from our own, his
voice seems to be directed to each of us living now.
He lived before the great social and military cata-
clysms of the 20th century, but he was prophetically
aware of their imminence. He was keenly and pain-
fully conscious of the spiritual malaise of modern
man, whom he saw as becoming progressively more
estranged from the sources of his being as he becomes
more and more masterful in scientific techniques.
Dostoevsky's portrayal of modern man's lostness and
of the possibility of his redemption retains its powerful appeal, even—and perhaps especially—with those
who do not adhere to traditional religious beliefs.
This intensely Christ-centered writer is still highly
regarded by Russian readers today, nurtured though
they are by the official atheistic philosophy.

233

This reading affords us a fine example of the continuing appeal of Dostoevsky to contemporary man. The theme is the real effect in the world of personal acts of love, humility, and confession. Working on this theme, this master novelist conveys in his master novel a simple, yet profound, portrait and interpretation of man's spiritual predicament.

This short reading is rich in ideas, such as these: that holy acts are like seeds which are dropped in the ground to come to ripeness at the proper time; that all things are connected, so that acts done here and now have their effect in remote places and times; that we are to love and rejoice in the whole world, animate and inanimate; that the monastic life shows the way to reach such joy and love; and that the Russian people have a holy mission to the peoples of the world.

All these ideas are conveyed to us through unforgettable persons and scenes: the saintly elder as a young officer, kneeling to beg forgiveness of persons he has injured; the confession of the mysterious visitor; and the conversation of the dying elder with his disciples. Here Dostoevsky gives us both the story and the commentary. They provide memorable experience and counsel.

Fourteenth Reading

I

Dostoevsky's religious ideas arise from the context of Russian Orthodox faith. Russian Orthodoxy is a form of Greek (or Eastern) Orthodox faith, which was the religion of Christians in the eastern half of the Roman Empire. Eastern Orthodoxy, centered at Byzantium (Constantinople), separated from the Roman Church in the Great Schism of 1054, because of conflicts about doctrine, ritual, and jurisdiction and because of basic cultural differences. The Catholic Church thereafter was divided between two institutions and two cultures—one Roman, or Latin, and the other Byzantine, or Greek. The Eastern Church considered itself the true faith ("orthodox"), and Byzantium, the Second Rome. After the fall of Constantinople to the Turks, Russia (a latecomer to the family of Christian nations) became the main stronghold of Orthodoxy. The idea was promulgated that Moscow was the Third Rome, and the tsar, the legitimate successor to the Byzantine emperor.

Russian Orthodoxy assumed many special characteristics. Religion and nation were fused; indeed, Russian Orthodoxy and the Russian nation developed at the same time, and to be a Russian meant to be Orthodox. The idea arose that Russia was a holy people with the special mission of establishing the reign of justice under Christ. But the state became more and more dominant over the church until the priests and the hierarchy became mere government functionaries. Popular sects and schisms arose in protest over the unspiritual state of the official religion and the abandonment by the state of its messianic role. By Dostoevsky's time the ruling and educated class had been permeated by modern Western ideas and had become estranged from the illiterate, pious peasantry. Socialism, which

Dostoevsky saw as the only real alternative to Christianity in the modern age, had begun to influence the intellectuals and the working class.

Monasticism played an important part in the Christianization of Russia, and the monks remained an important religious force down to modern times. Russian saints were chosen almost entirely from the monks rather than from the priests, who were generally regarded as lacking in ethical and religious virtue. From these monks came the *startzi*, or elders, a remarkable type of religious leader that exercised great spiritual influence in the 19th century.

The *staretz*, or elder, was a spiritual guide or teacher, who exercised authority through his personal character and holiness. The relation to his disciples, who could be fellow monks or laymen, was based on absolute personal trust. Father Zossima, in our reading, is a typical Russian elder of the time. His aide, Father Païssy, is absolutely certain that the dying elder will fulfill his promise to hold a last conversation with his disciples. No impediments of flesh, including death itself, can shake that absolute trust. Zossima is the human center of love and trust and guidance for the monks and novices who surround him. He is the incarnation, and hence the assurance, of holiness on earth.

II

The present reading consists of Book VI of *The Brothers Karamazov*, entitled "The Russian Monk." It is quite comprehensible apart from the rest of the book. However, its themes, as well as other religious ideas, are expanded throughout the work. For instance, Book I, Chapter 5, tells us about the Russian elders and about Father Zossima in particular (see pp. 11-15). And Book II has many important religious discussions; see especially Chapter 5, pages 28-32, on the state becoming a church. Book IV, Chapter 1, shows us Father Ferapont, the ultrarigorous ascetic and opponent of the laxer Father Zossima (see pp. 83-88).

Do not fail to contrast Zossima's sweetness and light with the nihilism and doubts expressed by Ivan Karamazov. In Book V, Chapter 4, Ivan proclaims his inability to believe in love of neighbors and his revolt at human suffering in a world supposed to be ruled by God (see pp. 121-127). The next chapter contains Ivan's composition *The Grand Inquisitor*—Dostoevsky's famous dramatization of the church's temptation to seize worldly power (see pp. 127-137). Our old friend, the Devil, appears in Book XI, Chapter 9, to carry on a theological discussion with Ivan (see pp. 337-346). And do not miss the ironical aftermath of Father Zossima's death and Alyosha's disillusionment, in Book VII, Chapters 1 and 2, pages 171-180.

III

"The Russian Monk" consists of three parts: an introduction setting the scene, Father Zossima's story, and Father Zossima's commentary on the story. We might say, in liturgical terms, that Zossima's story is the text and that his commentary is the homily, or sermon. But this text is from the book of his life, and the occasion of his narrative and commentary is his approaching death. His audience consists of his brother monks and disciples.

Father Zossima tells a story of redemption from evil. The story deals with three men who undergo this transformation: Zossima's brother, Zossima himself, and a mysterious visitor. The three "conversions" are bound together, and there is a dynamic increase in spiritual fall and rise from one to another. More and more evil, spiritual struggle, and ultimate transcendence are involved in each successive conversion. But at the end we are aware that the essential elements of all the experiences were present in the first, and that each has dropped into its successor like a seed, waiting for the moment of ripeness.

First Zossima tells of the time when he was a nine-year-old boy and his elder brother experienced a remarkable spiritual conversion. The transformation came to the older boy when he confronted his imminent death from an incurable disease. Previously he had expressed religious doubt, denial of the existence of God, and some profane remarks on the sacraments. In his new state he announced to his astonished family and friends the themes that resound throughout this story; joy in the world, responsibility for all men's sins, humility, and service and love toward all. This world is paradise, and we would have heaven here if we only opened our eyes. God's glory is in the animal and natural world around us. His final words to Zossima were: "Enjoy life for me, too."

This note of joy in the world—of the glory of God in the world and of the world in God—sounds triumphantly through the whole narrative. Zossima cautions against feeling superior to the animals.

Every blade of grass, every insect, ant, and golden bee, all so marvellously know their path, though they have not intelligence, they bear witness to the mystery of God and continually accomplish it themselves. . . . It's touching to know that there's no sin in them, for all, all except man, is sinless, and Christ has been with them before us. . . . the Word is for all. All creation and all creatures, every leaf is striving to the Word, singing glory to God, weeping to Christ, unconsciously accomplishing this by the mystery of their sinless life. . . . how good and beautiful is all God's work! (p. 153b-d)

The second act of the story tells us of Zossima's own conversion. It occurred when he was a shallow and selfish young officer, sowing his wild oats, and dominated by the conventional social attitudes of his class. His transformation was set off by a moment of pique and wounded vanity when a girl whom he thought he was in love with married someone else. Although the other man was the girl's long-intended betrothed and there had never been any understanding between her and Zossima, he decided to get "revenge." He insulted his "rival" in such a way that he forced him to accept his challenge to a duel. Then he went home and beat his orderly with vicious brutality.

When Zossima woke up the next morning (the morning of the duel) he felt low and vile. He realized it was because of what he had done to his servant the night before. As he beheld the rising sun and the greenery and the birds—the whole world rejoicing and praising God—his dead brother's words came back to him, and the seed that was dropped years before fructified at that decisive moment. He recalled his brother's protest that he was unworthy to be waited upon by another human being. Zossima realized that he, too, was unworthy of being served (degradingly) by a creature made in the image of

God, and he recognized his spiritual duty in the present situation.

He knelt down at the feet of the common soldier he had beaten and begged his forgiveness. With that "conquest" behind him, he went forth to his next deed—to beg forgiveness of his opponent in the duel. Knowing that he would be thought a coward and that his act would fail of its effect if he did it before the duel, he let the other man shoot at him without firing in return, and then begged his forgiveness.

As a result of his conversion, Zossima decided to become a monk. While awaiting entry into the monastic life, he encountered a prominent citizen of the garrison town who expressed great admiration for Zossima's remarkable act of moral courage. This man, a constant visitor of Zossima's, proclaimed the saving virtue of living, human example in leading men from the present period of self-centered isolation to the apocalyptic day when they will realize that they are all members of one another.

Sometimes even if he has to do it alone, and his conduct seems to be crazy, a man must set an example, and so draw men's souls out of their solitude, and spur them to some act of brotherly love, that the great idea may not die. (p. 159a)

One day this man suddenly confessed to Zossima that fourteen years earlier he had murdered the woman he loved because he was angry at her for choosing another man. He had not confessed (though a servant of hers was charged with the murder) and he regarded the whole thing as settled when the servant died shortly after his arrest. However, neither a career of public service and philanthropy nor a new life as a husband and father was able to still his conscience. He finally realized that only confession could heal his soul and give him peace, but he was too fearful of the consequences to go through with it. Zossima's great act of moral courage was the example he was waiting for. This incarnation of spiritual sublimity in a fellow human being close at hand convinced him that he, too, was capable of such an act.

But it was not so easy. The murderer went through a terrible struggle on the road to confession. For a whole fortnight he argued with Zossima that confession would ruin his wife and children, or that people would not believe him, or that they would not understand his gesture. Zossima said simply, "Go and confess." He cited two verses from the New Testament:

Verily, verily, I say unto you, Except a corn of wheat fall into the ground and die, it abideth alone: but if it die, it bringeth forth much fruit. (John 12:24)

It is a fearful thing to fall into the hands of the living God. (Hebrews 10:31)

The murderer, who had been angry and almost hateful toward Zossima during the discussion, was shaken by these "terrible" texts. He understood that he had been, for the past fourteen years, "in the hands of the living God," and that he must do what was necessary to make those hands let go of him.

The next day the murderer confessed his crime to a large gathering at his house.

"I cut myself off from men as a monster. God has visited me," he said in conclusion. "I want to suffer for my sin!" (p. 162d)

Nobody believed him, and he was considered mad. He fell into a fatal illness soon after his confession, and in a final interview with Zossima the dying man told of his present bliss, of the heaven in his heart, of his being able to love his wife and children freely and fully once he had shared his burden with mankind. He also revealed to Zossima that he had wanted to kill him the night before he confessed.

"I went out from you then into the darkness, I wandered about the streets, struggling with myself. And suddenly I hated you so that I could hardly bear it. Now, I thought, he is all that binds me, and he is my judge. I can't refuse to face my punishment to-morrow, for he knows all. It was not that I was afraid you would betray me (I never even thought of that), but I thought, 'How can I look him in the face if I don't confess?' And if you had been at the other end of the earth, but alive, it would have been all the same, the thought was unendurable that you were alive knowing everything and condemning me. I hated you as though you were the cause, as though you were to blame for everything. . . . The Lord vanquished the devil in my heart. But let me tell you, you were never nearer death." (p. 163c-d)

When he died a week later he was given the honorable burial due his high social position and good works. Zossima was the subject of popular resentment for a while, because he was believed to have caused the man to fall ill by his disturbing ideas and preaching. But later, people came to Zossima to get at the truth of the story, eager "to see the downfall and disgrace of the righteous." But Zossima remained silent, and soon after entered monastic life.

I V

Zossima's commentary, or sermon, on this moving story taken from his own life is directed to the monks who are his brothers and disciples. He finds in the story a sign and an inspiration to sustain them in their monastic vocation. To the harsh criticism of the monks as useless parasites who contribute nothing to the society they live on, Zossima replies that, on the contrary, they are preserving God's Word and the image of Christ for the moment of ripeness—"for the day and the hour, the month and the year."

In the story, Zossima's brother dropped a seed into Zossima's heart, and he in turn dropped a seed into his visitor's heart. He told how the Bible dropped "the seed of God's word into my heart"—how it came suddenly to him in a moment of worship service when he was a boy, and how it remained there, waiting to ripen, through all the days of his vain and profligate officer life.

This dropping of the seed, says Zossima, is what the monks can do for the Russian people, and so for all mankind. They can teach them the Bible and bring them close to its wonderful, terrible, and mysterious message. They can demonstrate, through their life of obedience, fasting, and prayer, the way to true freedom and joy. This is necessary for men's salvation in the present age, says Zossima, when the spiritual and higher part of man's being is denied and men hope to achieve fulfillment and human brotherhood by taking science as their guide and the satisfaction of material desires as their goal. It is the monks who, through their preaching and their practice, can save the presently moribund "idea of the service of humanity, of brotherly love and the solidarity of mankind."

It is the Russian people, the simple peasantry, that will respond to the call to build a true community based on love and faith. The star of redemption for a failing mankind will come out of the East. The "stone rejected" will become the cornerstone of the edifice of the human community. The Russian people will be the first to demonstrate the great human bond of mutual love and service, or true dignity and fraternity. And it is not the monks, but the rich and educated classes who are cut off from the people. The monks and the people naturally and traditionally belong together.

Of old, leaders of the people came from among us, and why should they not again? The same meek and humble ascetics will rise up and go out to work for the great cause. The salvation of Russia comes from the people. And the Russian monk has always been on the side of the people. We are isolated only if the people are isolated. The people believe as we do, and an unbelieving reformer will never do anything in Russia, even if he is sincere in heart and a genius. Remember that! The people will meet the atheist and overcome him, and Russia will be one and orthodox. Take care of the peasant and guard his heart. Go on educating him quietly. That's your duty as monks, for the peasant has God in his heart. (p. 165a)

It is in the context of this mission of the Russian people that Zossima discourses on love and sin, on prayer and forgiveness, and on joy in the world. Zossima realizes the tension that must arise between the law of love and the exigencies of actual life. How is one to practice Christian virtues in the present social order? Are people who have servants to treat them as equals, and even serve them? "Why not," answers Zossima, "sometimes at least?" And even while your servant is serving you, he can be to you a fellow human person.

It is impossible that there should be no servants in the world, but act so that your servant may be freer in spirit than if he were not a servant. And why cannot I be a servant to my servant and even let him see it, and that without any pride on my part or any mistrust on his? Why should not my servant be like my own kindred, so that I may take him into my family and rejoice in doing so? (p. 166c-d)

Are we expected to love all men, even hardened sinners, brutal criminals, the men who resist good and prevent its embodiment in the world? Certainly, answers Zossima; this is the true imitation of God, to "love a man even in his sin." We should identify ourselves with the criminal, not stand off and

condemn him. We are responsible for one another; we share
the burden of one another's sins. "There go I," we should say
about every condemned person, and our hearts and prayers
should go with him. Above all, do not fight evil with evil; do
not seek revenge, but seek suffering instead, as if *you* were the
guilty one. And do not be tempted to use force to fight against
sin.

Always decide to use humble love. If you resolve on that once for all,
you may subdue the whole world. Loving humility is marvellously strong,
the strongest of all things, and there is nothing else like it. . . . And even
though your light was shining, yet you see men were not saved by it,
hold firm and doubt not the power of the heavenly light. Believe that if
they were not saved, they will be saved hereafter. And if they are not
saved hereafter, then their sons will be saved, for your light will not die
even when you are dead. The righteous man departs, but his light remains. Men are always saved after the death of the deliverer. Men reject
their prophets and slay them, but they love their martyrs and honour
those whom they have slain. You are working for the whole, you are
acting for the future. Seek no reward, for great is your reward on this
earth: the spiritual joy which is only vouchsafed to the righteous man.
(pp. 167d, 169b)

Love and joy—these are the keynotes of Zossima's discourse.
We must love all things in God: every leaf; every blade of
grass; every grain of sand; and those sinless creatures, animals
and children. Through that love, we "will perceive the divine
mystery in things" and keep up our living bond with the
heavenly world where our roots are. Beware, warns Zossima,
lest you be cut off from the roots of heaven!

Much on earth is hidden from us, but to make up for that we have been
given a precious mystic sense of our living bond with the other world,
with the higher heavenly world, and the roots of our thoughts and feelings are not here but in other worlds. That is why the philosophers say
that we cannot apprehend the reality of things on earth.

God took seeds from different worlds and sowed them on this earth,
and His garden grew up and everything came up that could come up,
but what grows lives and is alive only through the feeling of its contact
with other mysterious worlds. If that feeling grows weak or is destroyed
in you, the heavenly growth will die away in you. Then you will be indifferent to life and even grow to hate it. (p. 168c)

Our roots are in heaven, says Zossima, but they bear fruit in
the life of this world.

Man, he says, was sent here to say, "I am and I love." We are sent to give love during this short earthly existence. This "moment of active *living* love" comes only once, and eternal existence becomes an endless consuming remorse for those who did not love and sacrifice in this life. Hell is "the suffering of being unable to love." There is no second chance; this life is our only chance. For the unloving, even the infinite, forgiving love of the righteous in Paradise can only evoke a "flaming thirst for responsive, active and grateful love which is now impossible." All the unloving can do is to accept humbly this love which they cannot return, and thus attain "a certain semblance of that active love which they scorned in life."

This utter frustration and impotence of the God-given faculty of earthly love, relieved by humility and acceptance, is the lot of those who recognize and regret their loss. It is a better state than that of the obdurate sinners possessed by Satanic pride.

Oh, there are some who remain proud and fierce even in hell, in spite of their certain knowledge and contemplation of the absolute truth; there are some fearful ones who have given themselves over to Satan and his proud spirit entirely. For such, hell is voluntary and ever consuming; they are tortured by their own choice. For they have cursed themselves, cursing God and life. They live upon their vindictive pride like a starving man in the desert sucking blood out of his own body. But they are never satisfied, and they refuse forgiveness, they curse God Who calls them. They cannot behold the living God without hatred, and they cry out that the God of life should be annihilated, that God should destroy Himself and His own creation. And they will burn in the fire of their own wrath for ever and yearn for death and annihilation. But they will not attain to death. . . . (p. 170b)

The elder Zossima dies shortly after this discourse, in the midst of conversation with his disciples, kissing the ground in joy before he gives up the ghost.

V

Can acts of love and humility produce real effects in the world?

Most of us are willing to grant the force of such living examples as Zossima's brother, Zossima himself, and his visitor.

In these cases, there was a chain effect of some persons' acts and words on the lives of other persons who experienced them. But Zossima's teaching points beyond conscious experience to an effect in the whole of being.

. . . for all is like an ocean, all is flowing and blending; a touch in one place sets up movement at the other end of the earth. (p. 168a)

And at the other end of time, too, Zossima would add.

But how are we to conceive the medium in which these acts of love and humility dwell constantly, with perpetual potency to affect the world? Are we to think of this realm psychologically, as a kind of collective or racial unconsciousness? Or is there perhaps a web of being, beyond human faculties, in which the personal intentions of the heart have substantial and perpetual reality, not merely an ephemeral sentimental value? Can our little "sometimes" acts have transforming power to the ends of space and time? Would the intention of the heart alone suffice, without being embodied in empirically obvious acts (for sometimes action is physically impossible; and at others, love and humility travel incognito)?

Do animals and inanimate things have religious value and significance?

What bearing does the nonhuman world have on the relation between man and God in the faiths rooted in the Bible? Does Genesis 1 indicate that animals and things perform a merely instrumental function in serving human needs? Or does the doctrine of divine creation imply the psalmist's conviction that God's glory is manifest throughout nature? (See Psalm 19, [D] 18) Does this imply the pantheistic idea that all things embody God? Or does it imply the quite different notion that all things are in God? If all things are in God, are they so in the same way? Do animals and things have a relation to God apart from man and his love for them? Would an indifferent, calloused, or merely exploitative relation of man to the natural world be irreligious? Or is religion only an affair between the human soul and God?

Does the religious idea of collective responsibility for sin conflict with the ethical notion of individual justice ("to each his due")?

Zossima advocates that we identify ourselves with the criminal and accept his acts as our own, no matter how righteous we may be or think ourselves to be. Does Zossima's stand rest on the notion of original sin: that we are guilty just by being men, no matter what we do; that there is a solidarity in sin as well as in holiness? Or does he advocate this identity as a transcendent act of love by actually righteous men, which alone can help to raise the sinner out of his sin? Does this do away with the notion of individual responsibility and the idea of the just allotment of punishments? Or does Zossima merely advocate condemning the sin rather than the sinner? Does he say that the criminal should not be punished, or that he should not be judged self-righteously and vengefully?

Zossima says that we are ultimately responsible for the evil deeds of other men and that we should undergo penance for their sins as if we were guilty ourselves. Notice that Zossima himself, in an earlier section of the book, advocates excommunication as the one sure way to reform the criminal. The hardest and most effective penance, he says, is being cast out of the body of the church. The aim is to regenerate and restore the excluded person (see pp. 30-31). Is there a distinction here between the action and responsibility of the individual member and those of the corporate body? Or is there both a distinction and a connection at the same time? See if you can discover Zossima's idea of the nature of the person and of the community, and of the right relation between them.

Can a nation or a people have a unique religious role?

Zossima's ideal of Russia as a holy people has a precedent in the Biblical concept of Israel as a priest-nation sent to proclaim God's will to the world: to work out the divine will in their national existence, and thus to bring about the kingdom (or rule) of God over all mankind. Modern thinkers usually split the religious, or spiritual, realm from the national, or political, realm.

John Locke is a typical example of the modern separation of religion and nation. What about Hobbes? Did he propound a unity of nation and religion? Wherein does the difference lie between Zossima's and Hobbes's conceptions of the relation between people and religion? Is Zossima's main concern with law and the state, or with love and the imitation of Christ? Does Hobbes put his total state-church under the rule of Christ and the law of love? Is Zossima's central interest in the nation religious or political? Is Hobbes's central interest in religion political or religious?

Notice the discussion earlier in the book, indicating that Zossima's idea is that the state should become the church, not that the church should become the state. (See pp. 28-32, and compare this with "The Grand Inquisitor" episode, pp. 127-137.) Does the assumption of a unique God-bearing status by one nation smack of idolatry or self-centered pride? Is the dichotomy between national existence and religious faith essential to Christianity?

Is the asceticism advocated by Zossima consistent with "joy in the world"?

Asceticism (the denial of physical and emotional needs) has played an important role in many religions, not only as a purgative way to a higher spiritual state, but as a normal and permanent discipline for select religious groups. Criticism has been directed at asceticism as fostering a dangerous form of spiritual pride in human strength and powers, and also as withering away essential parts of the human person and having baleful psychological effects. Defenders of asceticism retort that it is a demonstration of man's bond with a higher, spiritual world, as against the material world, the flesh, and the devil. In Christianity, asceticism is often considered the model Christian sacrifice, demanded of those who would imitate Christ. Opponents retort that God wants us to hallow the whole of human life—the vital and emotional as well as the spiritual—and not to sacrifice it or mutilate it.

Does Zossima advocate the monastic way of obedience, fasting, and prayer in order to deny the world and natural desires, or in order to free the spirit from the bondage of false desires so as to attain true freedom and joy? Does Zossima instruct his fellow monks to withdraw from the world and man, or to go out into the world? Does he counsel hate or love of the natural world and fellow creatures? Are the last words of Zossima's brother ("Enjoy life for me, too") in contradiction with Zossima's preaching? See also Zossima's final advice to Alyosha on page 148a.

Does Zossima advocate a this-wordly religion?

Zossima preaches that the roots of the human spirit are in "the other world," and that when "the heavenly growth" dies in us we grow to hate life. But in what sense are there a heaven and a hell? The literal notion of material hell-fire is utterly meaningless to Zossima, and he sees hell as "the suffering of being unable to love."

Is this a condition in this life, or an eternal state after death? What of the suicides whom Zossima laments? (See p. 170a.) Do they "reside" in hell? Is there a purgatory for Zossima as for Dante? Do Dante and Zossima put the same emphasis on love? If hell is being unable to love, what is heaven to Zossima— active and responsive love? Does Zossima promise an otherworldly reward for the righteous man? If not, what does he promise him?

The following questions are designed to help you test the thoroughness of your reading. Each question is to be answered by giving a page or pages of the reading assignment. Answers will be found on page 270 of this Reading Plan.

1 What one person does Zossima regard as most responsible for his conversion?

2 Whom does Zossima say we should pray for especially every day?

3 What political event did Zossima choose for insulting his rival?

4 Which book of the Bible does Zossima recall as having had a great effect on him when he was a boy?

5 What sin, or psychic state, should we most avoid?

6 Why did Zossima send his orderly back to the regiment after the duel?

7 Will belief in the Russian people lead to belief in God?

8 Who wrote down the account of Father Zossima's final conversation?

9 Which of the monks had accompanied Father Zossima on his journey?

FREUD

Civilization and Its Discontents, I-II

New Introductory Lectures on Psycho-Analysis, Lecture 35

Vol. 54, pp. 767-776, 873-884

The interpretation of religion in terms of psychological needs has a long and distinguished tradition. Lucretius and Hobbes saw the origin of religion in fear and ignorance, and Plato poked fun at people who sought solace in religious ceremonial and sacraments. But it is Sigmund Freud who has presented the most famous psychological interpretation of religion, and he has done this in writings of great literary power. His account of the workings of the mind and his view of human nature have left their mark on the modern mind. Thinkers in almost all areas of human culture have had to face the creative challenge of Freud's thought, whether they agreed with it or not.

No one has found a greater challenge in Freud than the adherents of traditional religious faiths. At first the reaction of religious spokesmen and thinkers to Freud was bitter opposition and condemnation. His theories seemed an even more insidious and mortal threat to traditional religion than those of Darwin and Marx. But in time, many religious thinkers came to accept Freud's theories, at least in part, and began to make constructive use of his insights and method.

However, apart from his general contributions to the study of the human mind, Freud's special view of religion still stands as a challenge to the spokesmen for traditional faiths. Before judging the value of Freud's interpretation of religion, we should first find out what he said and what he meant. To this consideration we address the final selections in this Reading Plan.

Fifteenth Reading

I

Sigmund Freud was the founder of psychoanalysis, a theory of the causes of mental disorders and a method for dealing with them. Simply speaking, it finds their causes in unconscious mental processes, in repressed or inadequately transformed instinctual impulses, especially erotic needs. Freud avidly applied his psychoanalytical insights to literature, art, and religion. Indeed, in his autobiography he calls his medical career a "detour" from the cultural interests which were his main concern.

In 1907, Freud wrote an essay comparing obsessive acts and religious ritual. It shows his early interest in religion and his typical interpretation of religious phenomena. He saw the obsessional neurosis (the compulsion to perform certain acts, and the resulting guilt and anxiety at not performing them) "as a pathological counterpart to the formation of a religion . . . a private religious system," and he saw religion "as a universal obsessional neurosis." In a later work, *Totem and Taboo* (1913), he applied his basic notion of the Oedipus complex (the son's desire to kill his father and take his mother as wife) to the origin of religion. He constructed the hypothesis of a primal prehistoric event in which the tribal father was killed by his sons. From the ensuing sense of guilt at this "original sin," said Freud there grew social order, moral restrictions, and religious ritual commemorating and expiating the primal crime. Freud saw this slain tribal father as God the Father walking the earth in human form, the prototype of all father-gods.

In spite of vigorous criticism of his thesis (as fanciful and unsupported by sound anthropological research), Freud adhered stanchly to it throughout his career and applied it in his final work, *Moses and Monotheism* (1939), to the origin of Judaism. Here Moses is the murdered father figure. Freud was undeterred by criticism from Biblical scholars and historians that he had constructed an imaginative fiction. He was not concerned with scientific scholarship in the conventional sense, but attempted by an intuitive method to grasp the deep underlying meaning of what he was studying. Note that he preferred to call his thesis of primal murder in *Totem and Taboo* a "vision" rather than a hypothesis. Freud held that scientific scholarship was not necessarily right when it contradicted him, and that it did not matter anyway, since he was only trying to fit together a psychoanalytically correct picture. "I am not an ethnologist, but a psychoanalyst," he said. "It was my good right to select from ethnological data what would serve me in my analytic work."

Some eminent psychoanalytical practitioners and theorists, as well as many religious thinkers, have tried to distinguish between Freud's view of the workings of the mind and his view of religious faith. They insist that two different levels of reality are involved—that one can accept Freud's theory of psychoanalysis, which is professional, without accepting his views on religion, which are merely personal.

Freud himself did not see it this way. In a preface which he wrote for a work on religious ritual written by a disciple of his in 1919, he said that we must not restrict the application of psychoanalytic insight to dreams and mental disorders. "Even the highest achievement of the human spirit," he said, must be subject to psychoanalytical interpretation. Indeed, in this preface, he saw analogies between hysteria and art, obsessional neurosis and religion, paranoia and philosophy. He considered the *asocial* response of neurotics and psychotics to their conflicts and needs to be similar to what is expressed, *with social sanction,* in poetry, religion, and philosophy.

In his vigorous attack on religion in *The Future of an Illusion* (1927), as well as in the texts discussed here, Freud admits that tracing religious beliefs back to psychic needs does not disprove their objective truth. He relies on the findings of the natural sciences for that. But he is not interested in abstract rational thought on religion, such as that of Plato, Aristotle, Aquinas, or Calvin. He frequently appeals to the faith of the ordinary man against the ideas of the philosophers. Freud is angry with what he considers pale abstractions which avoid the real emotional substance of religious faith. He appeals ironically to the God of Abraham, Isaac, and Jacob, in whom he does not believe, against the God of the philosophers. He wishes he were a believer so that he could say, "Thou shalt not take the name of the Lord thy God in vain!" (p. 771b) The ordinary man's religion, he insists, has to do with a personal heavenly father who is looking out for him and responds to his prayers if he is good. This is the only religion Freud is interested in, the only one which deserves the name, for him.

II

Let us glance briefly at Freud's own religious background. Freud was born a Jew in a Roman Catholic culture. His father migrated to Vienna from an orthodox Jewish ghetto community in the Austrian province of Galicia, but the father apparently discarded traditional religious beliefs and practices. Freud probably received no religious education, although he tells of having heard the Bible stories at an early age. He thinks they were a decisive influence in turning his interest toward human concerns rather than natural objects. His nursemaid, who was a Catholic, took him to church with her and put ideas of heaven, hell, and salvation into the young child's mind. However, she was dismissed when Freud was only two-and-a-half, and apparently had no lasting religious influence on him. Freud's biographer Ernest Jones says, "He grew up devoid of any belief in a God or Immortality, and does not appear ever to have felt the need of it."

As for Freud's attitude toward Judaism, he said in his autobiography, "My parents were Jews, and I have remained a Jew myself." But this does not mean that he considered himself a Jew in religion. He also said that he was "as little an adherent of the Jewish religion as of any other." And he often attributed crippling psychological effects to the instinctual restrictions demanded by the Jewish moral law.

Yet Freud was intensely proud of being a Jew—a "son" of the Jewish people, as he expressed it. He identified himself with what he considered typical Jewish character traits: tenacity, critical intelligence, and moral rigor. He responded to the anti-Semitism which he encountered in Vienna with firm resistance, refusing to consider himself a member of an inferior race. This militant counterattitude toward anti-Semitism played a great part in his attitude toward the Catholic Church, which was dominant in his country. In his youth he identified himself with Hannibal, "the Semitic commander" who almost conquered Rome—for Freud, the symbol of the Catholic Church. In his last work, on Moses, he calls the church the old enemy, as compared with the new enemy, Nazism. In that work, he considers the church not only the ancient persecutor of his people, but also "the implacable enemy of all freedom of thought," and hence of psychoanalysis.

This is Freud's religious and antireligious background. When he talks about religion, he usually means Christianity—specifically Roman Catholicism, with its basis in Judaism. His main animus against religion, from a psychoanalytic view, is that it represses the instinctual satisfactions of the individual, keeps him in a childhood state, and prevents him from developing an independent, mature self. In his work on group psychology, he treats the church, along with the army, as a typical authoritarian institution (see pp. 674-676). From his early writings on religion to his final work, Freud understood religion as being similar to a neurosis in the individual, and a repetition of—a throwback to—an early stage of the human race.

III

We have selected two texts for this reading. The first comprises the first two sections of *Civilization and Its Discontents,* the work in which Freud discusses the relation between the individual and his culture. The second is the final lecture in the *New Introductory Lectures on Psycho-Analysis,* Freud's last work on psychoanalysis for the general reader.

Freud provides a "psychogenetic" interpretation of religion, that is, he explains it in terms of its origins in certain psychological needs. He looks for the nature of religion in its psychological function. This function he finds to be the relief of the feeling of helplessness felt by the human individual when confronting the external world. This feeling of helplessness goes back to the childhood of the individual and the childhood of the race. It is relieved by the imaginative construction of a heavenly providence, in the image of a father-god who looks after his children. The childish feeling of helplessness develops into the feeling of dependence and trust directed toward an imaginary heavenly father.

The derivation of a need for religion from the child's feeling of helplessness and the longing it evokes for a father seems to me incontrovertible, especially since this feeling is not simply carried on from childhood days but is kept alive perpetually by the fear of what the superior power of fate will bring. (p. 770c)

The ordinary man cannot imagine this Providence in any other form but that of a greatly exalted father, for only such a one could understand the needs of the sons of men, or be softened by their prayers and placated by the signs of their remorse. (p. 771a)

This is the original situation, as Freud sees it, and it becomes more acute in a world where man experiences much suffering and frustration. Thus religion, the belief in an illusion, serves a very real function as a narcotic, a tranquilizer, a painkiller. We avoid awareness of our frustration in the actual world, says Freud, by constructing an imaginary world where we can be safe and happy. (Freud defines happiness as the avoidance of pain and the attainment of intense pleasure.) Thus, religion is nothing but the shared delusion of wish fulfillment.

. . . each one of us behaves in some respect like the paranoiac, substituting a wish-fulfillment for some aspect of the world which is unbearable to him, and carrying this delusion through into reality. When a large number of people make this attempt together and try to obtain assurance of happiness and protection from suffering by a delusional transformation of reality, it acquires special significance. The religions of humanity, too, must be classified as mass-delusions of this kind. Needless to say, no one who shares a delusion recognizes it as such. (p. 774c-d)

IV

Thus far Freud interprets religion in simple psychological terms—helplessness, dependence, suffering, frustration. But he recognizes that man requires something more than balm for wounded feelings and emotional stress, and that religion claims to fulfill this additional need. Freud alludes to this need in our first selection, where he notes that "only religion is able to answer the question of the purpose of life." (p. 772a) Indeed, he holds that the question, "What is the purpose of life?" is inextricably bound up with religion. Our second selection, entitled "A Philosophy of Life," deals with religion's claim to provide a *Weltanschauung*, that is, a coherent view of the world and human existence. This text compares the world view of religion with the world views offered by art, philosophy, and science. Its main purpose is to demonstrate the superiority of science to religion in furnishing a true picture of the real world.

Freud concedes at the start that religion is better able than science to offer psychological bolstering through a unitary world view which answers all the problems of existence.

When one believes in such a thing, one feels secure in life, one knows what one ought to strive after, and how one ought to organize one's emotions and interests to the best purpose. (p. 874a)

Freud concedes that the view of things provided by science may be inadequate, both in affording a full and coherent explanation of the world and in giving consolation and emotional strength to withstand the suffering and frustration of human existence. But that is not the purpose of science, says Freud. Its task is to find out the truth about the actual world, not paint a picture of an illusory one. The latter is what art, philosophy (to a certain extent), and religion do. No real knowledge or truth is obtainable by way of revelation, intuition, or inspiration. They lead only to illusion, which fulfills certain emotional demands at the cost of cutting us off from reality and from the real fulfillment that is possible for us in the actual world.

Religion alone, says Freud, still poses a serious threat to the scientific world view. Art is harmless, even beneficent, not pretending to be anything but illusion. Philosophy attracts only a small elite, even among intellectuals. Religion is the real enemy of science, for it both appeals to the deepest emotions of men and provides a coherent world view. Religion claims to satisfy fundamental intellectual, emotional, and social needs. It gives an account of the origin of the world, comfort and consolation in life and death, and ethical precepts to harmonize the relations between men.

After acknowledging the powerful attraction of the religious world view, Freud proceeds to demonstrate his "thesis that the religious *Weltanschauung* is determined by the situation that subsisted in our childhood." Why a cosmogony (an account of the creation of the world), he asks, that is strangely connected with emotional assurance and ethical precepts? What does the origin of the world have to do with right conduct? Freud answers that God the Creator is obviously nothing but God the Father. Looked at psychoanalytically, He is nothing but the actual father of our childhood, the apparently grandiose figure who protected and cared for us when we were small. The mature man, feeling a similar childlike helplessness and dependence in the face of the external world,

looks back to the memory-image of the overrated father of his childhood, exalts it into a deity, and brings it into the present and into reality. The emotional strength of this memory-image and the lasting nature of his need for protection are the two supports of his belief in God. (p. 876b)

This heavenly father is the creator of the world, as the earthly father was the creator of the child. He rules over the actions between human beings by the same system of rewards and punishments (of giving and withdrawing love) that parents use to bring up children to be decent social beings.

The child is brought up to know its social duties by means of a system of love-rewards and punishments, and in this way it is taught that its security in life depends on its parents (and, subsequently, other people) loving it and being able to believe in its love for them. This whole state of affairs is carried over by the grown man unaltered into his religion. The prohibitions and commands of his parents live on in his breast as his moral conscience; God rules the world of men with the help of the same system of rewards and punishments, and the degree of protection and happiness which each individual enjoys, depends on his fulfilment of the demands of morality; the feeling of security, with which he fortifies himself against the dangers both of the external world and of his human environment, is founded on his love of God and the consciousness of God's love for him. Finally, he has in prayer a direct influence on the divine will, and in that way insures for himself a share in the divine omnipotence. (p. 876c-d)

But rational appraisal informs us, says Freud, that there is no evidence for a beneficent power governing the universe through some system of rewards and punishments to see that justice is done. "Dark, unfeeling, and unloving powers determine human destiny." That is the verdict of rational and realistic interpreters of human existence.

Freud concludes that religion foists an illusion on the human race, keeps it in a state of childhood, and by no means assures it of bliss.

Religion is an attempt to get control over the sensory world, in which we are placed, by means of the wish-world, which we have developed inside us as a result of biological and psychological necessities. But it cannot achieve its end. Its doctrines carry with them the stamp of the times in which they originated, the ignorant childhood days of the human race. Its consolations deserve no trust. Experience teaches us that the world is not a nursery. The ethical commands, to which religion seeks to lend its weight, require some other foundations instead, for human society cannot do without them, and it is dangerous to link up obedience to them with religious belief. If one attempts to assign to religion its place in man's evolution, it seems not so much to be a lasting acquisition, as a parallel to the neurosis which the civilized individual must pass through on his way from childhood to maturity. (p. 878c)

Science, on the other hand, restricts itself to providing genuine knowledge of the real world and rejects illusions. The scientific world view may seem limited and meager compared with the religious, but it has the advantage of being true.

Those of our fellow-men who are dissatisfied with this state of things and who desire something more for their momentary peace of mind may look for it where they can find it. We shall not blame them for doing so; but we cannot help them and cannot change our own way of thinking on their account. (p. 884d)

If we go back to the first selection, we see that Freud even questions whether religion can make people happy by mass illusion. In the first place, he sees religion as forcing everyone to conform to one pattern—turning individuals away from love and action in the real world, although that may be the road to happiness for them. In the second place, religion, too, ends up with submission to the inevitable course of suffering and frustration, so the religious man sacrifices truth without attaining happiness.

Religion circumscribes these measures of choice and adaptation by urging upon everyone alike its single way of achieving happiness and guarding against pain. Its method consists in decrying the value of life and promulgating a view of the real world that is distorted like a delusion, and both of these imply a preliminary intimidating influence upon intelligence. At such a cost—by the forcible imposition of mental infantilism and inducing a mass-delusion—religion succeeds in saving many people from individual neuroses. But little more. There are, as we have said, many paths by which the happiness attainable for man can be reached, but none which is certain to take him to it. Nor can religion keep her promises either. When the faithful find themselves reduced in the end to speaking of God's *inscrutable decree,* they thereby avow that all that is left to them in their sufferings is unconditional submission as a last-remaining consolation and source of happiness. And if a man is willing to come to this, he could probably have arrived there by a shorter road. (p. 776a-b)

Freud contends that science is more wholesome emotionally, intellectually, and practically. It is better for the individual and for society. It does not place a ban on critical thought, causing severe mental inhibitions and emotional disorders. On the contrary, it relies on reason, the great uniter of men, which affords reasonable fulfillment to the emotions. Religion, with its ban on thought and its variety of special beliefs, is divisive and a danger to the future of mankind (see p. 880a).

It is interesting to note that Freud cites the way of love as an alternative to religion. Love, too, strives for inner satisfaction, says Freud, but by turning toward the world, not away from it. Unlike religion, it sets up a positive, full-bodied, emotional relation with the things and persons of this world.

. . . it, too, strives to bring about independence of fate . . . and with this object it looks for satisfaction within the mind, and uses the capacity for displacing libido which we mentioned before, but it does not turn away from the outer world; on the contrary, it takes a firm hold of its objects and obtains happiness from an emotional relation to them. Nor is it content to strive for avoidance of pain—that goal of weary resignation; rather it passes that by heedlessly and holds fast to the deep-rooted, passionate striving for a positive fulfilment of happiness. Perhaps it really comes nearer to this goal than any other method. I am speaking, of course, of that way of life which makes love the centre of all things and anticipates all happiness from loving and being loved. (pp. 774-775a)

Is this the same kind of love that is proclaimed by Father Zossima to be the heart of religion?

V

Are religious beliefs necessarily illusions if they satisfy human wishes and emotional needs?

Freud is very careful not to claim this. Notice that on page 878b he says, "This does not precisely imply a refutation of religion." What he does claim for psychoanalysis is a completion of critical knowledge about religion as a human enterprise, through a description of the role it plays in the psychological "economy." This, he says, contradicts the claim of religion to be of divine origin. As for the objective truth of religious doctrines, Freud thinks they either deal with large, metaphysical subjects which can neither be proved nor disproved through experience or reason, or that they refer to matters which can be checked and refuted by the empirical sciences.

Though Freud disclaims the power of psychological analysis to judge the intrinsic truth and value of religious doctrines, he thinks that if we are convinced that religion provides consoling illusions and ministers to our psychological needs, we are bound to doubt the truth of religious beliefs. Notice that at one point (p. 878c) Freud advises us to forget about the question of religious truth and concentrate on understanding the psychological role of religion in the development of the individual and of the race. We may say that just as Pascal's "wager" was a dialectical device against doubt, Freud's psychogenetic interpretation is a dialectical device against faith.

Does the interpretation of religion as the illusory fulfillment of psychological needs tend to cast doubt on religious doctrines in your mind?

263 FREUD: *Civilization and Its Discontents* 263

*Is it possible that wishes and needs may point to-
ward an objective reality beyond the human
mind?*

Freud sees religion as a "projection" of human needs and
desires on the blank, unresponsive screen of the universe.
Would it be just as likely that such wishes and exigencies
are a response to the reality that is really "out there"? For
the purposes of hypothetical investigation, could we think of
the psychological processes analyzed by Freud as analogous
to human hunger for food or sexual love? Of course, Freud
himself sees man's spiritual and cultural pursuits as "sublima-
tions" of instinctual needs. But we can ignore the "reductive"
interpretation for the moment, and accept the analogy.

Can we find in human thoughts and acts an intention of the
human being toward a reality that transcends the empirical
world and the human mind? Is there such a thing as metaphysical or religious hunger that is even more exigent than
nutritive or sexual hunger? Might such hunger be expressed
in wishes and images such as Freud describes? This hypothetical argument is not intended to demonstrate that "wishing
makes it so," but it suggests that wishing and needing may
point to what is so—to what fulfills the wish and satisfies the
need—ontologically (in reality, in being), not merely psychologically (in the mind alone).

There is a somewhat different way of approaching this
problem. If you will look back at the Guide to the Second
Reading, you will see that Plato puts a cosmic, and even a
world-transcending value on will and wish and purpose. (See
p. 26.) And one of the greatest of the ancient Vedic hymns
puts desire at the beginning of things. Plato and the Vedas
refer, of course, to what transcends human psychology and
the empirical world. Would it be legitimate to see some
analogy between human and cosmic desire, and to ascribe
some share in the value and meaning of the latter to man's
wishes and needs?

Does the "childishness" of a belief detract from its value, meaning, and truth?

Freud uses "childish" as a term of depreciation and "mature" as a term of appreciation. He regards it as a telling attack on religion to trace it to childish needs for trust and dependence. Are the childish and innocent necessarily inferior to the mature and experienced in all realms of human perception? Do all great thinkers regard childhood as an inferior state? You may remember Zossima's attitude toward children, expressing that of Dostoevsky. And perhaps you have read *Songs of Innocence* by the English poet William Blake. What does the New Testament have to say on the state of childhood? Does Christianity depreciate or honor a childlike relation to the world and God? Are childish views untrue in all things and all respects, or may children see deeper and more clearly into certain things than "experienced" adults?

How does Freud handle the notion of religious experience?

A good example of how Freud deals with religious experience is offered at the beginning of our first selection. The noted French writer Romain Rolland (who is not named specifically in the text) had revealed to Freud that he experienced a constant feeling of the infinite, eternal, or "oceanic." Rolland held that this feeling—an inner spiritual experience unconnnected with specific religious beliefs and practices —is the source of all religion. Freud is willing to admit that other men may have this experience, although he has never known it himself, but he cannot agree with Rolland's interpretation of it. Freud proceeds to link this feeling to the objective idea that the individual is an inseparable part of the cosmos; hence we have the "feeling of indissoluble connection, of belonging inseparably to the external world as a whole."

At this point Freud seems to have provided an objective basis for the "oceanic" feeling (although in doing so, he has finitized Rolland's infinite, and temporalized his eternity by reducing it to the material world). But this is not the case; by a psychological analysis of the development of the human ego, Freud finds the "oceanic" feeling to be a reflex or derivative expression of the more basic feeling of childish dependence and helplessness. This, as we know, he regards as the origin of all religion. Rolland's "oceanic" feeling thus turns out to be, for Freud, just another device of the human psyche to escape from the real dangers of the external world.

Freud interprets all that is offered as religious experience in purely psychological terms. He denies that such experience demonstrates a relation with a divine reality outside the human mind. How can Freud's objections be met? Is it possible to argue rationally for the possibility of immediate experience of divine power? Is it possible for one who has no similar experience of his own to judge this assumedly unique experience from the viewpoint of an outside spectator?

Freud is disarmingly frank about his innocence in such matters and also about his inner repugnance against dealing with such dark abysses of the human soul. "Who breathes overhead in the rose-tinted light may be glad!" he quotes Schiller (p. 771a). Would a critical interpreter of Freud be justified in applying psychogenetic analysis to Freud's innocence and repugnance in these matters?

How does Freud's analysis apply to the famous religious figures we have examined?

Think of the Old Testament figures we have discussed. Do Abraham, Moses, and Job project an image of a heavenly father to serve their infantile and neurotic emotional needs? Do they claim to bend the divine will to their purposes and to share in the divine omnipotence? Does Moses promise the children of Israel an otherwordly consolation for their suffering and frustration on earth? Does Psalm 19 ([D]18) fit Freud's analysis of the link between ethical precepts and a divine creator?

What of the New Testament? Which passages in it bear out Freud's thesis, and which deny it? Does the New Testament use God and eternity as consolation prizes for earthly frustration, or does it stress the doing of God's will in the world? Does the New Testament promise joy in the acts of the everyday world, or only in an otherworldly existence? What of Augustine and Pascal? Are they especially vulnerable to the Freudian critique? What of Aquinas and Locke? What of the churches and temples in your community? Do they promise good feeling, peace of mind, and family togetherness as the fruits of religion; or do they require the service of a divine will that may disturb rather than assure human tranquillity?

What is the philosophic basis for Freud's rejection of religion as an illusion?

Is Freud's view of religion as illusion a result of his psychological analysis, or does it rest on a basic intellectual slant that precedes his psychological investigations, though it is enriched by them? What is that basic slant? Is it his announced "scientific" view that the only approach to truth is through controlled observations, hypotheses, and concepts designed to fit the facts? Is it the common-sense view of not going beyond everyday experience? But does not Freud himself use intuition, imagination, myths, and fictions to understand psychological processes? And is Freud's scientific or common-sense view based on a previous metaphysical assumption that there is no special level of reality available to religious experience?

Reason tells us, says Freud, that there is no beneficent Providence and no moral world order, and that "dark, unfeeling, and unloving powers determine human destiny." Is the latter judgment the result of empirical inquiry and rational appraisal or the expression of Freud's own "theology," resembling the ancient Greek belief in the Fates?

What virtues does Freud extol as against the religious virtues?

We have seen above (p. 260) that Freud believes that the ethical precepts proclaimed by religion are necessary for man's social existence. He objects only to their being based on what he considers to be such unwholesome and insecure grounds. But an essential part of Freud's attack on religion is that it produces defects in mind and character. Can we deduce Freud's ideal of human character from a careful survey of the undesirable traits he ascribes to the influence of religion? What attitudes and what actions does Freud believe the individual should take toward himself, toward his fellow men, and toward the natural world? What should be a man's basic aim in life? Freud often spoke of the psychoanalyst as "a secular spiritual guide." What does that "spiritual guidance" consist of? What is Freud's image of man as he should be?

The following questions are designed to help you test the thoroughness of your reading. Each question is to be answered by giving a page or pages of the reading assignment. Answers will be found on page 270 of this Reading Plan.

1 According to Freud, what basic principle guides human life?

2 What Eastern religious practice may be connected with the "oceanic" feeling?

3 What is Freud's theory of the prehistory of religion?

4 What is the historical example for the mind's conservation of past stages?

5 How does Russian Marxism resemble religion?

6 What are Freud's objections to philosophy?

7 What are the two alternatives to religion indicated by Goethe's verse?

ANSWERS
to self-testing questions

First Reading
1. 40d-41a
2. 42c
3. 44c-45a
4. 47a
5. 47d, 49a
6. 51b

Second Reading
1. 193a
2. 196c-d
3. 758c
4. 765b
5. 770a-b
6. 770d-771a

Third Reading
1. Gen. 12:4-5
2. Gen. 17:17
3. Ex. 4:1:10
4. Ex. 14:10-12
5. Ex. 19:10-15
6. Ex. 20:23-26

Fourth Reading
1. 1:1
2. 4:18-22
3. 9:14-17, 11:18-19
4. 12:40
5. 15:21-28
6. 11:11-14, 17:10-13
7. 19:16-22

Fifth Reading
1. 90d
2. 91b-c
3. 101b-c
4. 101d
5. 102a
6. 106d-107a
7. 108c-d

Sixth Reading
1. Vol. 19, 5b
2. Vol. 20, 386a-b
3. Vol. 19, 9a-c
4. Vol. 19, 9d-10c
5. Vol. 20, 387d
6. Vol. 20, 400d-401a
7. Vol. 20, 401a

Seventh Reading
1. 146c-d
2. 126b-d
3. 143c-d
4. 112b
5. 135d-136b, 137a-138a
6. 106a
7. 134c
8. 111b
9. 126b

Eighth Reading
1. 228a
2. 242b-c
3. 80d
4. 163d
5. 170c
6. 209d-210b

Ninth Reading
1. 153d
2. 156a
3. 98b
4. 156c
5. 325c-d
6. 152d-153a
7. 155d

Tenth Reading

1. 99a
2. 145b-146a
3. 93b-94a
4. 136a-b
5. 96b, 113b, 114b
6. 150a
7. 111b-112a
8. 98a
9. 139b
10. 108a

Eleventh Reading

1. 224a-b
2. 213b
3. 206b, 218b
4. 222b
5. 220a
6. 217a
7. 211a

Twelfth Reading

1. 21a-22b
2. 4d-5a
3. 381a
4. 21a-b
5. 10b
6. 12b-c
7. 5a-b

Thirteenth Reading

1. 501a
2. 497a
3. 495d
4. 498d
5. 496c
6. 489c

Fourteenth Reading

1. 166b
2. 167b-c
3. 154d
4. 151b-d
5. 168b
6. 157c
7. 153a
8. 148c
9. 147a-b

Fifteenth Reading

1. 772b
2. 770d
3. 876d-877c
4. 769b
5. 883d-884b
6. 875a, 877b
7. 771c

ADDITIONAL READINGS

I. Works included in *Great Books of the Western World*

Vol. 5: AESCHYLUS, *The Suppliant Maidens; Agamemnon; Choephoroe; Eumenides*

7: PLATO, *Phaedo; The Republic,* Book VI, Book X; *Timaeus*

8: ARISTOTLE, *Physics,* Book VIII; *Metaphysics,* Book XII

12: LUCRETIUS, *On the Nature of Things,* Books I-III
EPICTETUS, *The Discourses,* Book I
MARCUS AURELIUS, *The Meditations*

17: PLOTINUS, *The Six Enneads,* Third Ennead

18: AUGUSTINE, *The City of God,* Books XI-XIII; *On Christian Doctrine*

19: AQUINAS, *Summa Theologica,* Part I, QQ. 44-49, "Treatise on the Creation"

21: DANTE, *The Divine Comedy,* "Purgatory"

31: DESCARTES, *Meditations on First Philosophy*
SPINOZA, *Ethics,* Part I

32: MILTON, *Miscellaneous Poems* (pp. 1-13); *Psalms; Samson Agonistes*

33: PASCAL, *The Provincial Letters*

35: BERKELEY, *The Principles of Human Knowledge*

40: GIBBON, *The Decline and Fall of the Roman Empire,* Chapters XV-XVI, XX-XXI, XXIII-XXV, XXVIII, XXXVII; "General Observations" (pp. 630-634)

41: GIBBON, *The Decline and Fall of the Roman Empire,* Chapters XLVII, XLIX, L-LI, LIV, LVIII-LXI, LXIX-LXX

42: KANT, *The Critique of Pure Reason:* "The Ideal of Pure Reason" (pp. 173-209); *The Critique of Practical Reason:* "Dialectic of Pure Practical Reason," Part I, Book II; *The Critique of Judgement,* Sections 85-91, and "General Remark on Teleology" (pp. 607-613)

II. Other Works

A. History of Religion

BETTENSON, HENRY S. (ed.), *Documents of the Christian Church*. New York: Oxford University Press, 1947

COCHRANE, CHARLES NORRIS, *Christianity and Classical Culture*. New York: Oxford University Press, 1944

DAWSON, CHRISTOPHER H., *Religion and the Rise of Western Culture*. New York: Image Books (Doubleday), 1958

HARRISON, JANE E., *Prolegomena to the Study of Greek Religion*. New York: Meridian Books, Inc., 1955

HOLL, KARL, *The Cultural Significance of the Reformation*. New York: Meridian Books, Inc., 1959

HUGHES, PHILIP, *A Popular History of the Catholic Church*. New York: Image Books (Doubleday), 1954

LATOURETTE, KENNETH S., *A History of Christianity*. New York: Harper & Brothers, 1953

NILSSON, MARTIN P., *A History of Greek Religion*, 2nd ed. New York: Oxford University Press, 1949

OESTERLEY, W. O. E., and ROBINSON, THEODORE H., *A History of Israel*, 2 vols. New York: Oxford University Press, 1932

ROTH, CECIL, *A Short History of the Jewish People*, rev. ed. New York: Meridian Books, Inc., 1953

SCHWARZ, LEO W. (ed.), *Great Ages and Ideas of the Jewish People*. New York: Random House, Inc., 1956

B. Bible and Talmud

ALBRIGHT, WILLIAM F., *From the Stone Age to Christianity*. New York: Doubleday Anchor Books, 1957

ALLEGRO, JOHN M., *The Dead Sea Scrolls*. Baltimore: Penguin Books Inc., 1956

BEWER, JULIUS A., *Literature of the Old Testament*, rev. ed. New York: Columbia University Press, 1933

BUBER, MARTIN, *The Prophetic Faith*. New York: The Macmillan Company, 1949

CHARLES, ROBERT H. (ed.), *The Apocrypha and Pseudepigrapha of the Old Testament*, 2 vols. New York: Oxford University Press, 1913

COHEN, ABRAHAM (ed.), *Everyman's Talmud*, rev. ed. New York: E. P. Dutton & Company, 1949

DODD, CHARLES H., *The Apostolic Preaching*. New York: Harper & Brothers, 1936; *The Parables of the Kingdom*. New York: Charles Scribner's Sons, 1936

ENSLIN, MORTON SCOTT, *Christian Beginnings*. New York: Harper & Brothers, 1938; also published in 2 vols. Harper Torchbooks, 1956

GASTER, THEODOR H. (trans. and ed.), *The Dead Sea Scriptures in English Translation*. New York: Doubleday Anchor Books, 1956

GOLDIN, JUDAH (trans. and ed.), *The Living Talmud: The Wisdom of the Fathers and Its Classical Commentaries*. New York: New American Library (Mentor Books), 1957

KNOX, RONALD A., *New Testament Commentary for English Readers*, 3 vols. New York: Sheed & Ward, Inc., 1954-56

OTTO, RUDOLF, *The Kingdom of God and the Son of Man*. Boston: Beacon Press, 1957

PEDERSEN, JOHANNES P. E., *Israel: Its Life and Culture*, 2 vols. New York: Oxford University Press, 1953

RICHARDSON, ALAN (ed.), *A Theological Word Book of the Bible*. New York: The Macmillan Company, 1951

SCHWEITZER, ALBERT, *The Quest of the Historical Jesus*. New York: The Macmillan Company, 1948

SCOTT, ERNEST F., *The Literature of the New Testament*. New York: Columbia University Press, 1932

SNAITH, NORMAN H., *The Distinctive Ideas of the Old Testament*. Naperville, Ill.: Alec R. Allenson, Inc., 1953

STRACK, HERMANN L., *Introduction to the Talmud and Midrash*. New York: Meridian Books, Inc., 1959

WELLHAUSEN, JULIUS, *Prolegomena to the History of Ancient Israel*. New York: Meridian Books, Inc., 1957

WILDER, AMOS N., *Eschatology and Ethics in the Teaching of Jesus*, rev. ed. New York: Harper & Brothers, 1950

C. Religious Thought

ADAM, KARL, *The Spirit of Catholicism*. New York: Image Books (Doubleday), 1945

ANSELM OF CANTERBURY, *Proslogium; Monologium;* etc., trans. by Sidney N. Deane. La Salle, Ill.: The Open Court Publishing Company, 1903

AQUINAS, THOMAS, *On the Truth of the Catholic Faith.* 5 vols. New York: Hanover House (Doubleday), 1955-57

BAECK, LEO, *The Essence of Judaism.* New York: Schocken Books, Inc., 1948

BARTH, KARL, *Epistle to the Romans.* New York: Oxford University Press, 1933; *Dogmatics in Outline.* Naperville, Ill.: Alec R. Allenson, Inc., 1955

BRUNNER, H. EMIL, *The Christian Doctrine of God.* Philadelphia: The Westminster Press, 1950

BUBER, MARTIN, *Israel and the World.* New York: Schocken Books, Inc., 1948

CALVIN, JOHN, *Institutes of the Christian Religion,* 2 vols. Philadelphia: The Westminster Press, 1949

D'ARCY, MARTIN C., and others, *Saint Augustine.* New York: Meridian Books, Inc., 1957

GILSON, ÉTIENNE, *The Spirit of Mediaeval Philosophy.* New York: Charles Scribner's Sons, 1936; *History of Christian Philosophy in the Middle Ages.* New York: Random House, Inc., 1955; *The Christian Philosophy of St. Thomas Aquinas.* New York: Random House, Inc., 1956

HUSIK, ISAAC, *A History of Mediaeval Jewish Philosophy.* New York: Meridian Books, Inc., 1958

KIERKEGAARD, SÖREN A., *The Sickness Unto Death.* Princeton, N.J.: Princeton University Press, 1941

LUTHER, MARTIN, *Three Treatises.* Philadelphia: Muhlenberg Press, 1947; *The Table Talk of Martin Luther,* ed. by Thomas S. Kepler. Cleveland, O.: World Publishing Company, 1952; *Commentary on Genesis.* Grand Rapids, Mich.: Zondervan Publishing House, 1958

MAIMONIDES, MOSES, *The Guide for the Perplexed.* New York: Dover Publications, Inc., 1957

McGIFFERT, ARTHUR C., *A History of Christian Thought,* 2 vols. New York: Charles Scribner's Sons, 1953

NIEBUHR, H. RICHARD, *Christ and Culture.* New York: Harper Torchbooks, 1951

NIEBUHR, REINHOLD, *The Nature and Destiny of Man*, 1-vol. ed. New York: Charles Scribner's Sons, 1947; *Faith and History*. New York: Charles Scribner's Sons, 1951

RICHARDSON, ALAN, *Christian Apologetics*. New York: Harper & Brothers, 1947

SCHECHTER, SOLOMON, *Studies in Judaism*. New York: Meridian Books, Inc., 1958

SCHLEIERMACHER, FRIEDRICH E. D., *The Christian Faith*. Naperville, Ill.: Alec R. Allenson, Inc., 1958

TEMPLE, WILLIAM, *Nature, Man and God*. New York: St. Martin's Press, Inc., 1953

TILLICH, PAUL J., *Systematic Theology*, 2 vols. Chicago: The University of Chicago Press, 1951-57

The "FATHERS OF THE CHURCH Series." New York: Fathers of the Church, Inc.

The "LIBRARY OF CHRISTIAN CLASSICS Series." Philadelphia: The Westminster Press

"WRITINGS OF THE ANTE-NICENE FATHERS Series." Grand Rapids, Mich.: Wm. B. Eerdmans Publishing Company, 1951

D. Religious Experience

BOEHME, JAKOB, *Confessions*, ed. by W. Scott Palmer. New York: Harper & Brothers, 1954

BROTHER LAWRENCE, *Practice of the Presence of God*. Westminster, Md.: The Newman Press, 1945

BROWNE, SIR THOMAS, *Religio Medici and Other Writings*. New York: Everyman's Library, 1951

BUBER, MARTIN, *I and Thou*, 2nd ed. New York: Charles Scribner's Sons, 1958

BUNYAN, JOHN, *Pilgrim's Progress*, rev. ed. New York: Everyman's Library, 1954

FOX, GEORGE, *Journal*. New York: Everyman's Library

FRANCIS DE SALES, *Introduction to the Devout Life*. New York: Image Books (Doubleday), 1959

FRANCIS OF ASSISI, *The Little Flowers*, etc. New York: Everyman's Library, 1951

GUILLAUME, ALFRED, *Prophecy and Divination Among the Hebrews and Other Semites*. London: Hodder & Stoughton, Ltd., 1938

HEILER, FRIEDRICH, *Prayer*. New York: Oxford University Press Galaxy Books, 1959

IGNATIUS OF LOYOLA, *The Spiritual Exercises*. Trans. by Louis J. Puhl, S.J. Westminster, Md.: The Newman Press, 1951

INGE, WILLIAM R., *Christian Mysticism*. New York: Meridian Books, Inc., 1956

JAMES, WILLIAM, *Varieties of Religious Experience*. New York: Modern Library, 1936

JOHN OF THE CROSS, *Ascent of Mount Carmel*, 3rd ed. New York: Image Books (Doubleday), 1958

KIERKEGAARD, SÖREN A., *Purity of Heart*, rev. ed. New York: Harper & Brothers, 1948

LAW, WILLIAM, *A Serious Call to a Devout and Holy Life*. New York: Everyman's Library, 1955

LEEUW, GERARDUS VAN DER, *Religion in Essence and Manifestation*. London: George Allen & Unwin, Ltd., 1938

MACMURRAY, JOHN, *The Structure of Religious Experience*. New Haven: Yale University Press, 1936

Meister Eckhart: a Modern Translation. New York: Harper Torchbooks, 1957

OTTO, RUDOLF, *The Idea of the Holy*, 2nd ed. New York: Oxford University Press Galaxy Books, 1950

PRATT, JAMES B. *The Religious Consciousness*. New York: The Macmillan Company, 1920

SCHOLEM, GERSHOM G., *Major Trends in Jewish Mysticism*, rev. ed. New York: Schocken Books, Inc., 1954

SÖDERBLOM, NATHAN, "Communion with Deity (Introductory)," *Encyclopaedia of Religion and Ethics*, ed. by James Hastings, Vol. III, pp. 736-740. New York: Charles Scribner's Sons, 1911; "Holiness (General and Primitive)," *Op. cit.* Vol. VI, pp. 731-741

FRIENDS OF GOD, *Theologia Germanica*. Cleveland: The World Publishing Company, 1952

TERESA OF AVILA, *The Way of Perfection*. Westminster, Md.: The Newman Press, 1947

THOMAS À KEMPIS, *The Imitation of Christ.* New York: Pocket Books, 1953

UNDERHILL, EVELYN, *Worship.* New York: Harper & Brothers, 1937; *Mysticism.* New York: Meridian Books, Inc., 1955

WACH, JOACHIM, *The Comparative Study of Religions.* New York: Columbia University Press, 1958

E. Philosophy of Religion

BERGSON, HENRI, *The Two Sources of Morality and Religion.* New York: Doubleday Anchor Books, 1954

BUBER, MARTIN, *Eclipse of God.* New York: Harper & Brothers, 1952

BURTT, EDWIN A., *Types of Religious Philosophy,* rev. ed. New York: Harper & Brothers, 1951

CORNFORD, FRANCIS M., *From Religion to Philosophy.* New York: Harper & Brothers, 1957

EMMET, DOROTHY M., *The Nature of Metaphysical Thinking.* New York: The Macmillan Company, 1953

FEUERBACH, LUDWIG A., *The Essence of Christianity.* New York: Harper & Brothers, 1957

FORSYTH, THOMAS M., *God and the World.* New York: The Macmillan Company, 1953

FRANK, ERICH, *Philosophical Understanding and Religious Truth.* New York: Oxford University Press, 1945

HARTSHORNE, CHARLES, *Man's Vision of God and the Logic of Theism.* New York: Harper & Brothers, 1941

HEGEL, GEORG W. F., *Early Theological Writings.* Chicago: The University of Chicago Press, 1948

HOCKING, WILLIAM E., *The Meaning of God in Human Experience.* New Haven: Yale University Press, 1912

HUME, DAVID, *Dialogues Concerning Natural Religion.* New York: Hafner Publishing Company, 1948

JAEGER, WERNER W., *The Theology of the Early Greek Philosophers.* New York: Oxford University Press, 1947

KANT, IMMANUEL, *Religion Within the Limits of Reason Alone.* LaSalle, Ill.: The Open Court Publishing Company, 1934

KAUFMANN, WALTER A., *Critique of Religion and Philosophy.* New York: Harper & Brothers, 1958

LEIBNIZ, GOTTFRIED W., *Discourse on Metaphysics*, etc. La-Salle, Ill.: The Open Court Publishing Company, 1937

MARCEL, GABRIEL, *Being and Having*. Westminster, Md.: The Dacre Press, 1949

MARITAIN, JACQUES, *Science and Wisdom*. New York: Charles Scribner's Sons, 1940

NEEDHAM, JOSEPH (ed.), *Science, Religion, and Reality*. New York: George Braziller, Inc., 1955

NIETZSCHE, FRIEDRICH W., "The Antichrist," in the *Portable Nietzsche*, ed. by Walter Kaufmann. New York: The Viking Press, 1954

SANTAYANA, GEORGE, *Interpretations of Poetry and Religion*. New York: Harper & Brothers, 1957

SCHLEIERMACHER, FRIEDRICH E. D., *On Religion: Speeches to Its Cultured Despisers*. New York: Harper & Brothers, 1958

SPINOZA, BENEDICT DE, "Theologico-Political Treatise," in *The Chief Works*. Vol. 1. New York: Dover Publications, Inc., 1952

TURNER, JOHN E., *Essentials in the Development of Religion*. New York: The Macmillan Company, 1934

WHITEHEAD, ALFRED N., *Religion in the Making*. New York: The Macmillan Company, 1926